Follow the Money

How Much Does Britain Cost?

PAUL JOHNSON

abacus
books

ABACUS

First published in Great Britain in 2023 by Abacus
This paperback edition published in 2024 by Abacus

3 5 7 9 10 8 6 4 2

A CIP catalogue record for this book
is available from the British Library.

Paperback ISBN 978-0-349-14466-5

Typeset in Minion by M Rules
Printed and bound in Great Britain by Clays Ltd, Elcograf S.p.A

Papers used by Abacus are from well-managed forests
and other responsible sources.

Abacus
An imprint of
Little, Brown Book Group
Carmelite House
50 Victoria Embankment
London EC4Y 0DZ

An Hachette UK Company
www.hachette.co.uk

www.littlebrown.co.uk

Contents

Introduction

Following the Money

Total UK spending (2023/24): £1.19 trillion[1]

It is now more than half a century since the break-in by supporters of US president Richard Nixon into the Democratic Party headquarters at the Watergate Complex in Washington, DC. According to the film *All the President's Men*, 'follow the money' was the advice given to the investigative reporters Bernstein and Woodward by their source, known as Deep Throat – a reference to the contemporary adult film actor Linda Lovelace. Deep Throat finally unveiled himself in 2005, at the age of ninety-one.

It was Mark Felt, back then assistant director of the FBI – and it was he who met the reporters in the underground car park in Rosslyn just over the state line in Virginia. Not that there is any evidence he actually uttered those words. They were more likely invented for dramatic effect.

Let me say straight away that I am not implying that, when you have followed the money through the maze of taxes and government spending that defines the British state, you will find anything criminal. We are not following money towards corruption, though some of that may exist. We will, though, discover rather too much lazy thinking, a good deal of timidity, a pervasive failure to focus on the long or even medium term and, too often, a lack of both technical expertise and understanding of the actual effects of decisions on real people.

What hope then for the rest of us as we pay our taxes, receive our pensions, and use the schools and hospitals that our taxes pay for? What hope have we of holding our governments to account for the decisions they make that shape all our lives, if we can't judge the quality of the decisions they are making? That is the idea behind this book. To follow the money. To provide an explanation of where that money comes from, where it goes to, how that has changed and how it needs to change.

By following the money, I want to show how the choices governments make really do change the way we live and the sort of society we live in. Government decisions determine the welfare of the poor and the elderly, the state of the health service, the effectiveness of our children's education, and our preparedness for the future – whether for a future pandemic or the effects of global warming. As a society, we are a reflection of what the government spends.

In the last twenty years we have lived through the relative plenty of the period up to 2008, the financial crisis itself, austerity in the 2010s, Brexit, the Covid pandemic and the associated biggest spending splurge in peacetime history, the resurgence of inflation and an associated cost of living crisis. The government borrowed more during the pandemic year, 2020/21, than at any time in history outside of the First and Second World Wars. It borrowed again on a vast scale to manage rising energy bills. Debt has ratcheted up, and spending on debt interest payments is at its highest level in a generation. Demands for spending on public services and welfare are only going to go in one direction. Tax is following. The tax burden is at its highest sustained level in more than seventy years. An ageing population, and consequent need for more spending on health, social care and pensions, means that, whatever the politicians may tell you, there will be more tax rises, if not soon then certainly within the decade.

So, we must start by looking at how taxation works. That matters. How could it not when nearly four pounds out of every ten we earn goes, one way or another, to the taxperson? What are the combined effects of these decisions to take hundreds of billions from us every year and then dish it out again?

The rest of the book covers the welfare state, the big beasts of government spending: pensions, social security, health, social care, education, and local government. Defence spending will get a walk-on part in the concluding chapter, which will also contemplate the public finances more broadly alongside future challenges, not least those associated with climate change.

This is where the big money is. These are also the issues with which I concern myself every day of my working life. If you glance at the references you'll see that most of what's here is based on the work of my colleagues, at the Institute for Fiscal Studies. The idea is to stick to what I know, what I really know.

My perspective

It's probably worth knowing a bit about me before you embark on this book. I'm trying to offer an objective assessment but I will inevitably bring my own experiences and prejudices to bear. You'll have learnt something from the last paragraph. I am only going to write here about things I really know about.

I have been a working economist for the past three decades, both in and out of government. I have been a director responsible for public spending at the Treasury. I was a senior official in the Department for Education. For a decade, now, I have been director of the IFS, an independent research institute where we busy ourselves looking at just what this book is all about: how government raises and spends a trillion pounds a year. It's a privileged position, not least because it allows me to draw on the wealth of extraordinary analysis and research done by my amazing colleagues.

Part of the need for this book reflects the failure of we researchers, think tankers and academics to communicate what we know. It also arises from the existence of a yawning chasm between the work of most academic social scientists and the work of government. The cultures, the incentives, the values are utterly different, the mutual incomprehension often astonishing to behold.

Both worlds remain far too insular. Too many policymakers and politicians – and therefore civil servants – are focused on the short term and are shockingly ignorant of advances in the research world. Too many researchers are dismissive of the needs of government and equally ignorant of the policymaking process. The two communities are far less than the potential sum of their parts. It is hardly surprising then that the public doesn't really know where to turn or whom to believe.

The government employs literally thousands of economists,

statisticians, social researchers and others carrying out good and important work. They are constantly analysing data, building and running models and advising ministers. In many areas of policy, more analysis happens within the relevant government department than in all external bodies combined. Yet little of it ever sees the light of day, and if it does it is often wrapped in a party-political blanket. What a dreadful waste of resources and what a drag on the quality of public discourse and of public policy. Meanwhile, far too few academics engage properly either with policymakers or the public.

'Earth to economists: your ivory tower isolation is not an option', said a headline in the *Times Higher Education Supplement* in 2014.[2] I agree. It is our responsibility to explain what we can, and hold the government to account wherever possible. Without real understanding of the genuinely difficult decisions politicians have to take all the time, a breakdown of trust is inevitable. Without the sort of rigorous external holding to account which we at the IFS attempt to achieve, the politicians will get away with half-truths, elisions and dubious claims.

In the end the discipline of economics and the markets creates some constraints. The precipitous fall in the value of the pound, and increase in the cost of government debt, which followed the massive unfunded tax cuts announced by then chancellor Kwasi Kwarteng in September 2022, is evidence enough of that. But that is not enough. This book is designed to fill at least some of the huge gap left by the politicians, the civil servants and the academics. To explain the necessary compromises and unnecessary mistakes, the successes and failures.

I have been hugely fortunate to spend the majority of my career at the IFS outside the constraints of politics. In all we do, we try to be objective. We are determinedly independent, have no political axe to grind and certainly no political affiliation. As you'll see, that doesn't preclude a willingness to take a view about what is likely to work and what effects policy might have, but these views are based on the evidence as best as we can understand, analyse and synthesise it.

My first stint there began in the late 1980s when it was an even smaller organisation than it is today, occupying rather shabby offices above a sewing shop in London's Tottenham Court Road. I was immediately pitched among the most extraordinarily talented bunch of people, far cleverer than I. Many have gone on to glittering careers in academia, the media and – yes – politics. I'm sure the same will be true of many of my current colleagues.

I returned in 2011 after a stint in government. The IFS is a small charity, a think tank, which exists by happenstance, and survives thanks to the phenomenal work of my predecessors and colleagues. I could not be prouder to work with such people and in an institution in which we are all devoted to the furtherance of knowledge and the improvement of public policy. Drawing on the work of the IFS and my thirty years of work on the nation's finances, this book is an opportunity to sit back and look at what government is doing with our money: what it is doing right, what it is doing wrong and why it will probably soon need more of it.

Cometh coronavirus

Imagine the river Thames in London – held back a little by what, in those days, were the twelve piers of London Bridge – freezing solid for three months. It might be fun experiencing a frost fair on the ice, but after a few weeks the novelty would begin to wear off. That was what happened at the end of 1708 and well into March 1709. The French called it *Le Grand Hiver*: the 'great winter'. We called it the

Great Frost. That was probably the last time our national income collapsed as much as it did in 2020. The only other year to come close was 1919, the year of the last great pandemic, Spanish flu.

It's a long time since 1709. Imagine Christopher Wren putting the finishing touches to St Paul's Cathedral or William Pitt the Elder emerging into the world, up the river in Westminster, a couple of weeks before everything froze. And if 2020 came close to marking the end of the fossil fuel-driven industrial age, 1709 saw its beginning.

It was in 1709 in Coalbrookdale that Abraham Darby discovered how to use coke in a blast furnace to smelt iron. The year was even more important for a stranded pirate called Alexander Selkirk – supposedly the original of Robinson Crusoe – who was rescued from his South Pacific desert island when the Great Frost was at its height.

Back in freezing England, it was so cold that people would wake to find themselves frozen to their bedsheets, and some had to slice their bread with an axe. Those who were lucky enough to have any bread. When the Thames finally thawed in the spring, widespread flooding and famine followed. National income having collapsed even further just three years before, thanks to the outbreak of the War of the Spanish Succession, it is hardly surprising that it took a good decade for the economy to recover.[3]

At the other end of the fossil fuel era, UK economic activity fell by a fifth in the second three months of 2020, following the pandemic and government-imposed lockdown.[4] This time, however, the government had the wherewithal not only to prevent famine, but to protect the incomes of millions. In March 2020, then Chancellor Rishi Sunak had to take on the immense task of protecting our living standards in the face of this unprecedented closure of the economy.

'Today I can announce that, for the first time in our history, the government is going to step in and help to pay people's wages,' Rishi

Sunak told a roomful of journalists and cameras on 20 March. 'I am placing no limit on the amount of funding available for the scheme ... We're paying people's wages up to 80 per cent so someone can be furloughed, rather than laid off, to protect their jobs.'[5]

He was to spend tens of billions on a furlough scheme which at one point saw the government paying the wages of nine million workers, more than one in three of all those employed in the private sector. He came back again and again, renewing the furlough scheme and spending tens of billions more on schemes to support businesses and the self-employed.

He increased benefits for the unemployed. He found tens and tens of billions for 'test and trace' and personal protective equipment (PPE). He gave more to the NHS, bailed out the railways and local government. The spending seemed never to stop. All the usual rules were suspended.

For the second time in little more than a decade, the power of government to mobilise resources way beyond the capability of the private sector was demonstrated. The time before, in 2008 and 2009, it was all about bailing out the banks and making sure that the financial system didn't implode. This time it was about responding to a pandemic, protecting our incomes and propping up public services. Total additional spending topped £300 billion – a staggering amount of money.

Intervention on that scale probably prevented mass unemployment and poverty. But the trillions of pounds, dollars and euros printed and spent across the western world to deal with Covid played their part in exacerbating the next big challenge: inflation.

President Putin made that far worse when he invaded Ukraine and precipitated huge increases in energy prices. Again, government stepped in with a splurge of spending to hold down all our energy bills. All that spending cushioned us from their immediate effects, but make no mistake, Covid and the energy price surge have both made us worse off. Governments can spread the pain between people and across time. They can't make it disappear.

In fact, it's payback time already. Government debt is at its highest level for more than 60 years. The Bank of England raised interest rates fourteen times in a row until it finally paused in September 2023. We are now spending more on debt interest than at any time in decades, and more than on any public service other than the NHS. That's a shock because for more than a decade, from the financial crisis through to Covid, rock-bottom interest rates had meant that interest payments on that debt had been at their lowest levels in history.

If there is one thing we must all learn it is that nothing is forever. The early 2000s now look like some kind of economic nirvana. People who should have known better thought that the economy had been tamed. That boom and bust was gone for good. Then came the banking crash, financial crisis and associated recession. Policymakers and central bankers had to look into economic history to understand what had happened and know what to do.

Then we had austerity – the most dramatic period of spending cuts in modern history – as the subsequent governments tried to wrestle both the deficit and the debt down. Accompanying austerity was also the loosest monetary policy – the lowest interest rates – in history.

The Bank of England was founded in 1694. Never in all its 300+ years had it reduced interest rates to such a low level. Until the middle of 2021 it looked like rock-bottom interest rates and low inflation were here to stay. Instead, everything has changed again.

During Covid the Bank of England effectively printed hundreds of billions of pounds. It now holds almost half the two trillion or so of UK public debt. Observing this curious money-go-round it was tempting to think the rules and economics of public spending had been completely upended. Money seemed to be, literally, free. If we could spend hundreds of billions then, why should we worry about constraints on what we can spend to improve our health and education and social care services tomorrow?

The short answer is because economic and fiscal realities really haven't changed. Ukraine, of course, made it worse, but inflation was on its way up in any case. It hit 7 per cent – more than three times the Bank of England's target rate of 2 per cent, in March 2022, *before* the effects of the Russian invasion of Ukraine could be felt. As Andy Haldane, outgoing chief economist at the Bank of England, rather presciently wrote, the combination of big government spending, ultra-low interest rates, rapid recovery in consumer demand, and ongoing constraints in supply, were always likely to result in a resurgence of inflation.[6] If we just increase spending now, without accompanying tax rises, we'll get even higher interest rates and more inflation, as well as more debt.

It's OK to borrow in order to see us through difficult times, but we can't have debt rising inexorably during normal times. We learnt a hard lesson in the autumn of 2022 when Liz Truss and Kwasi Kwarteng, briefly prime minister and chancellor respectively, announced some £45 billion of tax cuts, without even allowing the independent Office for Budget Responsibility to provide a forecast of their fiscal consequences, let alone providing any sense of how they might be paid for. Had those cuts been implemented, public debt would have been put on an unsustainable path. Because it looked like billions were about to be pumped into an economy in which inflation was high, the labour market tight, and interest rates rising, the value of the pound fell, the cost of borrowing rose, and rose more quickly than almost ever before. We looked over the precipice. Another new chancellor, Jeremy Hunt, had to undo almost all the announced tax cuts within weeks of the ill-conceived 'mini Budget' in which they had been announced.

If there are two central messages of this book they are first, there are no simple solutions to the tough problems of public policy. And second, there are nearly always trade-offs and choices to be made. You can't just cut taxes and expect all to be fine, any more than you can just increase spending without both managing the spending carefully and increasing taxes to pay for it.

One of the truths that politicians are not keen to utter is that some things make us worse off. Covid will make us worse off in the long run. Of course it will. Energy prices going up will also make us worse off. Government is there to mitigate the pain, to spread it over time and to protect the poorest. It can't magic away global changes and crises that make us poorer. The Office for Budget Responsibility made that all too clear in November 2022 when it predicted that household incomes would fall further over two years than they had ever done in the more than seventy years since comparable statistics have been published.

Although it's not the subject of this book, government can do a lot to make us better off in the long run. It can design taxes so as to minimise their economic cost. It can invest in infrastructure and education. It can put appropriate laws and regulations in place. It can get trade and competition policy right. It can reform planning laws to get more houses built where they are needed.

It *can* make a difference. Government's dirty secret is that it chooses not to. It often chooses not to do the right thing because it is scared of us voters. Tax reform, planning reform, change, are not always popular. Government needs to be brave, but so do we.

The changing state

The size of the state, whether measured by the tax that governments raise, or the spending they do, changed remarkably little
in the seventy years up to 2020. Spending fluctuated between 35
and 40 per cent of national income, tax between 30 and 35 per
cent.[7] That has now changed. Spending is settling at getting on
for 45 per cent of national income. The tax take is heading for its
highest ever level.

In the UK we are around average in the developed world in
terms of the size of our state. We tax and spend rather less than
most of our Western European neighbours but rather more
than the US, Canada and other non-European members of the
Organisation for Economic Co-operation and Development
(OECD), sometimes called the club of rich nations. There is nothing in economics which says we can't have a bigger state. France,
Germany, Sweden and the Netherlands are all successful economies which raise a lot more in tax than we do, and spend a lot
more as well. What we can't have are American levels of tax and
European levels of public spending.

The size of the state may not have altered much, but its shape has
changed dramatically. For one thing, government no longer owns
the car manufacturers, airlines, coal mines, steelworks and power
stations which were such a large part of its business in the 1950s,
'60s and '70s. Nor does the public sector any longer build houses:
house building by local authorities peaked at over 250,000 in 1953.
In 1967, the year of my birth, it hit 200,000 again. It reached a nadir
of just 130 completed dwellings in 2004 before creeping back up
to 4,000 in 2018.[8] Housing associations, not formally part of the
public sector in any case, have taken up only a small fraction of the
slack, never reaching even 40,000 completions in a year.

The big story, though, is of the ever-expanding welfare state. Spending on social security – pensions and working age benefits together – doubled from 5 to 10 per cent of national income between the mid-1950s and the present. One pound in every ten created in the UK economy is taken from us and given straight back to us as cash. At any one moment, the payers and the payees tend to be different people. But over a lifecycle a lot is recycled. Those of us currently on the tax side of this equation will eventually be recipients of state pensions.

Meanwhile health spending has risen from less than 3 per cent of national income to around 8 per cent. In 1955 it accounted for less than £8 in every £100 spent by government. Today it is nearly £20 in every £100. Over the same period defence spending has fallen from more than 20 per cent of the total to less than 5 per cent.

Over recent years Labour and Conservative governments have been united on one thing – spending on the NHS trumps everything else. It rose as a fraction of the total whilst the total was rising fast in the 2000s. It continued to rise as the total was squeezed in the 2010s. It is rising again in the 2020s.

As we will see in the following chapters, recent years have seen working age welfare benefits shrink as pensions have risen. Education has not shared in the growth enjoyed by other parts of the welfare state, especially health. Local government has gradually been stripped of its powers and has increasingly become a vehicle for delivering social care and not much else. The devolved governments in Edinburgh, Cardiff and Belfast, on the other hand, have gained control over spending, and some taxes.

Meanwhile, the tax system as a whole remains largely dependent on income tax, National Insurance and VAT, as it has been for decades. It is – we are – increasingly dependent on the taxes paid by the very rich. It also remains complex, inefficient and inequitable, treating similar forms of income and spending very differently. It helps mess up our housing market, it doesn't play the role it should in meeting climate targets, and it penalises employees relative to rentiers. It needs reform.

Choices have been made, ones that are often not transparent to us, the voters. And the choices are only going to get tougher. 2023 saw arguably the biggest fiscal announcement of my lifetime, outside of crises at least. You might not even have noticed it. It was the announcement of an NHS workforce plan. Much needed, only 75 years too late, but better late than never. As we'll see in Chapter 5 though, it will, if implemented, *by itself* raise public spending by about 2 per cent of national income – £50 billion or so in today's terms – by the mid-2030s. That's how much taxes will have to rise, or other spending cut, to pay for it. £50 billion is, coincidentally, also the scale of the income tax increase that is currently being visited upon us. Again, you might not have noticed it. That will be the additional revenue raised as a consequence of freezing in cash terms for six years the personal allowance – the point at which income tax starts to be paid – and the higher rate threshold at which the 40 per cent rate of income tax kicks in.

Neither that tax rise nor the increase in the rate of corporation tax from 19 per cent to 25 per cent is being implemented because government enjoys raising taxes. We are paying for the costs of high debt, poor growth, and a welfare state which is struggling to deliver what we citizens want.

To repeat the refrain: there are no easy solutions to the problems we face. Tax cuts do not pay for themselves. Debt cannot rise forever. Spending implies taxing. Economic constraints are real. Grown up and effective government requires an acknowledgment and understanding of these facts. Countries which have tried to deny them have always paid a heavy cost.

As for spending, the challenges – both immediate and over the longer term – are going to be huge. A decade of austerity has left many public services struggling. The 2010s really were completely unique in history for the scale of spending cuts. The justice system, the prison system and the social care system – three public services which are hidden from most of us most of the time – suffered the most. Local government spending was slashed by a fifth. School spending per pupil fell. Health spending rose, but at its slowest rate since the formation of the NHS. Teachers and nurses saw their wages fall in inflation-adjusted terms. Benefits for the unemployed and for low earners were cut, for some dramatically.

So even before Ukraine, before inflation, before Covid, the pressure for more public spending was becoming unstoppable. There is going to be no getting away from ever-increasing pressures on the state. More money will be needed to deal with climate change. The need to keep feeding the NHS with more cash is not going to disappear. If there is one long-term consequence of Covid which worries me beyond anything else, it is the need to mitigate the loss of education suffered by a generation of children, especially the poorest. Surely, we will end up spending more there too. More pensioners will mean more spending on pensions, and on social care. And we are inventing new legs to the welfare state. In 2023 a new right to free childcare for all children of working parents from nine months old was announced. That'll cost another £5 billion a year or so. The list, it seems, is endless.

Yet where is the debate about how to raise the tax and how best to spend the money? We have to make choices. If we want better public services we will have to raise more in tax. If we want to cut tax we have to be honest about which parts of the welfare state we are happy to spend less on. There are no short cuts, no easy answers. Those who claim there are, are taking us for fools. Hard choices are everywhere, and it's the failure of our leaders, our failure, to face up to them which is largely responsible for landing us in some of the problems that now beset us – everything from feeble economic growth to burgeoning NHS waiting lists, from the squeeze on the living standards and prospects of the young, to the disastrous social care system facing the elderly.

Hence this book. I'm hoping to at least shine a light on some of the facts, the trade-offs and the tough choices that are the inevitable territory of the politician and the policymaker. Especially those which they want to keep us in the dark about.

Lest you think understanding doesn't matter all that much, just remember the two great referendums of our generation, on leaving the EU and on Scottish independence. Arguments about public spending were at the centre of both. I don't need to be anti-Brexit to say that the claim that membership of the EU cost us £350 million a week was a lie. It was a straightforward lie, cleverly used. Nor am I making a statement against Scottish independence if I point out that billions flow from the rest of the UK to support Scottish public services, billions that would be lost to the Scots if they did become independent.

There are far more important considerations than these which should and do determine people's votes, yet the fact that these simple truths were contested is evidence enough that they matter. What matters even more is the availability and quality of the public services we all consume and the fairness and efficiency of the taxes we all pay.

Let us therefore brace ourselves ...

I hope this sets the scene for this book. It is a forensic look at some of Britain's annual budget, which has now burst through the £1 trillion a year mark. Where does the money go to? Who does it come from? Where did it emerge from in the first place? Along the way it will also look at some of the things that matter to the size and shape of the state – the distribution of income and wealth, our changing demography, our economic performance.

For we can understand nothing of current and future decisions without understanding what has happened to incomes, wealth and inequalities; more than a decade of stalled productivity, and the worst decade for earnings growth since the onset of the industrial revolution; the collapse in homeownership among those in their twenties and thirties; the growing importance of wealth and inheritance; the sixty thousand individuals whose incomes of over £650,000 put them in the top 0.1 per cent; the huge inequalities in health and education. All these are both products and determinants of government action.

Having read this, I hope you, the reader, will end up understanding just a little more about the coming debate and the big choices we will have to make. Choices over the size and scope of the state, the overall levels of taxation and spending; choices over which taxes we get the money from, and which parts of spending we prioritise; and, just as important, choices over exactly how we structure those taxes and deliver and manage that spending. Few things are more important to our wellbeing and to shaping the kind of society in which we wish to live.

1

Getting Our Hands on the Money

National Accounts taxes in 2023/24: £915 billion, of which . . .
Income tax: £264 billion
National Insurance contributions: £172 billion
VAT: £162 billion[1]

Big taxes

It is hard to know quite what to make of William Pitt the Younger, more than two centuries after his death. He was clever – and very young. Not only was he our youngest prime minister, but when he got the keys to Downing Street, at the age of only twenty-four, he had already turned the honour down twice before and had already lived at Number Ten as chancellor of the Exchequer. He would go on to become our second-longest-serving prime minister.

He was also capable of drinking prodigious quantities of port. You might well have caught him throwing up behind the Speaker's Chair. Or giving the clerk a headache with his wine-laced breath. Or 'oscillating' all the way back to his carriage.

He died in office at the age of just forty-six, having run the country at one of its most difficult periods – under 'mad' king George III and through most of the French Revolutionary and Napoleonic wars. 'A sight to make surrounding nations stare, A kingdom trusted to a schoolboy's care,' read the satire The Rolliad.[2] The cartoonist Gillray depicted Pitt's political opponent, Charles James Fox, as a schoolmaster whipping a student Pitt.

Our interest in Pitt is that it was he who first introduced income tax in the UK. He didn't invent it – that place has to go to the Roman republic, or the Xin dynasty in ancient China. In England it had precursors of sorts including Henry II's 'Saladin Tithe' of 1188, eventually used to help fund the Third Crusade under Richard the Lionheart.

Pitt became an MP at twenty-one, immediately before the battle of Yorktown in 1781 made it clear that the American Revolution had succeeded and the British had lost. By then, the country's finances were in a desperate state. Out of annual tax revenues of about £13 million, £8 million went on just the interest on the national debt of £234 million. Most of the money came from peculiarities like a gin tax. The authorities aimed to avoid direct assessment of people's income – a damned unEnglish idea, as they used to say.

Pitt, influenced by Adam Smith, whose Inquiry into the Nature and Causes of the Wealth of Nations had been published just a few years earlier, planned to sort out the financial muddle with new taxes which fell principally on the well-off. These included new 'assessed taxes' on male and female servants, on horses, on carriages (varying according to whether four-wheeled or two-wheeled) and on houses. He managed to invent taxes on everything from gaming licences to dogs and hair powder, and came up in 1797 with the brilliant idea of the 'triple assessment', which assessed taxpayers on the basis of what they had paid the previous year and tripling it – actually, more than tripling it. Let's not remind the Treasury about that one ...

But then came the crisis: war with France. Suddenly the army and the navy both needed major expenditure, necessitating unprecedented borrowing and increased taxation. And so it was that in the Budget of 1798 income tax was introduced, coming into effect the following year. All annual incomes over £200 were to be taxed at 10 per cent. Those earning between £60 and £200 were taxed at a graduated rate from just under 1 per cent upwards. No one was taxed on incomes below £60, which, given that an ordinary soldier's annual income was about £14, was itself quite a hefty sum. This was a very different tax threshold from the £12,570 we have today, a threshold that ensures that everyone in full time work pays income tax.

At first, the tax was highly unpopular and was widely evaded, particularly among merchants and manufacturers. It only raised 60 per cent of what Pitt had hoped. It was thought to be too intrusive into people's private financial circumstances. But in time, it came to be seen as a patriotic duty for winning the war against Napoleon.

When a lasting peace was finally achieved after Waterloo, income tax was abolished – and there was even a symbolic public burning of the government records relating to the tax. It was brought back by Robert Peel in 1842 and despite repeated promises to abolish it by both Tories and Whigs, and by both Disraeli and Gladstone, it has remained with us ever since. At least nowadays we don't have to sit through the sort of five-hour-long Budget speech which Gladstone, as chancellor, delivered in 1853 in which he outlined his seven-year plan to do away with income tax. The Crimean War put paid to that.

Pitt died in 1806, a few months after his great contemporary, Horatio Nelson. He may have managed the nation's finances through crises even worse than those we face today, but he was famous for handling his own personal finances rather badly. In fact, he left behind a huge personal debt of £40,000 – many millions in today's terms. A grateful government paid it, and gave him a state funeral to boot.

Times have changed rather since the days of Pitt, or indeed of Gladstone. Even following austerity, Covid, and the cost-of-living crisis, we don't hear much about a patriotic duty to pay our taxes to support the welfare state. The Victorians, though, remained allergic to high levels of taxation, and it took the best part of the nineteenth century to pay down the huge debts accumulated during the Napoleonic wars. Even by the turn of the twentieth century, the UK government took less than a tenth of national income in taxes. That had jumped to a fifth by 1920 in the aftermath of the First World War, and to a third by the time the Second World War came to end.[3] The tax burden today is not so much higher than that, though heading now for over 37 per cent of national income – the highest we have borne since the late 1940s. That's around the OECD average, and considerably less than in many Western European countries including France and Germany.

Just as the Napoleonic and Crimean wars played a crucial role in the birth of income tax, and the First and Second World Wars saw the tax burden ratchet upwards, it looks like the recent crises – Covid and the energy price shock – will see another upward ratchet. Instability in tax policy is such that one cannot be sure quite what will happen but, as of autumn 2023, corporation tax is rising to take an historically unprecedented share of national income, while a six-year freeze to the income tax personal allowance – the point at which you start to pay income tax – and other thresholds should end up raising a cool £50 billion a year. Both constitute direct reversals of years of Conservative policy which saw corporation tax rates fall and the income tax allowance rise. These are but two of the innumerable examples of a complete lack of any principle or strategy behind our tax policy.

When the taxperson takes more than a third of what we earn, we can be sure that the *way* they take it matters. It matters for social inequality and for economic efficiency. It affects who works and how they work, how companies are organised, the price of houses and the cost of renting, whether saving in a pension is worthwhile. Even whether I buy Jaffa Cakes or chocolate digestives to eat with my tea. It affects whether our children will be able to afford a home.

Where the money comes from these days

The chancellor may stand up every year on Budget day and assure us he (it has so far always been a he) is making big and important changes to the tax system. But the truth is the system as a whole has proved remarkably hard to shift. There are so many ways in which it could be improved, yet in so many ways, not much changes. Its complexity certainly grows. The tax code runs to millions of words. But the system we have today is a still recognisably similar to the one that I first studied in the 1980s.

Now, as then, we get most (nearly two thirds) of our revenue from just three taxes – income tax, VAT and National Insurance contributions. There are dozens of other taxes, some of which we will look at in the next chapter, but if you want serious money, you have to look to the serious taxes. You might well want to change them for other reasons, but faffing around with taxes on tobacco or inheritances or capital gains will never raise enough money to make a real difference to the size or scope of the state.

Many of these sources of revenue have another purpose, some of them at least as important as the raising of money. For tobacco taxes, that's obvious. For income tax, it is to smooth out and redistribute some of the huge economic inequalities in our society. Some of them, like National Insurance, once had a clearer role than they do now. But let's focus on their role as revenue raisers, because in the end that is the main reason for having taxes: to pay for all the things we're looking at in the rest of this book.

In this chapter we'll look at the big three – income tax, NICs and VAT. Chapter 2 will look at some of the rest.

Income tax

Let's start with income tax. It accounts for more than a quarter of the total tax take. It is on a gradual upward trajectory. By the middle of this decade around 10 per cent of national income will be paid in income tax.

The basics of income tax are relatively simple. You've got a personal allowance of £12,570 (as of 2023) on which no income tax is payable. That is enough to make sure that some 40 per cent of adults don't pay income tax at all in any given year: they might be students, pensioners, part timers, unemployed, or looking after children. They might not be poor – their spouse might have a high income or, in the case of students, they can expect a higher

income later on in life. Even so, it's a statistic worth holding on
to when thinking about the distribution of incomes in the UK.
Around four in ten adults – more than 20 million of us, or the
population of three Londons – have personal incomes of less than
£12,570 a year.

If you are one of the 32 million or so who do pay income tax,
then it's charged at 20 per cent on the next £37,770. For the roughly
six million of us with incomes over £50,270 we pay at 40 per cent
on income above that level. The basic rate of income tax has been
falling for decades – it was 33 per cent in 1979.

The point at which the higher rate kicks in has also been coming
down. Being a higher rate taxpayer used to be quite unusual. By
the mid-2020s, nearly eight million people, about a quarter of all
income taxpayers, are likely to be paying 40 per cent tax.

There will also be nearly two million paying at either 60 per
cent or 45 per cent. The 45p tax rate is quite well known. It's the
rate payable on the highest incomes, over £125,140 as of 2023,
having been payable only on incomes over £150,000 for more than
a decade before that. Why that very specific number £125,140?
Because that's where the 60 per cent rate runs out.

Mad but true: your tax rate rises from 40 to 60 per cent and
then falls back to 45 per cent as your income rises from just under
£100,000 to just over £125,000. Of course, that's not how the 60
per cent rate is described. It's described as the tapering away of the
personal allowance: a policy put in place back in 2009 by the then
chancellor, Alistair Darling.

If you're married, and you pay tax at the basic rate and your
spouse doesn't pay income tax, then you're entitled to an extra tax-
free allowance of £1,250. Which you lose as soon as your income
hits the higher rate threshold of £50,270. That means you can get a
pay rise and become worse off. If your income goes up by a pound
and tips you over the £50,270 mark, you lose the whole of that
allowance immediately. This is, of course, not sensible.

If you have children, then your child benefit gets taxed away once your income rises over £50,000. If you have three children this will mean an effective tax rate of 68 per cent on incomes between £50,000 and £60,000.

Income tax is a tax on income. But what is income? That's a question that economists, and tax lawyers, have spent a lot of time debating. If I get paid in gold rather than cash, that should definitely count as income. And so it should count if part of my remuneration comes in the form of a company car. If my wealth rises because the value of something I own – maybe my own company, maybe a painting – rises, shouldn't that count as income too? You can see the difficulties already. We don't count capital gains or gifts or inheritances like other income for tax purposes. That naturally provides opportunities for 'tax planning'.

And that's before we worry about *whose* income it is. Until 1991, we used to add the incomes of husbands and wives together and tax the total. Now we largely treat them entirely separately for tax purposes, though quite definitely not separately for the purposes of determining eligibility for welfare benefits. Joint taxation was problematic not just because it afforded no privacy within marriage, but because it could disincentivise the second earner – usually the wife – from working. She might have had to pay a high rate of tax on the first pound earned because her husband was a high earner.

The current system has its own problems. It means that a couple where both earn £40,000 pay a lot less tax than a couple where one earns £80,000 and the other nothing. Though you might think that appropriate: a two-earner couple where both are working full time on £40,000 will be worse off in terms of free time than a single-earner couple with gross earnings of £80,000. If one spouse sets up a company and pays half the dividends to her husband that can mean a lot less tax than if she just paid them to herself.

The really big issue, though, which has exercised economists for decades, if not centuries, is what to do about savings. If I'm putting money away in a pension, say, should the money I save be counted as income today? I'm not spending it now, I'll spend it later when I draw the pension. If you count it as income today *and* when I withdraw it, then that really is a form of double taxation.

Subject to limits, you can put money in a pension today and not pay any income tax until you withdraw it. So, your taxable income today is your total income *less* your pension contributions. It works the other way around with Individual Savings Accounts (ISAs). You put money in today after you've paid tax, but then pay no tax, including on any interest or capital gains, when you withdraw it. That's sort of also how we tax owner-occupied housing. Buy the house out of taxed income, but pay nothing when you sell it, even if you've made a whopping capital gain.

Because the ISA/housing route allows people to make huge gains untaxed, the pension tax route is the better one: don't tax savings when they're saved, tax them when they're withdrawn and used. That doesn't penalise savings, but it does make sure that you get taxed appropriately if you happen to do very well.

Inevitably things are more complicated than that simple picture suggests. Pensions are more tax privileged than that. You pay no National Insurance contributions either when the money goes in or when it comes out if the pension contribution comes from your employer. (Surprisingly enough most pension contributions come from the employer.) You can also take a lump sum of a quarter of the accumulated pot completely free of tax up to a maximum of just over £250,000. That we offer the most generously pensioned such an enormous tax-free bonus is a scandal. Not as much of a scandal as the way pensions are treated for inheritance purposes. Don't much need your pension? Use it as a vehicle for the avoidance of inheritance tax instead.

Of course, the government over the last decade has done

exactly the wrong thing. Instead of limiting these egregious reliefs, they have limited the amount you can save in a pension at all. Though this is another area of inconsistency over time. The annual allowance was reduced from over a quarter of a million pounds to £40,000, then raised to £60,000 but tapered away for high earners. The lifetime allowance was cut to £1 million, then in another policy reversal, abolished in 2023. If you want to limit pension savings this is again exactly the wrong policy. It might be reasonable to limit the amount benefiting from tax relief over a lifetime, but why on earth would you want to limit how much people save in any one year? And if any area of tax policy needs to be consistent then surely it is this. Decisions over pensions are long term and need to be taken with some idea as to what the tax system will be like.

Never mind. The principle of saving free of tax and then paying tax at the end is right. Eminent economists, including Nobel laureate James Meade, who wrote a huge report for the IFS back in the 1970s, and even more persuasively John Kay and Mervyn King (respectively my predecessor-but-three at the IFS and a future governor of the Bank of England) have been making that case for years. Unfortunately, the tax system has been going in the other direction. Chancellors tend to be greedy. Why wait for the tax revenue until people withdraw their pensions or savings when you can have it now? You can put far less into a pension than used to be the case, but far more into an ISA.

Before we move on to the other two tax behemoths – NICs and VAT – a word about the role of income tax in redistribution. Within the tax system as a whole, income tax does the heavy lifting when it comes to reducing inequality. The richest pay at a marginal rate of 45 per cent. More than a third of adults pay no income tax at all. We are now in the remarkable position whereby the top 1 per cent of income taxpayers contribute 30 per cent of all income tax. That top 1 per cent, those with incomes over around £190,000, tend to be male, middle aged, and living in and around London.[4]

The top 5 per cent pay half of income tax, and the top half pay 90 per cent of it. Which means that the bottom half pays just 10 per cent. Given how many don't pay income tax at all that means that 90 per cent of income tax is paid by just a third of the population. The rest, a little more than two thirds, pay just 10 per cent between them.

That is partly a result of the structure of the income tax system, but mainly a function of the UK's very high level of income inequality. The rich pay such a large share of income tax because they receive such a large share of total income. The top 10 per cent of adults receive just over 40 per cent of all fiscal income – that is income which counts for tax purposes. That's around the same amount that flows to the bottom 80 per cent. The top 1 per cent, meanwhile, receive 15 per cent of all fiscal income; the same share that flows to the bottom 55 per cent. The top 0.1 per cent (a group of just over 50,000 people with incomes in excess of around £650,000) meanwhile, receive 6 per cent of total fiscal income – sixty times greater than their share of the population.

Right in the stratosphere of the income distribution, the super-rich look quite different to the rest of us, not just in how much income they have, but in where they get it from. Most of us ordinary mortals get most of our income in the form of wages (or pensions, which we can think of as deferred wages). Not so the rich. Here we're talking not about the top 1 per cent. They tend to be like the rest of us: wage slaves, but with higher wages (over £190,000 or so). Once you get to the top 0.1 per cent, though, those with over around £650,000, business income starts to play a bigger role, accounting for more than a third of their income. Business income can include the income individual owners of a business receive, or the income that, say, equity partners in law firms get to enjoy, or income from stocks and shares. Either way:

guess what? This sort of income is taxed much less harshly than normal earnings.

This all matters far more than it used to, because inequality is much greater and the rich are much richer. Of course, inequality has always existed, but it really took off in the 1980s. The decades after the last war saw the differences between the top and the bottom gradually fall. The 1980s were different. The closure of much old industry, technological change, creeping globalisation, the neutering of the trades unions, and the deregulation of finance – the famous big bang in the City of London – all these contributed to a massive increase in inequality of pre-tax incomes. At the same time, cuts to benefits and taxes added to the growth in inequality of post-tax incomes.

On the whole inequality hasn't changed much since then. Since 1990, the poor have got no poorer relative to the middling well off. They, in turn, have fallen no further behind the really pretty well off. The top 1 per cent, on the other hand, continued to pull away right up to the time of the financial crash. After that they fell back a bit, but have recovered most of the ground since. Post Covid, for the first time in more than a decade, the richest are pulling away once more, with financial services once again leading the way.[5] The dominance of our financial sector is one reason that inequality in the UK is higher than in most comparable countries.

'It took watching his son being paid 225 grand at the age of twenty-seven, after two years on the job, to shake [my father's] faith in money,' wrote Michael Lewis about his time on Wall Street in the late 1980s.[6] Meanwhile, our reliance on the very richest has been growing over time. Forty years ago the top 1 per cent paid only about a tenth of total income tax. It was a fifth twenty years ago, a quarter a decade ago and about 30 per cent today. The big increases up to 2010 were down to big increases in income. Since 2010, the rich haven't actually got richer, but the income tax system has become more progressive.

The point at which the top 45 per cent rate kicks in was stuck at £150,000 for more than a decade before being cut to just over £125,000 in 2023. The numbers paying it more than doubled to nearly half a million even before the threshold was cut.[7] Pension tax relief for the highest earners has also been slashed.

Could we get more from top earners? George Osborne cut the rate on those with incomes over £150,000 from 50 per cent to 45 per cent in 2013, arguing that the cost of doing so would be negligible because people respond to rates as high as 50 per cent by avoiding tax. Robert Chote, then head of the Office for Budget Responsibility fiscal watchdog said we were 'strolling across the summit of the Laffer curve', a reference to the famous curve drawn by American economist Art Laffer, showing that at some point the tax rate can get so high that you could raise more revenue by cutting the rate.[8]

Obviously if you tax at 100 per cent nobody is going to bother earning or declaring any income because they get no benefit from doing so. At some point tax rates can get so high that cutting the rate really will bring in more tax revenue. This is particularly plausible when looking at those super rich, who take income in dividends, and can alter the form and timing of the income they receive. That happened on a huge scale when the 50 per cent rate was introduced.

The evidence on the revenue maximising top rate of income tax is inconclusive. For what it's worth my take on it is that one could modestly increase revenues by returning to a top rate of 50 per cent, but by a small number of billons at best. You might well want to do this to reduce inequality. It won't make a big difference to tax revenues. And it genuinely could reduce revenue.

A more general word of caution. Great though it is to know that someone else – the top 1 per cent – is picking up more of the bill for public spending, it does make us very dependent on them and their behaviour. What if they all head off to other countries and take their tax payments with them? Once upon a time I would have dismissed that as an absurd notion, but not so much nowadays. In recent ground-breaking work, my colleague Arun Advani has, with co-authors, used data from the HMRC to show that a quarter of those in the top 1 per cent of income taxpayers were actually born abroad, rising to a third if you look right into the stratospheric parts of the income distribution.[9] They *chose* to live here, in other words. They can choose not to. In large part, this again reflects the importance of the financial services sector in the UK and the international nature of its workforce. Those jobs, and those people, really could move abroad if we make the UK less attractive. By, for example, leaving the European Union.

National Insurance contributions

Everyone is familiar with income tax. But we have another tax on income (well, earnings actually), which is also huge: National Insurance contributions. These are, in 2023, paid by employers and by employees on earnings above £175 a week (employers) or £242 a week (employees).

In the weird world of NICs, it is weekly earnings that matter (if you're paid weekly, monthly earnings if you're paid monthly), not annual ones. As of late 2023 employers pay at 13.8 per cent and employees at 12 per cent, falling in the latter case to 2 per cent on earnings above £967 a week. The self-employed pay a lot less than that – they pay at 9 per cent with no employer contribution.

Your tax alarm bells should be ringing at this point. If there's a lot less tax on the earnings of one group – the self-employed – than on another – employees – you might expect rather a lot of effort to go into tax avoidance. Have you noticed how keen Uber, for example, were to make sure that their drivers counted as self-employed? Well, there's one of the reasons. An awful lot less tax for Uber to pay if that's how they are defined. (See the next chapter for how HMRC has been pursuing BBC presenters like Gary Lineker for turning themselves into companies. Since NICs are not payable at all on anything not defined as earnings, it makes a lot of sense to define your income as something other than pay.)

A lot of self-employed people get rather upset when I suggest that they should pay the same taxes, including NI, as employees. They no longer get anything less out of public services or the welfare and pension system. But, they argue, they don't have the employment protection, paid holiday, sick pay, and other benefits enjoyed by employees. This is true. But it is not relevant to the design of the tax system.

Employment rights are not a benefit given by the government to employees, they are not like state benefit entitlements. They are a benefit that the government requires employers to give to their employees. Employment rights make employment more attractive (relative to self-employment) to the worker. But they simultaneously make it less attractive for employers to choose employees over the self-employed. Employment rights do not favour employment over self-employment overall – they redistribute from employers to employees. Overall, they do not act to skew the labour market in favour of employment relative to self-employment.

In contrast, the National Insurance system does skew the labour market in favour of getting work done through self-employment. That is, it leads to more work happening through self-employment than would otherwise be the case. So, the result of preferential headline tax rates for the self-employed is to bias the labour market in favour of self-employment, not to level the playing field between employment and self-employment.

In an article entitled The First Thing We Do, Let's Tax All the Lawyers, (tax lawyer) Dan Neidle makes the point thus:

- A City law firm has £100m of profits to share between 100 partners. The tax consequence: each partner has gross income of £1m on which they pay £435k income tax, plus £35k national insurance. So the lucky partners take home £530k, and lucky HMRC collects £47m.
- A bank has £100 million of profits to share between 100 traders. The tax consequence: the bank pays employer's 13.8% national insurance of £13.8m. Each banker has a gross income of £862k, on which they pay £373k income tax and £24k national insurance. So the poor bankers take home £465k, and even more lucky HMRC collects £53.5m.[10]

The lawyers have an overall effective tax rate of 47 per cent; the bankers' rate is 53.5 per cent. That is an odd and irrational result.

The reason for the difference is that the partners in the law firm are just that, partners, not employees. We pay more tax so that millionaire partners in law firms can pay less.

And yet it is to NICs that both Gordon Brown in 2002 and Boris Johnson in 2021 turned when they wanted more money for the NHS (though Johnson's proposed increase was never actually implemented in the end). It is absolutely clear that raising the same amount of money by increasing income tax would have been both fairer and simpler. It would have spread the burden wider, and affected those with incomes from all sources, not just the workers. As rates of income tax have fallen, so NIC rates have risen, increasing the wedge between the taxation of earned and unearned income, benefiting pensioners and rentiers at the expense of workers.

This all stems from relatively ancient history. NICs were supposed to be something close to genuine insurance payments to cover the unemployment benefits, pensions and sickness benefits put in place in the 1940s following the Beveridge report (on which more in Chapter 3). They were originally paid at a flat rate in return for earning the right to receive a flat-rate benefit. Gradually they became earnings related. The Upper Earnings Limit, the point at which the rate for employees falls to 2 per cent, is a vestigial reminder of that old flat-rate contribution system.

The link between what you pay in NICs and what you are entitled to in benefits is now completely severed. Not only are there no earnings-related elements in the benefit system, there are almost no benefits for which your record of actually paying NICs matters. So long as you have lived in the UK for long enough it is now very hard to avoid building up rights to a full state pension (see Chapter 4). Whatever their origin, they are now simply another tax on earnings. They don't pay for pensions, the NHS or anything else that people seem to think they pay for, any more than any other tax does.

Life would be much simpler, fairer and better if we could just recognise this and merge the systems to make sure that all income, whether earned or not, was taxed at the same rate. That would mean a basic rate of tax of over 40 per cent including the employer element of NICs. And it is important to consider the employer element. In the end it is largely incident upon the employee: take home pay is reduced by employer NI just as surely as it is reduced by employee NI. You see the problem. That's how much our earnings are taxed – employer NI, plus employee NI, plus income tax. It doesn't sound anything like so bad to have a basic rate of income tax of 20 per cent, does it, even if we know there is National Insurance to pay on top?

Value Added Tax

Tax economists and finance ministers love VAT. Here's what the IFS said about it when we launched the Mirrlees Review back in 2011:

Since its introduction in France in 1954, it has proved an exceptionally successful form of taxation and has been adopted by many countries worldwide, including all OECD countries other than the USA ... unquestionably the most successful fiscal innovation of the last half-century ... perhaps the most economically efficient way in which countries can raise significant tax revenues.[11]

So, something else to lay at the door of the French. Tax accountants may love VAT for other reasons – mainly perhaps because it gives them plenty of work. Finance directors, including mine at the IFS, are less keen. It may be a great idea in principle, but it is fiendishly complex in practice.

It is a great idea in principle for two reasons. First, it taxes spending as it happens, which gets around that problem of how you deal with savings. It's rather like that way of taxing pensions. If we charged VAT on all spending it would be just like a proportional income tax with a tax relief for anything not spent – or saved, in other words.

Secondly, the way it works should make it fairly robust. As its name suggests, it is a tax on the value added at each stage in the production process; bits of it are paid as goods move up the value chain. So even if one firm in the chain tries to evade it, most of it should still get paid. By contrast, a much simpler sounding tax like a 'purchase tax' which just imposes tax when a good is sold to the consumer, is much more open to abuse. That's why virtually every country in the world, with the notable exception of the USA, has migrated to a VAT in recent decades.

So far so good. Of course, it isn't quite so straightforward in practice. In part that's because VAT is not charged on everything at its normal full rate of 20 per cent. Most food, children's clothes, and public transport, for example, is zero rated for VAT purposes. VAT is charged at just 5 per cent, not the full 20 per cent, on domestic gas and electricity use. That saves us, and costs the government, tens of billions relative to a world in which we taxed all spending, rather as we – broadly speaking – tax all income. It also creates rather a lot of complexity, and not a little weirdness. If you tax some things and not others you create boundaries and someone has to decide what is at either side of those boundaries. Let me illustrate with perhaps my favourite thing in all of tax literature: the fur skin flow chart. This is genuinely published by HMRC to 'help' people work out what VAT they have to pay on items of clothing which contain some fur or animal skin.[12]

After asking you to determine whether the item in question is actually clothing – not straightforward in itself – it goes through a series of questions aimed at deciding whether VAT is payable. This depends on an astonishing range of specifics about the nature of the fur or skin used in the item, how much of it is covered in fur/skin and the nature of the item of clothing.

For most of the way through, there is a kind of logic about it. If the cost of the fur to the manufacturer is 'greater than the cost of the other components' (question 6), then it is clearly luxury and you probably should be paying VAT on it. Unless, that is, the fur comes 'from rabbit, woolled lamb or sheep' (question 8), in which case it is probably just for keeping warm. So, probably no VAT. Question 9 asks 'Is the fur skin from bovine cattle (including buffalo), horses etc, pigs (including peccary), chamois, gazelle, deer or dogs? Yes – Go to Question 10. No – Go to Question 11.'

If that sounds a little surreal in a tax manual, then try question 12. Here we end up considering clothes which have fur/skin from goats or kids as opposed to any other animal and, at this point. 'Does the goat or kid originate from Mongolia, Yemen or Tibet?' If yes, VAT is payable, if not there is no VAT. What the tax authorities have against Yemeni goats I do not know.

My second favourite piece of VAT guidance also concerns animals. It is advice on what animals and animal food are subject to

VAT.[13] Honeybees are not VATable, bumble bees are. If you want a pet, get a rabbit. Most pets are subject to VAT. Because rabbits are edible, they are not.

The same goes for gingerbread men (or women) – not in this case whether they originate in Mongolia, but whether they have chocolate buttons or belts. If the only chocolate they contain are chocolate eyes then there is no VAT, but any more chocolate decoration and the price goes up 20 per cent because VAT is applied. That's because chocolate-covered biscuits are subject to VAT, and plain biscuits aren't. But there's no VAT on cakes, chocolate covered or not. Which brings me to Jaffa Cakes.

The Jaffa Cakes dilemma came to a head in 1991 when McVitie took the Inland Revenue to a VAT tribunal to challenge the decision that Jaffa Cakes were to be considered glorified chocolate biscuits. (Chocolate covered biscuits are subject to VAT, chocolate covered cakes are not.) McVitie won. You can see why it was confusing. Where do you find Jaffa Cakes? The biscuit aisle. How do you eat them? With fingers – who eats Jaffa Cakes with a fork? On the other hand, McVitie's lawyers argued that they go hard if you leave them out, just as a cake does. Also, biscuits are hard and snap – whoever snapped a Jaffa Cake? This appears to have been the crucial factor. The tribunal decided in favour of McVitie. Jaffa Cakes really are cakes, which happen to be sold rather like biscuits. Similar contention has arisen over flapjacks and cereal bars.

As the tax lawyer Dan Neidle has written, 'any sufficiently detailed VAT rule is indistinguishable from satire'.[14]

'So it is that a group of VAT experts will spend a good part of their working week eating small food stuffs and discussing among themselves whether the texture is more that of a cake or a biscuit, or pulling out the bust of a tiny T-shirt to decide if it should qualify as children's clothing or is in fact designed for young women headed to Ayia Napa.' Such were the recollections of Damian

McBride, pugnacious former adviser to Gordon Brown, on his time working on VAT policy. In an attempt to avoid more exceptions, he reports civil service resistance to the idea of reducing the VAT rate on tampons. They apparently argued that to do so would be sexist. If applied to tampons for women, what about beard trimmers and Jewish circumcision knives?[15]

Don't blame the lawyers, it's the politicians – and ultimately us voters – who are to blame. A furore erupted after George Osborne's 2012 Budget, dubbed the 'omnishambles' Budget, after he proposed to impose VAT on food bought warm but designed to cool down, like sausage rolls and pasties.

VAT on hot takeaway food like fish and chips was introduced by Nigel Lawson in 1984, ending an exemption which had been written into the legislation at the start of the 1970s.

In a plaintive letter to *The Times* Hugh Mainprice, one of the team of lawyers who drafted the original VAT legislation, explained that they were instructed to zero rate 'the working man's fish and chips'.[16] The lawyers asked whether this zero rating should also apply to Dover sole and French-fried potatoes served in the grill room of the Savoy, to which the answer was no. Thus arose the zero rating for hot food served to be eaten off the premises.

'This gave rise to the question,' Mainprice went on, 'what were the premises from which the supply came. At a wedding reception was the supply made by the caterer from his premises or at the place where the wedding reception was being held?'

Happily, it's not just a British problem. As I write this, an Irish court has ruled that the bread served at Subway, the US-based sandwich chain, is not in fact bread. For VAT purposes, it contains too much sugar and is therefore confectionery. Making it liable for VAT in Ireland.

These are all slightly trivial examples of a much wider point. If you treat similar things differently for tax purposes – whether it be different foodstuffs, different clothes or different forms of income or employment – then you create complexity, inefficiency and unfairness. In the context of VAT, that leads most economists to a deeply unpopular conclusion. It should be charged at the full rate on everything we buy – food, books, children's clothes, household gas and electricity. The lot.

Obviously, if you moved from where we are to that system you would make a whole lot of people a lot worse off. And because food and household fuel make up an especially large part of the spending of poorer people, you would have a particularly big impact on the poor. But in practice you could raise so much money you could easily more than compensate the poor on average by cutting other taxes and raising benefits. Don't forget that while poorer people spend a larger *fraction* of their budgets on these currently zero-rated goods, it's the rich who spend more in total. In cash terms, VAT zero rating is a bigger benefit to the rich than to the poor. Especially if they happen to like Jaffa Cakes.

The obvious objection is that you couldn't compensate everyone who is poor. If there are people on low incomes spending especially large amounts of money on food or, more likely, heating, then some would be left worse off than they are today. But we should ask ourselves why we might want to subsidise them *at the expense of* others on low incomes with different spending patterns and preferences? One person's tax break is another person's bigger tax bill, after all. In the same way, the self-employed would be made worse off by aligning taxes between them and employees. But remember: the fact that they pay less now is effectively penalising employees.

This is a real political problem. Tax changes that create losers are not popular. The attempt to introduce VAT at the then full rate of 17.5 per cent on domestic energy consumption back in 1993, even with a comprehensive set of compensation for the poor, was one of the policies that precipitated the decline in popularity of John Major's Conservative government, eventually resulting in that party's worst defeat in more than fifty years. As the then chancellor

Norman Lamont later wrote, his Budget in spring 1993 was his best from an economic point of view, but helped his party lose the next general election.[17]

He did introduce VAT on energy at 8 per cent, subsequently reduced to 5 per cent by the Blair government. We continue to effectively subsidise consumption of gas, and indeed bags of coal, by charging VAT at that reduced 5 per cent rate rather than at the standard rate of 20 per cent. That's worth repeating. We are aiming at net zero greenhouse gas emissions, yet we are, through the tax system, subsidising the burning of fossil fuels.

As with so much else in the tax system, today's oddities – including the different treatments of cakes and biscuits – have very long histories, reaching back to the days before VAT. Its predecessor, Purchase Tax, was introduced in 1940, specifically on luxury goods, and with the stated aim of reducing wastage of raw materials during the Second World War. Many of the differences were maintained when Purchase Tax was superseded by VAT on our joining the Common Market in 1973. And that's why VAT in the UK applies to a narrower range of goods and services than VAT in just about any other advanced economy.

It is true that moving towards a flat-rate VAT would bear more heavily on the poor than on the rich. But the question then arises as to why you might want VAT, specifically, to be redistributive. The important thing about the tax and benefit system is that it be redistributive *overall*. We don't need every individual bit of it to take from the rich and give to the poor, so long as that's what the whole system does. And there are much better ways to redistribute than through the VAT system – via income tax and social security benefits for example. From an economic and indeed a fairness point of view, the case for a flat-rate VAT is unanswerable. The case against from a political point of view, as Norman Lamont will tell you, is probably unanswerable too. And, of course, the politics wins.

Raising a bit more

The arithmetic of taxation means that when chancellors want serious amounts of money they have to take aim at income tax, NICs or VAT. That's where two thirds of the revenue is. That's why 2021 saw announcements of an increase in NICs and, through freezing the personal allowance, an increase in income tax. The former may not have survived long, the latter has done.

In an inflationary environment, freezing tax thresholds can raise a lot of additional revenue in a politically easy way. More income gets dragged into the tax net, a higher fraction of everyone's income becomes subject to tax. When Chancellor Rishi Sunak announced in March 2021 that income tax allowances and thresholds would be frozen for four years he expected that this would increase revenues by £8 billion a year come 2025. Inflation is now turning out so much higher than expected, it looks like it will in fact raise nearly six times that.

Freezing the personal allowance drags more people into paying income tax, while freezing the higher rate threshold creates more higher rate taxpayers. There will soon be nearly eight million people paying at the higher, 40 per cent, rate of income tax, around three times as many as there were little more than twenty years ago. The number paying the additional 45p rate had already tripled between 2010 and 2022 as the £150,000 point at which it started to bite had never been indexed.

What no chancellor has done in half a century is raise the main rates of income tax. Indeed, they have been moved ever downwards. The one blip on that trend was the introduction of the 50 per cent – now 45 per cent – rate of income tax for the highest earners after the financial crisis. But as we've seen, that doesn't mean that income tax overall has been cut. It still raises as much as ever. The cuts in the headline rate have been more than made up for by the effects of fiscal drag, and the abolition and restriction of various reliefs and allowances. Meanwhile NI rates have risen. This is opaque, inefficient and inequitable.

Looking further back the three biggest tax increases between 2010 and 2020 were the increase in the rate of VAT from 17.5 to 20 per cent, an increase in the main rate of NICs, and the restriction of income tax relief on pensions. Gordon Brown's biggest tax rise was an increase in NICs. In 1991, the Conservatives fixed the poll tax fiasco by raising VAT. And during the 1980s, NICs were increased year after year. Don't just take my word for it, look at the last forty years. If you want serious revenue these are the only three taxes that can make a serious difference.

In the next chapter we'll go on to look at some of the dozens of other taxes which raise a lot less money than these three.

Before we do, though, one word of caution. The truth is, the bill for health and other public services in the years to come will fall on you and me. If, as I think is inevitable, we will in the next decade or so need to raise taxes by another couple of per cent of national income, raising £50 billion or so a year, on top of the increases already in the pipeline, then we are going to have to do what all other countries which have bigger tax burdens than we do. We will have to have higher taxes on the bulk of the population, on those with middling sorts of incomes. For it is not the case that those countries, in Western Europe (especially), which have higher taxes and spending than we do, raise those taxes from the rich or companies or 'someone else'. They raise them by having higher taxes on average earners.[18]

2

Getting Our Hands on Even More Money

National Accounts taxes in 2023/24: £910 billion, of which . . .
Onshore corporation tax: £82 billion
Capital gains tax: £18 billion
Inheritance tax: £7 billion
Council tax: £44 billion
Business rates: £30 billion
Property transaction taxes (mainly stamp duty): £13 billion
Alcohol duties: £13 billion
Fuel duties: £24 billion[1]

Little taxes

The notorious window tax was first imposed in England in 1696, by the government of William III, the asthmatic Dutch protestant who was the main beneficiary of the 'Glorious Revolution' which deposed James II in 1688. It was intended to be a progressive tax. Houses with a smaller number of windows, initially ten, were subject to a two-shilling house tax, but exempt from the window tax. Houses with more than ten windows faced extra taxes which increased in line with the number of windows they possessed. The idea was that the poorest, those who were more likely to live in houses with fewer windows, would therefore be taxed less.

This idea worked pretty well when it was applied to the rural poor, but it failed miserably to help the urban poor. As still happens all too frequently today, those designing the policy forgot to engage with the real world. Or, indeed, with the basic principles of economics. In the real world, even in the eighteenth century, poorer people often lived in huge, subdivided tenement blocks, and they were defined as one dwelling house under the terms of the tax. So their homes got heavily taxed.

That was supposed not to be a problem, because the tax had to be paid by the landlord, not the tenant. But as any economist will tell you, the person who ends up paying the cost of a tax is not necessarily the same as the person who remits the tax to the government – or upon whom it is 'formally incident', to use the jargon of the tax world. VAT is remitted by the retailer, but it is largely us, the consumers, who pay it. In the same way, landlords just added the tax to the rent. As any economist will also tell you, taxes can also incentivise changes in behaviour. In this case, landlords boarded up the windows, or built new tenements for rent without enough light or air.

The local health committee have 'witnessed the very evil effect and operation of the window tax,' said an 1845 report from Sunderland. 'And they do not hesitate to declare that it is their unanimous opinion that the blocking up of the numerous windows caused by the anxiety of their owners to escape the payment of the tax, has, in very many instances, greatly aggravated, and has even ... in some cases been the primary cause of much sickness and mortality.'[2]

So it was that, in 1766, when the tax was extended to include houses with seven or more windows, the number of houses in England and Wales with exactly seven windows reduced by nearly two-thirds. The reason some rooms and buildings are labelled as such in older, larger houses is because rooms that especially needed air, like dairies, cheese rooms and milk houses, were exempted as long as they were clearly labelled.

We've all probably heard of the window tax. Both history, and the present day, are littered with examples of many more taxes than the familiar. Pitt himself fell foul of the bricks tax introduced in 1784 to help pay for the army in North America. It outlasted the clock tax which survived only nine months (people stopped buying clocks and watches, throwing the clockmakers into crisis – though incidentally encouraging the erection of numerous public clocks).[3] Of course, a tax on bricks, which depended on the number of bricks your house was made of, was easily avoided. You simply use bigger bricks, or wood instead of bricks. Which is precisely what happened. You can see it in the walls in Measham in Leicestershire, where brickmaker Joseph Wilkes used massive bricks he called 'gobs'.

So, in the game of cat and mouse between tax authority and taxpayer that has been going on for centuries, regulations were introduced on the size of bricks, and different rates of tax were applied to bricks of different sizes. This sort of behaviour is exactly replicated today as more and more complex regulations are used to clamp down on tax avoidance, which is itself made possible by poor tax design in the first place.

There are plenty of examples of much weirder taxes than that. In 1705, the Russian Tsar decided that beards were uncultured, and imposed a beard tax in an effort to discourage people from growing them. Note, of course, that the more successful such a tax is at achieving what it sets out to achieve the less revenue will be forthcoming. No beards = no tax. You could say the same to those today who want to replace income taxes with green taxes. If the green taxes work, they won't raise much.

Our current excise duties are some of the closest direct descendants of taxes from previous eras. Taxes on beer date back to 1643, raised to finance the parliamentary armies in the English Civil War. In the intervening centuries hats, playing cards, salt, and coffin nails have been among a host of goods subject to such duties. They were the main source of government revenues through to Victorian times.

They were not wildly popular. Samuel Johnson in his famous dictionary defined them thus: 'Excise ... A hateful tax levied upon commodities, and adjudged not by the common judges of property, but wretches hired by those to whom excise is paid.'[4]

Duties on films, televisions, matches and mechanical lighters are of more recent vintage. The last of them wasn't abolished until 1993. While much diminished in total, those we still have play an important role. Duties on petrol, alcohol and tobacco were due to raise about £24 billion, £13 billion and £10 billion respectively in 2023/24. Vehicle Excise Duty (road tax) raises a further £8 billion or so.

In the last chapter we looked at the big three taxes. It's hard to say exactly how many other taxes we have in the UK. Some accountants have suggested a hundred or more. I struggle to count beyond about thirty of them – from the insurance premium tax, to the apprenticeship levy and the soft drinks levy – but that's still plenty.

Many, despite being levied on us today, are probably still less well known than the window tax. With that number of taxes, we encounter yet more complexity and many additional absurdities – absurdities which stop us moving house, encourage us to drink strong cider, persuade companies to use debt to finance themselves, and give us incentives to hold on to assets until death and beyond.

Of those other taxes, the biggest is corporation tax, the onshore element of which will raise around £77 billion in 2023/24, about 5 per cent of total revenue. Council tax brings in another £44 billion and business rates £30 billion. Other than the excise duties on petrol, diesel and alcohol, only two others break the £10 billion mark – stamp duty on property transactions, and capital gains tax. We'll consider all of those here, plus inheritance tax, which bring in around £7 billion. For the rest, I'm afraid we shall have to remain silent for now.[5]

Corporation tax

Of any taxes, corporation tax is one of the more popular. After all, it's a tax on the profits that companies make, rather than on you or me. And we all love a tax which somebody else has to pay. 'Don't tax you, don't tax me, tax that fellow behind the tree,' as the saying goes. Even better if it's a faceless corporation and not a person at all.

To state what I hope is the bleedin' obvious, it can't be a corporation that pays tax in the end. In the end it has to be real people who pay tax. In the case of corporation tax, that could mean the people who own the company – the shareholders (including you and me if we have money invested in the stock market via our pensions, for example). It could mean customers – companies may raise prices to maintain profits. It could mean the owners of land and natural resources. Or it may mean the company's employees, whose wages might end up lower than otherwise.

If you think about it for a moment, there is nobody else who could be paying, nowhere else for the money to come from. The fact that it is a little opaque as to who actually ends up worse off when corporate taxes rise is good news for governments wanting to raise money without too much of a fuss. Less good from the point of view of transparency.

In some respects, corporation tax is rather a good tax. To the extent that it taxes what we economists call economic rents – bigger than normal profits resulting from having a monopoly, for example – then it's great. It raises money without doing any harm at all. Think about taxes on North Sea oil. When there was a lot of it about and the companies extracting it were making big profits, the rates of tax on their profits were very high indeed, and the exchequer benefited to the tune of many billions a year. But there was still plenty of money to be made, and plenty of investment was forthcoming.

The energy profits levy announced in May 2022 is really just another iteration of this North Sea regime, charging higher tax rates on windfall profits earned in the wake of huge increases in the price of oil and gas.

But corporation tax also has its downsides. When profits are low or uncertain, taxing them can put companies off from investing at all. If they need a return on their investment of 10 per cent to make the investment worthwhile, and corporation tax takes the return below 10 per cent, then it will stop the investment happening. And that can be very damaging. Indeed, a study for the OECD ranked corporation tax as the most harmful of all taxes when it comes to economic growth.[6]

There is an additional consideration in a world in which a lot of investment is made by multinational companies who can choose where to invest. A high level of corporation tax in one country can lead investment to be diverted elsewhere. While nobody would argue that the rate of corporation tax is the only, or even the main, determinant of these choices the evidence that it does make a difference is clear.[7]

Those sorts of worries were why, in the midst of austerity through the 2010s, the British government waived billions in corporate tax revenues by cutting the corporate tax rate again and again – from 26 per cent down to 19 per cent.

We know that having a very low tax rate has been important to the Irish economy in attracting inward investment. Dublin has become the go-to location for American firms looking for a European HQ – IBM, Microsoft and Google's European operations are all run from the so-called Silicon Dock.

More minor changes to the UK rate, in an economy which is much bigger and more profitable than the Irish one was when its low rate was introduced, will have a less clear cut and less transformational effect. So that bet on cutting corporate tax rates was a big one. As chancellor, Rishi Sunak decided it was a bet that had not paid off. The headline rate is back at 25 per cent from April 2023 – after a few shenanigans along the way as that increase was called off and then reinstated through a few chaotic weeks in the autumn of 2022.

Whatever the right level for corporation tax, this is a terrible way to make policy. One thing we do know that companies (and the rest of us) want from tax policy is that it be reasonably stable and predictable. I'm probably being too generous to then Chancellor Sunak by suggesting that he decided to raise the corporation tax rate because he found the evidence unconvincing. The truth is he found himself needing to raise some money, and decided that raising corporation tax would be the most politically palatable way of doing so, whatever the economics. An increase of that scale will likely bring in a fair amount of cash; perhaps not the full £16 billion he was hoping for, but we are without question still living in the normal world where raising rates of tax raises you money.

Those who point to the fact that CT revenues have increased over the last decade while tax rates have fallen, and drawn the conclusion that cutting rates increases revenues, are confusing a lot of things that are going on at once. Most importantly, profits were always going to recover after their post financial crisis nadir. We have also broadened the tax base – the *effective* rate of corporation tax did not fall by anything like as much as the headline rate.

Taking the headline rate of corporation tax back to 25 per cent will still leave it relatively low by G7 standards, and pretty average by OECD standards. But it will bring our effective rate of corporation tax, and the revenue we get from it, to high levels both internationally and by UK historical standards. For as the headline rate fell over time, from over 50 per cent in the 1970s down to 19 per cent in 2022, the base on which the tax is levied was gradually broadened. This allowed revenues to be maintained, but has meant that the system is far less competitive and investment friendly than a simple comparison of tax rates would suggest. We are now likely to see corporation tax revenues reach their highest sustained level in half a century and reach levels which are among the highest in the developed world.

Whatever the intricacies of the evidence for higher or lower rates of CT, you are probably more interested in the 'scandal' of why Google, Amazon and the like pay so little in this country. Facebook, for example, paid a reported £37 million of UK corporation tax in 2020 on recorded profits of £190 million. Their revenue was £1.4 billion.[8] In 2020, the corporation tax contribution by Amazon UK Services – the group's warehouse and logistics operation, which is believed to employ the majority of the group's UK workforce – was just £18m, and that was 26 per cent up from the year before.

Is this really a scandal? These companies may sell tens of billions worth of stuff in the UK, but corporation tax isn't a tax on sales – it's a tax on profits. And under the current international framework for corporate taxation they have a lot of choice over where they declare those profits. Big multinationals, especially the US tech giants, have shifted some activity and a lot of profits into countries with low rates of corporation tax: Ireland, the Netherlands and Singapore have been among the winners in this race to the bottom. Shareholders have been bigger winners. Other governments have lost out.

The companies are generally telling the truth when they say they are following the law. The problem lies deep in the roots of the international corporate tax system. It works on the principle that profits should be taxed where the profits are made. Sounds good. It might have been fine back in the 1920s when the international treaties governing these issues were first negotiated. But in today's world, where the research and development might happen in the US, components manufactured in half a dozen countries, the final product assembled in China, and then the sales happen in the UK and across the world, who is to say where the profit was made? Is the profit down to the R&D, the assembly, the sales, or some combination? And who's to say *what* combination?

Amazon and others would argue that the profits that arise from the billions of sales in the UK come not from UK based activities – largely storage and delivery services – but from technology that was designed and is managed in other countries. It's a self-serving argument, but a hard one to disprove in the courts.

There is an answer that in principle could unpick the whole unholy mess. Change the international rules and levy tax not in that unknown place where the profit is generated, but in that known place where the sales occur: in the jargon, move from an *origin* basis to a *destination* basis. That would be clean and efficient and would cut through all the problems of the current system. My former colleague Mike Devereux, now professor of business taxation at Oxford University, has been making this argument for years.[9] A move in this direction may eventually be inevitable as the current system creaks under the weight of its own contradictions and complexities. It would be a bold step though, for the UK to go it alone and withdraw from the current international system, and impose a zero rate of tax on profits arising from investment in the UK while effectively adding an additional tax on sales. If the world were to go down this route some countries would gain a lot of tax revenue and some would lose. Getting international agreement would be tough.

Then again, the world might be beginning to make progress on the different formidable challenge of shoring up the system we have. Hammered out after years of work at the OECD and in finance ministries across the world, and finally championed by the Biden administration in the US, the proposals are relatively straightforward in principle, but mind-blowingly complex to implement in practice.

One part of the proposals would allow countries to tax a small fraction of the profits of the world's hundred or so biggest companies on the basis of their sales in that country. These are largely American companies and many of them operate primarily online. A system like this would essentially layer a second system of corporation tax on top of the ones that currently exist within countries. The second element of the plan is for a global minimum rate of corporation tax of 15 per cent. As far as the Americans are concerned, that's the quid pro quo. Other countries get some rights over tax revenues from big US companies, but a new global minimum rate will ensure the US gets more revenue in total.

If successful this could shore up our – and the world's – corporate tax systems for a while longer. Don't get too excited, though. If it happens, and despite the huge investment in developing it that is looking less likely by the day, this might make for a better system and it could mean a bit more money being paid in the UK. But not much.

All of that said, one of the great tax surprises of the last four decades is that, despite cuts in tax rates and the incessant pressures of international tax competition, corporation tax revenues have held up pretty well. At more than 2.5 per cent of national income, revenues in the immediate pre-pandemic years were well above the average of the last forty years, and higher than at any time since the dotcom bubble at the turn of the century.

That is, frankly, a surprise. Those predicting the demise of this particular form of tax revenue – and serious people have been in that game for a long time now – have, at least until now, been proved spectacularly wrong. The Treasury will be mighty relieved at that.

When you think about corporation tax, it's almost certainly getting money out of these corporate behemoths that you have in mind.

At the other end of the scale, corporate tax is also what is paid by the very smallest companies. I could incorporate myself. That is, instead of taking the modest sum I'm being paid for writing this book as self-employment income, I could declare myself a company and take it as corporate income. There is absolutely nothing to stop me doing that. I would then pay corporation tax on my profits and, if I were to withdraw those profits, I'd pay income tax on the dividends. In this case, no National Insurance contributions at all would be payable. I would also have the option of keeping the money in the company and then paying capital gains tax on it after winding the company up. In general, I would have plenty of options to pay less tax than if I took the money in self-employment income. Which, if you remember, involves less tax than what I'd pay as an employee. Not surprising, perhaps, that the number of one-person companies has grown rather rapidly in recent years, leading the Office for Budget Responsibility at one point to warn of the cost of this trend in lost revenues.[10]

The number of company owner-managers has more than doubled from under a million back in 2000 to around two million today.[11] The proportion of these businesses with any employees at all is just 15 per cent, down from over 40 per cent a few decades ago. Much of this incorporation behaviour is driven simply by the tax system. We think of small companies as the investors for the future, the drivers of economic growth. The vast majority are in fact just individual workers getting on with providing accountancy or window cleaning or plumbing services. Nothing wrong with that, but not the foundations for an economic renaissance.

In one particularly odd case the TV presenter Lorraine Kelly won an appeal against a £1.2 million tax bill which HMRC tried to impose on the basis that she was really an employee of ITV. She had been contracting her services via a company. Part of the thinking behind the ruling appeared to be that Ms Kelly was not appearing on our screens as herself but rather as 'a persona of herself'.[12] In another case, HMRC pursued Gary Lineker for £3.6 million in income tax and £1.3 million in National Insurance because they say he should have been taxed as a direct employee of the BBC, where he presents *Match of the Day*, and the sports channel BT Sport. Instead, he has worked as a contractor through Gary Lineker Media, a company he set up in 2012 jointly with his ex-wife Danielle Bux. HMRC claimed he was a 'disguised employee'.[13] Lineker eventually won the case. As you can see, though, the sums potentially at stake can be very large.

Despite reams of legislation the definition of exactly what constitutes an employee is inevitably imprecise. Governments have tried and tried again to bolster their position by shoring up the legislation. But the problem is more fundamental. Working for someone as an employee, self-employed, or through a company is economically similar, but they are taxed in very different ways. The answer is not to add thousands of lines to legislation that is already almost inoperable. It is to sort out the tax system so that it doesn't provide such egregious incentives.

If you are going to have a tax system like our current one though, you should at least try to police it properly. There are rules about when you should and should not be able to claim to be providing your services through a company rather than as an employee.

They are known as the IR35 rules – a name which, rather bizarrely, refers to the press release which originally announced the legislation back in 1999. Because too many people were simply ignoring these rules, in 2017 the government made it incumbent upon the employer to determine the tax position and liability of contracting parties. That did not change tax liabilities, it simply changed the collection mechanism to make it more effective.

As part of his disastrous 'mini Budget' in September 2022 then chancellor Kwasi Kwarteng abandoned this system of ensuring compliance with the law.

It is hard to think of a more scandalous decision. This was not a change in the rules, just a change in the enforcement of those rules and a change which the Treasury itself believed would cost north of £2 billion a year. That, to be clear, is £2 billion that would have been lost, deliberately lost, to those who set out to play fast and loose with the law and, in many cases, to deliberately defraud the exchequer. In an article in the *Financial Times*, Edward Troup, former head of HMRC, was as excoriating as I can remember any former senior mandarin being about a government policy:

Choosing how to tax citizens and businesses is the legitimate right of elected politicians. Deliberately opting out of the proper collection of tax is not.

Chancellor Kwasi Kwarteng's backtracking on the enforcement of the so-called IR35 rules in his 'mini Budget' raised a cheer from those happy to sidestep the proper payment of tax on employment. But by reopening opportunities to exploit tax rules it does nothing for growth and undermines the wider integrity of the tax system.

In bowing to pressure to abandon these rules, rather than continuing the hard work of making them work better, government has mistaken partisan lobbying for a legitimate business concern. It has seen an easy opportunity to appear pro-business,

> when in reality the only business that is being supported by this
> change is the business of the tax avoider.
>
> This is not merely a nod and a wink to avoiders and evaders:
> it's a WELCOME HERE sign.[14]

Thankfully, this was among the many measures announced in that scandalous statement that was swiftly reversed after Mr Kwarteng was fired.

It seems they will never learn. Of course, we all like small business people and entrepreneurs. That's one reason why, as chancellor in 2002, Gordon Brown decided it would be a great idea to charge corporation tax at zero per cent on profits of less than £10,000. He then watched in apparent amazement as the number of new companies being formed rocketed past 10,000 a week, not because of some sudden awakening of the entrepreneurial spirit among the British population, but rather as a result of the traditional response to seeing a foolproof way of putting one over on the taxperson. He soon had to execute a screeching U-turn.

Taxing wealth too?

By far the most tax revenue in the UK, and indeed in all developed countries, comes from taxing income and spending. All of the levies we've discussed so far tax one or the other (even corporation tax is a tax on corporate income). Very little comes from taxing wealth. Which may seem surprising. There is a lot of wealth around. Nearly £15 trillion of it according to the Office for National Statistics.[15] Compared with our national income, that is a lot more than it used to be – about seven times national income, as against three times national income in the late 1980s. Despite that, taxes on wealth have not risen as a share either of overall taxation or of national income.

What wealth there is, is also very unequally distributed indeed, much more so than income. The richest 1 per cent of households probably own about a quarter of all the wealth – though since the seriously rich don't tend to answer surveys about wealth, and we don't hold a register of wealth in order to tax it, these sorts of estimates are inevitably a little rough. We can say for sure that there is vast inequality here. And unlike income, the concentration of wealth at the top has been growing in recent years.[16] So perhaps you could kill two birds with one stone here – raise a lot of money *and* reduce inequality at the same time.

Inevitably, that is easier said than done. Outside of the top 1 per cent, most of that wealth is tied up in the houses we live in and the pension savings we have put aside for our retirement. If I have saved money out of taxed income, why should I be taxed again? Taxing pensions and housing wouldn't be terribly popular. It's really only the seriously wealthy, those with, say, £5 million plus, who have substantial wealth in assets other than pensions and housing. They can also afford good lawyers and are often able to move their assets abroad.

Should we nevertheless try to tax more of that wealth? Should we introduce a wealth tax? A good place to start is to look at the taxes on wealth we already have.

Council tax is a sort of wealth tax, being based on the value of property (albeit the value in 1991, which was the first and only time properties in England have been valued for the purpose of determining council tax). On the other hand, it is paid by the occupant of the property and not the owner. The same is true of business rates. As we'll see in Chapter 9, on local government, they definitely need reform. We should be levying council tax based on the current value of properties. It is absurd that we have a tax based on values from thirty years ago.

We should also be levying the tax at least in proportion to those values (equally obviously in my view). Not only is council tax capped such that the same is paid on multi-million-pound mansions as on much more modest properties, but even within the normal range of properties it is regressive. The most valuable properties in 1991 (Band H) attract just three times as much tax as the least valuable properties (Band A), despite being worth at least eight times as much in 1991 money and most likely even more now, since prices have risen most in areas where they were already highest.

Sorting that out would be a good place to start if we are really interested in taxing wealth. It would also, by the way, be a good place for a government concerned about 'Levelling Up' to start. We currently over-tax less valuable properties, predominantly in the north, and under-tax more valuable ones in London and the south-east. A quarter of all properties are in the lowest band, band A, meaning they were worth less than £40,000 in 1991. The vast majority of those properties is substantially over-taxed. Government and opposition both know this.

Of all the tax reforms that are needed, this has to be one of the most obvious. A complete no-brainer. The numbers have become ridiculous. The average property in Westminster pays council tax worth 0.06 per cent of its value and the average in Kensington and Chelsea 0.1 per cent. At the other end of the country, the average council tax in Hartlepool is levied at 1.3 per cent of the property's value – thirteen times as high as in central London.

Politicians are far too scared to do anything about it. Change would create vociferous losers, especially among the better off and the older generation who are more likely to live in more valuable properties. Does the fault lie with politicians for being weak and cowardly? Or with us voters for punishing any sign of bravery?

There's another aspect of the taxation of housing that needs changing. Stamp duty is levied on the purchase of residential property. It has a long history, about the longest of any tax still in existence, being first introduced in 1694 during the reign of William and Mary, and intended as a temporary tax to help fund war against France. Sound familiar? At that time few other potential taxes were straightforward to implement, whereas the transactions on which stamp duty was levied were easy to identify and to measure.

The case for maintaining it today is much weaker, but rather than phasing it out successive chancellors have increased it. In 2023, there is no stamp duty on property value below £250,000. It is charged at 5 per cent on value between £250,000 and £925,000, rising to a distinctly immodest 12 per cent on anything over £1.5 million. It may sound like a nice progressive tax on wealthy home buyers. But its main effect is to gum up the housing market. Such transactions taxes are particularly inefficient. By discouraging mutually beneficial transactions, stamp duty makes sure that properties are not held by the people who value them most. It creates a disincentive for people to move house, creates inflexibilities in the labour market and encourages people to live in properties of a size and in a location that they may well not otherwise have chosen. It should be phased out and the revenue lost made up through a reformed council tax.

Then there's capital gains tax. The idea, as the name suggests, is to tax capital gains. In other words, if you pay for something and then sell it later for more than you bought it for, you should pay some tax on the gain you made. It's important to have a tax like this if only to make sure income tax gets paid. Those of us of a certain vintage remember headlines in which private equity executives boasted about paying a lower rate of tax than their cleaners. That boast was made possible by another of Gordon Brown's dreadful tax policies. He had inherited a perfectly sensible CGT system, in which the rates of CGT were aligned with the rates of income tax. In an effort to promote 'long-termism' in investments, he decided to cut the rate to 10 per cent for assets held for more than a year. A lot of very rich people were delighted.

The current version of CGT is a bit more sensible than that, though higher rate taxpayers still only pay tax at 20 per cent on most assets, and then only on gains above £12,300 in any year. (That allowance is coming down to £3,000 in 2024.) Once you take account of other taxes that might have already been paid (like corporation tax), 20 per cent isn't quite as low as it seems, but it is still low enough to make capital gains more attractive than income for a lot of the rich. On the other hand, tax is paid on purely inflationary gains. In other words, if the value of your asset rises only in line with general price increases, you still pay tax on that completely imaginary increase in value.

There is an especially egregious part of the system which charges a rate of just 10 per cent on gains of up to £1 million on disposal of business assets. Until 2020, the limit was an eye-watering £10 million. A married entrepreneur can double up on their allowance by getting their spouse to hold some of their share of the business. This was, and remains, a huge tax break for the very wealthy. Before its restriction in 2020, each year it was worth an average of £300,000 in tax relief to just 6,000 very wealthy individuals realising an average of £3 million in gains per person. That fact, eventually, forced the chancellor into action.

The cut in the allowance from £10 million to £1 million was welcome, but I enjoyed the name change even more. In one of my favourite pieces of tax trolling, when Rishi Sunak reformed the relief in 2020 he changed its name from the rather attractive-sounding Entrepreneur's Relief to the rather less attractive sounding Business Asset Disposal (BAD) relief.

There is one final absurdity to pile upon all the others when it comes to CGT. It is forgiven at death. If I were to buy, for example, a property to rent out, and it were to grow dramatically in value, and I were to sell it I would, quite rightly, be charged tax on the capital gain I had made. If, instead, I were to keep that property until I died, all such tax liability would be wiped out. My heirs could sell it free of tax. Unsurprisingly a lot of assets are held way beyond the point at which there is an economic advantage in people holding on to them. They are kept only so that tax can be avoided.

There are some very obvious changes that need to be made to CGT. Get rid of BAD relief. Charge only on real gains. Charge at death. And align rates with those of income tax. Charging at death apart, this would take us back to broadly where we were in 1997.

You might note that I've not included the biggest CGT loophole of them all in my list of absurdities – the exemption on gains made on owner-occupied housing. HMRC estimates that exemption costs in the order of £25 billion a year.[17] Given the scale of capital gains that those of a certain generation have been lucky enough to make on their houses, it is perhaps unsurprising that the figure is so big.

This looks like, and is, a big and unmerited windfall for a lucky generation. Could CGT in fact be levied against them? Unlikely. Most of the gains are already made, so any effective tax would need to be retrospective. The real problem is a political one. One would need absolute political consensus – otherwise anyone thinking of selling their house would simply wait for the other lot to be elected, bringing the housing market to a grinding halt for years. Very few countries charge CGT on owner occupied housing.[18]

Reforming CGT ought to be a priority for any government wanting both to tackle inequality and to raise revenue. What about inheritance tax? Bringing in less than £7 billion a year, it would seem barely to warrant a mention. But it is a tax which attracts a disproportionate amount of both attention and opprobrium.

> I see nothing objectionable in fixing a limit to what anyone may acquire by mere favour of others, without any exercise of his faculties, and in requiring that if he desires any further accession of fortune, he shall work for it.[19]

This, from John Stuart Mill, has for more than a century been the central liberal case for a substantial and effective inheritance tax. The logic seems compelling. Gifts and inheritances come not as a result of effort or desert, but rather of blind luck. They reduce the incentive of the lucky recipient to work hard. They concentrate both economic and political power in an undeserving elite.

As we enter a second gilded age of great wealth inequality and the accumulation of great fortunes, Mill's case is surely at least as relevant today as it was in the nineteenth century.

Yet across the western world, there are few taxes as unpopular as inheritance tax. Sweden and Norway, often considered beacons of social democracy and equality, have abolished their inheritance taxes entirely. Meanwhile, estate taxation in the United States has produced the rallying cry 'no taxation without respiration', surely the best fiscal slogan since the Boston Tea Party.

Why? You can't deny the force of Mill's arguments. Looked at from the perspective of the recipient generation, inheritances appear random, unjust, an obvious basis for taxation. Looked at from the perspective of the bequeathing generation, though, bequests appear simply as an exercise in property rights. I have earned, and paid my taxes, and saved; it is my right to dispose of my assets as I see fit, and in particular to support my children.

Few human emotions run deeper. Deep enough certainly that people will go to considerable lengths to avoid inheritance tax. They even go as far as not dying. On 1 July 1979, Australia abolished federal inheritance taxes. There was a noticeable dip in the number of deaths in the last week of June as thrifty Aussies hung on to life for just a little longer to make sure their heirs could inherit tax-free.

If most of your wealth is tied up in your home, there is relatively little you can do to avoid inheritance tax – unless your partner inherits. If you have serious money, then avoidance is not hard at all. The simplest expedient is to give away your assets more than seven years before you die.

Or you can buy agricultural land, on which no inheritance tax is payable, or various kinds of business assets. Or you can make clever use of trusts. Or, if you have special 'foreign dom' status, you won't have to pay either. A good lawyer can save your heirs a lot of money. It remains as true today, as when my predecessor at the IFS was writing thirty years ago, that inheritance tax 'favours the healthy, wealthy and well advised'.[20]

As the Office of Tax Simplification has pointed out, the average effective tax rate paid by estates valued at around £2 million is 20 per cent. The average tax rate on £10 million estates is half that.[21] Here's tax lawyer Dan Neidle:

> Bob is a seventy-year-old with £5m of investments which he wants his children to inherit. But he'd like to avoid the £2m of inheritance tax. He asks his tax adviser for advice on how to avoid the tax, and is expecting a long, complicated memo, proposing a tax avoidance scheme involving seventeen companies, three tax havens, two trusts, and large fees. What he actually gets is written on a postcard:
>
> Step 1: Sell your existing investments and replace them with shares listed on the Alternative Investment Market. Either assembling a diversified selection yourself, or paying someone else to do it.
>
> Step 2: Make sure to live at least two years.
>
> Step 3: Drop dead, happy in the knowledge you've avoided inheritance tax.
>
> There is no Step 4.[22]

In 2016, the 6th Duke of Westminster – owner of the vast Grosvenor estates which cover much of central London – died.

His son, Hugh Grosvenor, found himself at the age of twenty-five not only the 7th Duke of Westminster but instantly catapulted into ninth place in the *Sunday Times* Rich List.

He became Britain's youngest billionaire. As the vast bulk of his inheritance was held in trusts, almost no inheritance tax was payable. To be fair there are tax charges on the trusts. But combine their relatively light taxation with the reliefs for agricultural land and other assets held by the Duke, and the charges on the estate won't have come close to reaching the more than £3.5 billion which would have been the straightforward charge on his inheritance of around £9 billion. (That is, had the estate paid the full 40 per cent rate that most people passing on the family home to their children end up paying on anything above £500,000.)

All of which makes the tax's unpopularity more comprehensible even to those who take Mill's view of the ethics of it.

Just as there is plenty we can do to make council tax, pensions taxation and capital gains tax a whole lot more effective, so it is with inheritance tax. The route best loved of economists and many others who have looked at it is to move to a tax on the recipients of gifts and inheritances. That, after all, is consistent with the reason for having the tax in the first place – to tax the undeserving recipient rather than the donor.

It also ensures that estates which are inherited by several people are taxed less heavily than those which go in their entirety to a single heir. It would mean that money received as a gift would be treated in the same way as money received as an inheritance. That is the system we should move to.

If that is deemed too radical, or too difficult, there are two other possible routes. One option is to take the current system, or something like it, and try to make it work. That means closing as many loopholes as possible, while sticking to the current 40 per cent tax rate on estates of more than £500,000. The risk is that the incentive to avoid the tax is too great and the game of cat and mouse between tax authority and the wealthy is one that the HMRC is bound to lose. An alternative solution would be to do away with nearly all the reliefs and allowances and impose the tax at a lower rate, so as to reduce the incentive to invest time and effort in avoidance. That might look like throwing in the towel. But maybe it is the best we can do. The status quo with all its burdensome inequities certainly should not be allowed to persist.

Partly reflecting all these problems with existing taxes, along-side that huge gulf in wealth holdings between rich and poor, and between old and young, there have been growing calls for a wealth tax. Now, that could mean many different things.

A wealth tax on holdings, including house and pension, of over £500,000 is a very different beast to a tax on those with over £10 million. A one-off levy is quite a different proposition from an annual tax.

The latest and best in-depth analysis of the options came from the Wealth Tax Commission.[23] Their report, authored by my colleague Arun Advani, LSE law academic Dr Andy Summers and tax barrister Emma Chamberlain, came out against an annual tax. Nowhere in the world has an annual wealth tax worked well. It is too complicated to collect, too easy for the rich to game the system, and too much open to special pleading and an accumulation of reliefs and allowances that create new unfairnesses.

They did, however, support the idea of a one-off wealth tax. They conclude: 'A well-designed one-off wealth tax would raise a total of £260 billion at a rate of 5 per cent over £500,000 per individual or £80 billion at a rate of 5 per cent over £2 million per individual, payable at 1 per cent per year over five years'[24]

That looks like a serious amount of money, but only because the tax they propose would fall on pensions and homes and would be levied on assets over £500,000. I would hazard that is a non-starter practically and politically. A large fraction of people in their forties and above have that sort of wealth, but entirely wrapped up in their house and pension.

Rather than get lost in this debate we should start by sorting out the wealth taxes we already have. They are ineffective, inefficient, inequitable, and absurdly favourable to the very wealthy. It doesn't sound as exciting as proposing a whole new wealth tax. But that would be the properly radical, and effective, way forward.

Excise duties and environmental taxes

When I was growing up, the headlines after Budget day were always about how much the taxes on beer and cigarettes were going to go up. Maybe it's because I understand more of what's going on that these seem rather less important nowadays, maybe it's because tobacco tax took a large part of the family budget when I was a child. High taxes on cigarettes are certainly among the reasons that smoking has declined so much. This is probably the only tax which is clearly on the downward sloping part of the famous Laffer curve – raise the tax rate and you get less revenue.

Even so, tobacco duties still bring in a relatively handy £10 billion or so each year as smokers do their bit for the public finances by both coughing up a lot of tax and dying early – as my mother did, of lung cancer, after more than half a century of heavy smoking. Personally, I do my bit by contributing to the £13 billion or so that alcohol duties bring in. The Japanese are reportedly encouraging younger adults to drink more, explicitly to increase tax revenues.[25]

With duty in the UK of around £3 on a bottle of wine, you can see how little goes into actually making the wine when you buy cheap plonk. Duty works out at about £7.50 on a 70cl bottle of spirits and getting on for a pound on every pint of beer.

There is a good economic case for taxing alcohol and tobacco. These are addictive and damaging substances. Consumers create costs for the rest of society (externalities), and for themselves (internalities). If that was the only reason for the tax, then when it comes to alcohol you'd expect the tax rate to be proportional to the amount of alcohol, or to the amount of harm associated with a particular drink. That is, I'm afraid, not how alcohol taxes are actually designed.

Per unit of alcohol, wine with a high alcohol content is taxed less than lighter wines. That's because the tax is levied per unit of drink not per unit of alcohol, creating an obvious incentive to produce and consume higher alcohol wine. Cider is treated the same way. Strong cider attracts less tax per unit of alcohol than any other drink, which may explain its popularity among some of the poorest and most addicted of alcoholics. Because they tend to be used more by heavy drinkers, there is a case for a higher tax per unit on spirits.

Reforms that were announced in 2021, made possible by a genuine freedom created by Brexit, should rationalise the system somewhat. Cider, though, will remain less heavily taxed than any-thing else, and hence presumably will remain the tipple of choice for too many of our indigent alcoholics.

First introduced in the Finance Act of 1908, taxes on petrol and diesel bring in £25 billion or so – more than alcohol and tobacco duties combined. As an economist, I'd like to say that they were introduced for the very good economic reason that driving creates externalities – costs imposed on others – because of the pollution and congestion that it causes. Taxing petrol is rather a good way of dealing with those externalities, by making driving more expensive.

In fact, fuel duties were introduced simply as a way of raising revenue – quite a lot of it. They now raise rather less than in the past. For more than a decade, chancellors have baulked at keeping fuel duty rising even in line with inflation, meaning that relative to other things we buy, and relative to national income, it has become much smaller. In 2000, fuel duties made up over 7 per cent of HMRC revenue. By 2019, that had fallen to only 4 per cent.[26] This is by far and away the biggest 'green' tax. It has been systematically reduced.

If, as we have committed to, we move to net zero greenhouse gas emissions by 2050, those revenues will inevitably fall to zero as we all start driving electric cars. That is an awful lot of money for the Exchequer to lose.

It will also mean that the biggest 'externality' created by driving won't be taxed. The biggest cost we impose on our fellow citizens by driving is not the local pollution we cause, or even the carbon dioxide emissions – it is the congestion we create on the road. That's why, for decades now, economists have been keen on the idea of road user charging, with charges varying according to how congested the roads are where you drive.

Technology now makes something like this much more plausible than in the past. There is also a fiscal urgency about making some kind of change along these lines. An easier alternative would be to tax according to the amount of electricity used or simply the distance travelled. Either way, we need to get a move on. The current plan is that new petrol and diesel cars will no longer be sold from 2035. We will need a new tax system for driving in place well before that. Either that or, inevitably, higher taxes elsewhere.

Given political pusillanimity on road fuel taxes I am not optimistic about other possible environmental taxes. The climate change levy raises an inconsequential £2 billion or so a year and various other environmental levies another £7 billion.

There is an overwhelming economic case for a carbon tax levied according to greenhouse gas emissions created irrespective of source – whether that's from driving, flying, heating our homes with gas or running electric appliances. We have no such thing and there seems little prospect of it. In fact, as mentioned above, we subsidise gas consumption by imposing VAT on it at just 5 per cent.

As we decarbonise electricity, by making the consumer pay, we make it more expensive relative to more environmentally damaging gas consumption. Our incoherent approach also means that, per unit of greenhouse gas emission, flights are taxed much less heavily than driving, with long-distance business-class flights especially lightly taxed.[27]

To reach net zero we need much more than a universal carbon tax. But failing to introduce one will just make getting there more expensive. And less likely to happen.

Reforming tax

One thing should be obvious from what you've read so far. We should be able to do better – to raise taxes in a way which is fairer on the one hand and causes less economic damage on the other. That we don't do better is not just the fault of politicians, though they certainly bear much of the blame – it's our fault too. We citizens tend to kick up quite a fuss when changes are mooted.

Perhaps more than in any other area of policy, tax suffers from a tyranny of the status quo. The tax system is riddled with contradictions and unfairnesses. But try to get rid of them and some lobby group or another – the pasty producers, the landowners, the self-employed, employees, pensioners, the over-paid, the corporates, the renters, the rentiers, the homeowners, the landlords, somebody – will cry foul.

Because every one of those current unfairnesses and contradictions benefits somebody. And human nature being what it is, making anyone worse off, even if they are undeservedly benefited by the current system, causes a ruckus. But cause a ruckus we surely must. Political bravery is required.

Things are not getting any better. Recent chancellors have made the system more and more complex. They seem to have gained great pleasure from introducing new taxes which, just within the last decade, include the apprenticeship levy, the soft drinks industry levy, the plastic bag tax, the bank levy, the bank surcharge, the diverted profits tax, and the digital services tax.

There are some good reasons for some of these. Between them, though, they serve to increase complexity. As does the proliferation of exemptions, allowances and incentives that chancellors feel bound to add to year on year.

Within income tax we have added the marriage allowance, the high-income child benefit charge and the pensions annual allowance taper. Additional reliefs, rates and allowances have been added to business rates, stamp duty, corporation tax, capital gains tax, and inheritance tax. The mess we are in is not just a left-over from history. Whole new systems of stupidities have been introduced into the tax system very recently.

We have also suffered from the most absurd lack of consistency. With the same party in power since 2010 we have had corporation tax slashed from 26 per cent to 19 per cent followed by an announcement that it would return to 25 per cent, then that it wouldn't, and then that it would. We had years of the government boasting about increasing the income tax personal allowance. Now it is cutting it again. Even more than in any area of government spending there is no sense of strategy or direction.

Government produces reviews and strategies with monotonous regularity for almost every area of public spending. It has literally never published a strategy for tax. This is all wrapped up in the silly way that too much tax policy gets made: in complete isolation within the Treasury building, to be announced to an expectant world on Budget day. Great theatre. A terrible way to make policy.

We can do better. This is not the place to set out a detailed blueprint for tax reform. With Nobel Laureate Sir James Mirrlees and others, I did that in a rather long book back in 2011.[28] We summed up by saying that we should aim for a progressive, neutral tax system. The word 'system' is important. One of the great failures of tax policymaking is that it happens in a series of silos. One tax is tweaked here, another is increased over there, with no regard for what the overall impact might be. We also shouldn't look for every tax to do everything. As long as the tax and benefit system as a whole is progressive, not every tax needs to be, just as not every tax needs to promote a green agenda, so long as the system as a whole works to do that.

Then there's neutrality – meaning treating similar things similarly. Lack of neutrality is where a lot of the problems we face come from. If you tax self-employment income differently from employment income, or capital gains differently from earnings, or biscuits differently from cakes, you are asking for trouble. You might as well put up a big sign saying PLEASE AVOID TAX HERE. Then enormous complexity is created because of all the efforts to reduce that avoidance. It's the brick tax over and over and over again. Most of these departures from neutrality are also just plain unfair, favouring one group over another.

As for being progressive, we will all have our own views as to how much more the rich should pay than the poor, but that the tax and benefit system *should* redistribute is surely not open to dispute. Again, not every tax needs to be progressive to achieve this – taxes on cigarettes are quite definitely not progressive. Poor people are more likely to smoke. But that doesn't make them bad taxes. Within the tax system it's income tax which does the heavy lifting on making sure it is progressive.

Simply sticking to that short imprecation – a progressive, neutral system – would get us a long way. Getting tax policy right, fixing some of the problems we have identified, adhering to these strictures, is only going to become more important. Whether we like it or not, whether politicians like it or not, unless there is some remarkable change in the direction of public spending, taxes are going to rise over the coming decade.

We can raise taxes. Our tax burden is still not especially high by western European standards. But if we are going to, we would do well, first, to sort out the mess that our system has become.

3

Poverty and
Working Age Welfare

Benefits and tax credits to working age people and
children: £124 billion in 2022/23[1]

The Jobcentre Plus office is the most visible aspect of Britain's benefit system. More than six hundred of them can be found across the
country with most town highstreets having one. But it is no longer
really at the heart of Britain's welfare state.

In recent decades the unemployment rate has fallen from
close to 10 per cent to under 4 per cent. And as worklessness has
fallen, the nature of poverty in Britain and the benefits system has
shifted. The Jobcentre is no longer at the centre of welfare policy

because unemployment is now such a small part of what drives welfare spending.

Few elements of our welfare state are as misunderstood as the benefit system. The common perception, often fuelled by politicians and media, is that most of the more than £100 billion we spend each year on benefits for people under state pension age goes to the unemployed. Nothing could be further from the truth. Only a tiny fraction of the total goes to people who are officially unemployed – that is, who are out of work and looking for a job.

About £16 billion goes on benefits for people who are judged too sick to work. A further £22 billion or so goes on disability and carer benefits, largely on Personal Independence Payments, paid to people in respect of a disability but not linked to whether or not they are in work.[2] We spend a total of £18 billion a year paying the rents of people of working age. In total, well over £60 billion of annual benefit spending goes to households with at least one person in work.

As these numbers suggest, dependence on these benefits is not a minority sport. Once Universal Credit is fully rolled out, more than one working age family in four will be entitled to it at any moment in time, and probably at least half of us will be eligible at some point in our lives. The benefit system is vast; it is far reaching, it is vital in ameliorating poverty and supporting the poorest. It is also often inadequate, damaging to work incentives and intrusive.

Despite spending well over £100 billion per year, not to mention the money that goes on pensions, on official measures, about one in five of us lives in poverty at any one time. Of those, a majority are in work, or live with someone who is in paid work. Of course, we can disagree about exactly what level of income constitutes a poverty line but – to put it another way – more than half of people towards the very bottom of the income distribution now are in work or live with someone who is in work.

If that's a surprise, that's probably because it's a relatively new phenomenon. Twenty years ago, most of the poor were, as you might expect, out of work. Two things have happened to change this, one good, one bad. The good thing has been a huge reduction in the number of workless households. The fraction of lone parents not in work, for example, has halved.

But there are bad reasons too. More people in work have very low incomes. Earnings have risen a lot less at the bottom of the distribution than towards the top. Some of the highest-earning households today have total gross earnings 60 per cent or 70 per cent higher than similar households twenty years ago. At the bottom, the growth has been only about 10 per cent.[3]

A lot, though by no means all, of that is down to changes in hours worked rather than in hourly earnings. More women are working and working full time in better-off households and, for the first time ever, a lot of low-paid men are working part time.

Even more important has been housing. You can't begin to understand poverty in this country without understanding what has been happening to housing costs. They have risen far faster for poorer households than for richer ones. The young and the poor increasingly live in privately rented accommodation. Falling interest rates, at least until 2022, have kept housing costs of older and richer households down. As the average homeowner has got older, and low interest rates have allowed mortgages to be paid down, for the first time in generations there are now more homes owned outright than there are homes owned with a mortgage. At the same time, rising rents and falling homeownership rates have sent costs soaring for the younger and the poorer.

This is a change by no means confined to the poorest. One of the most important *political* facts of the last two decades has been the collapse in homeownership among working age families on middling sorts of incomes. Two decades ago, like the rich, they were mainly homeowners. Today, like the poor, they are mainly renters.

As recently as the mid-1990s renting was something young people did – a waiting room until they coupled up, had kids and stepped onto the property ladder. Just one in five families with children rented privately in 1995. Nowadays more than two in five do. Almost one third of people aged thirty-five to forty-four in England now live in rented accommodation compared to just 10 per cent at the turn of the millennium.

In London and the south-east of England many graduates earning well above the national median wage struggle to save for a deposit large enough to get a mortgage. All that, combined with rising rents and falling mortgage rates, means that low-earning households have housing costs a good 50 per cent higher than they were twenty years ago, while housing costs for the highest-earning households have not risen at all, on average.

Of course, that average hides a lot of variation, but the lessons are stark. Largely through a series of accidents, our housing market has rewarded the better off and punished the poor. We're not going to be able to fix in-work poverty without doing something serious about housing.

I've been talking about the period since the mid-1990s. Most of the increase in in-work poverty happened between 1995 and 2008 as rents rose and household earnings became more dispersed. It would have grown a whole lot more if the tax credit system hadn't become a great deal more generous. Gordon Brown's largesse held back the tide.

Since 2010, by contrast, benefit cuts have been largely responsible for the continuing increases in in-work poverty. Remember, though, that for most the in-work benefit system is still much more generous today than it was before 1997.

On the bright side, poverty rates (on official definitions poverty means having income less than 60 per cent of the median) have at least not risen since 2010, though they have been on the rise for families with children, especially families with three or more children who have borne the brunt of benefit cuts.[4] Even for families with children there was, at least until 2022, some good news. The number of families saying they were unable to afford a range of necessities fell quite sharply over the 2010s.

The disaster of the last decade, though, has been the almost complete lack of growth in living standards across the board. The number of people with incomes below 60 per cent of the median, the official poverty line, hasn't grown since 2010 largely because the median has barely grown. A decade without an increase in living standards is bad enough for most of us. For the poor, especially those living on benefits whose real value has been cut, it can be a catastrophe.

A little history

It wasn't meant to be like this.

I mean, obviously we didn't want a world in which so many people were in poverty and dependent on benefits. But in particular they weren't supposed to be dependent on *means-tested* benefits. We still look back on the Beveridge report as the founding document of our welfare state.[5] But his vision failed. We will see in the next chapter how it failed for pensions. For working age benefits it failed even more comprehensively.

A rather cantankerous academic turned civil servant, Beveridge's famous report was published in November 1942, just at the turning point of the Second World War, around the time of Alamein, Stalingrad, Guadalcanal and Operation Torch (or 'the end of the beginning,' according to Churchill). It isn't an easy read – even when he talks about the Five Giants of Want, Disease,

Ignorance, Squalor, and Idleness, that he is setting out to slay – yet it sold 100,000 copies in its first month. Her Majesty's Stationery Office (HMSO) is said not to have had anything quite as hot for another twenty years, when they published the Denning Report on the Profumo scandal. Beveridge became a national hero overnight, rather to his surprise. It felt 'like riding an elephant through a cheering mob,' he said.[6]

Like many who had witnessed the household means test of the early 1930s, under which a grandparent receiving a pension or a child taking a paper round could result in a loss of benefit, Beveridge hated the idea of means testing. It was to George Orwell 'an encouragement to tittle-tattle and the informer'. So he designed a system which was supposed to eliminate it on any serious scale.

Under his scheme, benefits would be available as of right, and without a means test, to those unable to work because of unemployment or sickness, so long as they had contributed through a system of national insurance. The system was to be based on flat-rate benefits – not earnings related, in other words – paid for via flat-rate contributions.

For 'abnormal' cases, who didn't qualify for contributory benefit, means-tested National Assistance was to be put in place. But, since the contributory benefits themselves were only ever set at or close to 'subsistence' levels, and by definition the means-tested minimum had to be enough to subsist on, there was never much difference in generosity between the two.

Add to that what Beveridge called 'the problem of rent' and means testing was baked in from the start. The problem of rent is still with us: no flat-rate benefit can deal with wildly differing rental costs. Back in Beveridge's day about three quarters of the population were renters rather than owner occupiers. So a means-tested system of rent rebates was tacked on from the off. Housing-related benefits for people of working age now cost around 1 per cent of national income, or about £20 billion a year,[7] a staggering amount and more than we spend on entire public services such as the police.

Beveridge also took it as a given that work would be enough to lift a family from poverty: it was axiomatic that anyone in employment would have enough resources to support a wife and a child. With family allowances at a level high enough to support second and subsequent children, there could be no problem of the working poor.

None of his assumptions survived contact with reality and social change. Means testing gradually became more important as new groups of welfare recipients emerged, notably huge increases in the number of lone parents from the 1970s onwards, who were simply not covered by his contributory system.

Policy changes since the 1970s have essentially ended the contributory system altogether. The problem of rent only got bigger as council rents started rising from the 1980s and increasing numbers of claimants were again in the private rented sector from the 1990s onwards. And, of course, the idea that you couldn't be in work and poor has proven quite wrong as growing rates of in-work poverty all too clearly demonstrate.

At any given moment it has proven too tempting to cut the generosity of, and restrict eligibility for, contributory benefits. If you're looking to save money, then why have benefits which aren't means-tested? That just means some money goes to those who don't really need it. That is essentially the story of a policy pursued consistently by governments of all stripes since 1979.

And while the generosity of contributory benefits was being curtailed and eligibility criteria tightened, so means testing was on the rise. What started as a meagre Family Income Supplement for poor families in work, became the somewhat more meaningful Family Credit and then, under New Labour, the vastly more generous system of tax credits supporting families on a means-tested basis.

At the end of the 1970s, we were spending about twice as much on contributory benefits as on means-tested ones. Today the ratio is something like ten to one in favour of means-tested benefits. If not quite dead, the contributory system is well on its way to the morgue.

Beveridge envisaged a system of non-means-tested, flat-rate, contributory benefits for those unable to work. What we have is a system of means-tested benefits largely paid to those in work, with support for the sick and disabled mostly paid according to their income or level of disability rather than with any reference to contributions.

Towards Universal Credit

By the mid-2000s, a smorgasbord of benefits existed to support the unemployed, the sick and the poor: Income Support, Housing Benefit, Council Tax Benefit, Jobseeker's Allowance, Employment and Support Allowance, Working Tax Credit and Child Tax Credit.

All means-tested. All received by millions. Each with their own rules and conditions and separate means tests. If you moved into work, you would move from one benefit to another then back again if you lost your job. Because of the way they interacted, you could easily lose 96p of any extra pound earned as you lost eligibility to tax credits and housing benefit. It was messy, cumbersome, expensive, and often damaged incentives to work.

The whole system was made all the more unwieldy because tax credits were never properly integrated with anything else. Gordon Brown wanted to portray them as a tax cut, not a benefit.

'Instead of the state paying out benefit through the social security system to working families on lower incomes, in future they will receive cash directly through the tax system,' he told Parliament in his 1998 Budget.[8] A noble objective, but one at odds with reality. Tax credits are welfare benefits, they are not part of the tax system.

Like benefits, and unlike tax, they are calculated on the basis of family income. Following the autumn 2021 Budget, Chancellor Rishi Sunak tried the same rhetorical trick, claiming the reduction in the rate at which Universal Credit is withdrawn as a tax cut. It's not – it's a benefit increase.

One could write an entire book about the chaotic implementation of tax credits. There were overpayments on a grand scale. They were clawed back, leading to misery among many of the families which the system was intended to help. Expensive fixes were put in place to sort out the problems. Their legacy though was a social security system vastly more generous, expensive and redistributive than the one which New Labour had inherited in 1997.

Benefits for families with children rose dramatically. Tax credits were payable to people on well above average incomes. They were enough to hold back what would otherwise have been a decade of rising inequality. Outside the stratosphere, where the top 1 per cent live, *income* inequality did not rise, despite an increase in *earnings* inequality.

That success at holding back growing inequality came at a cost, and not just a financial one. The complexity of the system made it desperately hard to navigate, and the overlapping benefits meant many people in work would keep just a few pence of any extra pound earned as extra income triggered a loss of tax credits, housing benefit and council tax benefit.

So, by the mid-2000s, starting in think tanks and academia, and gradually infiltrating the thinking of some ministers and civil servants, the idea of replacing the whole caboodle with a single benefit began to take root. There were, arguably, two turning points. One came when the then Work and Pensions Secretary

James Purnell worked with former banker David, now Lord, Freud (and great-grandson of Sigmund) who wrote a landmark report on welfare reform proposing a single unified working age benefit.[9] The idea was stymied by Gordon Brown's resistance, and Purnell's resignation. Yet Freud, perhaps uniquely, got the opportunity to see through the recommendations of his independent report when he was made a minister in the subsequent coalition and Conservative governments.

The second had its origins a good seven years earlier, in 2002. The then Conservative leader Iain Duncan Smith had visited the notorious out-of-town estate Easterhouse in Glasgow. He was shocked by what he described as the effects of 'illiteracy, desertion and addiction'. Duncan Smith, a right winger and former Scots Guards officer, is said to have experienced an 'Easterhouse epiphany'. For him the Conservatives had to become 'the natural party of those who want to make a better life for themselves and their children'.[10]

Two years later, out of his leader's job, his new thinktank the Centre for Social Justice (CSJ) published its report, Breakdown Britain.[11] The report helped to fuel the debate – mainly in the more abstruse policy circles, it is true – that eventually merged six benefits (Jobseeker's Allowance, Income Support, Housing Benefit, Child and Working Tax credits, and Employment and Support Allowance) into just one: Universal Credit.

When Duncan Smith arrived at DWP in 2010 the CSJ had already spent years modelling the details of how such a benefit might be designed. With Freud as minister for welfare reform, rarely had the civil servants in a Whitehall department been faced with brand new ministers so knowledgeable about the policy agenda and so clear about what they wanted to achieve. So many of them were reminding themselves about Iain Duncan Smith's views that day, that the Centre for Social Justice website crashed.

There is one key disagreement about the initial meeting with civil servants at the DWP. Did they tell the new Secretary of State, as the Duncan Smith camp says, 'We believe we can do it, and that it will cost less than you think'? Or did they, as the other side remembered, say, 'We believe we can do it, but it will cost a bit *more* than you think'?[12] The senior official who described it at the time as 'the mother and father of all challenges' was certainly on the money.[13]

But set about it they did. From the moment Freud and Duncan Smith set foot in the offices of the DWP back in 2010, delivering Universal Credit became the number one priority for the department. Nearly a decade and a half later, it remains a work in progress.

Universal Credit is now a reality. Though even in 2024, it is far from fully rolled out. Its implementation suffered from the sins that so often beset UK governments: wildly unrealistic timetables, rows with the Treasury over money, and inconsistent leadership.

But it is important to remember why it was considered worth the money and hassle. And it did survive the most extraordinary test when claims rose to a staggering 700,000 in a single week in March 2020 as Covid and lockdown took hold. The system worked. It is inconceivable that the predecessor systems could have coped with such an extraordinary surge in demand. Whatever the success of the furlough scheme, had UC not worked back then the consequences for hundreds of thousands of families could have been calamitous.

Unfortunately, the introduction of UC has become synonymous with the imposition of welfare cuts. The version being rolled out is much less generous than the one originally planned and modelled back in 2010 and 2011. We had the curious spectacle of several George Osborne budgets banking savings from cuts to a benefit which didn't yet exist. Lord Freud later wrote about his first six months as minister, and being 'profoundly disillusioned' with the Treasury:

My perception was that the average age of the department was twenty-nine and many were arrogant, as only twenty-nine-year-olds out of their depth can be. The staff turnover rate was running at 25 per cent. They didn't own the policies they had forced on us. They had done their job once the spreadsheet was cleared by the Office for Budget Responsibility and many would be off to fresh pastures shortly thereafter.[14]

UC as it currently exists is, on average, neither any more nor any less generous than the range of benefits that it is replacing. The cuts were to benefits in general and would have happened whether or not UC was being introduced. 'On average' is doing a lot of work here, though.

Once it is fully in place, millions of families will be better off than they would have been had it not been introduced, and millions will be worse off. Analysis by the IFS suggests that around 17 per cent will lose at least £1,000 a year from the transfer to Universal Credit, while 14 per cent will gain at least as much.[15] That's a deliberate part of the policy design. In general, people with some savings or who own their house, as well as many self-employed, will get less from UC than from the so-called legacy benefits. On the other hand, a lot of people paying rent and some who are disabled will be better off.

As ever with these transitions, protections are built in. If you move onto UC from other benefits and your circumstances don't change, then you won't suffer a cash-terms cut in your benefits. But so many things do count as a change in circumstances, including having another child, gaining a partner or splitting from one, or moving in or out of a job, that the protection won't last long for most.

There *have* been big cuts over the last few years. They just don't have anything specifically to do with UC. The cuts have been across the social security system. We can't say we weren't warned. The 2015 Conservative manifesto promised £12 billion of cuts within two years. I'm on the record as saying that wouldn't happen – cuts on that scale would just be too painful. I was precisely right but completely wrong. We didn't get £12 billion of cuts over two years. But we did within five.

The biggest cut was the easiest to make, the least obvious, and the most invidious. For four years the benefits payable to some of the poorest in the land were frozen in cash terms. That meant a cut in purchasing power of 6 per cent. In March 2020, a single unemployed person was supposed to be able to live on just £325 a month. That was increased by £20 a week for the duration of the coronavirus crisis – a top-up that was withdrawn in October 2021, returning basic benefit levels to their same real terms level as they were fifty years ago. Over the same period earnings and general living standards have much more than doubled.

Our benefit system is extremely ungenerous to the unemployed, especially those without children. We offer much less than almost any other developed country. A single childless worker on average earnings in the UK can expect to receive 15 per cent of her in-work income when she loses her job; across the OECD the average is 55 per cent (if she had been in work for some time).[16] The contrast with the furlough scheme which ran through the Covid crisis – offering 80 per cent of previous earnings to those laid off – could hardly be more stark.

Another cause of hardship has been the way in which housing benefits have failed to keep pace with rents. After 2012, the limits on what rent the state would cover, for those renting in the private sector, rose only in line with prices, not with local rents. Then, from 2016, the limits were frozen altogether. They rose during the pandemic, but have been frozen again at their 2020 levels. The result is that, as rents rise, the maximum amount that can be covered by benefits does not increase, and so more of those on the lowest incomes need to find more money from other benefits, or any earnings, to cover part of their rent. Year by year this leaves people worse off. By 2023, with rents rising fast, only one in twenty private rental properties advertised on Zoopla were covered by housing benefit, down from nearly one in four just three years earlier. Nearly four in every ten private renters receive some housing benefit.[17]

The policy change that will have the biggest impact on individual families, and a direct, laser-like effect of increasing child poverty, was the introduction of the two-child limit on tax credits and Universal Credit. The more children you have, the higher your needs. Until 2017 the benefit system had always recognised that. But for most third and subsequent children born since April 2017 families will no longer get any additional means-tested support; that's a loss of over £50 per week per child.

This policy was sold on the basis that the unemployed shouldn't be able to revel in incomes higher than those available to many workers, and should have to make the same choices and trade-offs that the rest of us do. That also underlies the benefit cap which, as of 2023, for couples and lone parents, limits the total benefits they can receive to just over £22,000 a year (if outside London) irrespective of their circumstances.

Three in five households affected by the two-child limit have at least one adult in work. In her brief stint as secretary of state for work and pensions, Amber Rudd, who later resigned as Home Secretary and then as a Tory MP, scored one small victory on this front, ensuring that the limit would not apply to children born before the policy was put in place.

Even so, the numbers affected are now rising rapidly. By 2020, poverty rates among children in families of three or more were already, at nearly 40 per cent, double those of children in smaller families. Not least because many of those affected weren't aware of the policy, or became entitled to benefits only after their third child was born, recent research from the LSE led to the conclusion:

Over the past five years, the two-child limit has only had a small effect on whether families had a third or subsequent child. Instead, the policy has withdrawn significant resources from larger families living on a low-income, which was putting their mental health and wellbeing at risk, even before the recent cost of living increases.[18]

Alongside all this, with its delayed introduction and teething problems, Universal Credit won for itself a dreadful reputation.

'There is no doubt that the introduction of UC by the Department for Work and Pensions (DWP) caused, and in some cases is still causing, real hardship,' wrote Nick Timmins in a report for the Institute for Government in 2020.[19] 'The nominal five or six weeks wait for payment too often turned out to be ten or twelve weeks, or even more. Rent arrears rose. In the most extreme cases, people became homeless and even lost their jobs – the exact opposite of the policy's intention.' Things have improved since then, and UC has proved its worth during Covid, but the damage to the brand is likely to last.

Its painfully long gestation period hasn't helped. A policy originally scheduled to be fully up and running by 2017 will now not be completed until the second half of the 2020s. The complexity of the task was vastly underestimated. The DWP simply did not have the capability back in the early 2010s. In its first four years, it went through no fewer than six senior civil servants in charge. 'That merry-go-round did immense damage,' wrote Nick Timmins.[20]

This stopped in September 2014, when Neil Couling took charge. He had previously run the UK's Jobcentres, so understood the system and what had to happen. Under his calm stewardship, the programme is running about as smoothly as it could have done, but oh so much more slowly than its original gung-ho proponents had hoped.

Duncan Smith left in the run-up to the Brexit referendum. The

DWP then went through a period of six secretaries of state in four years: Stephen Crabb, Damian Green, David Gauke, Esther McVey, Amber Rudd and Thérèse Coffey. That is an average tenure of about eight months or so; none of them could have begun to get to grips with such an enormous project before moving on.

The good news is that despite all this, and thanks in no small part to Neil Couling and his team of unsung heroes, Universal Credit has been getting there. In January 2017, only half of new claims were being paid in full and on time. By July 2019, 93 per cent were getting their money on time.[21] When it is fully rolled out, there should be around seven million families getting Universal Credit.[22] At least a quarter of all working-age households will be receiving it, with roughly half of those being in work.

What has been delivered is what was designed. For the unemployed it is meagre. The five-week wait for benefits, ameliorated though it has been by the availability of loans, has created hardship. Benefits are still withdrawn sharply as incomes rise, creating an effective marginal tax rate which would be inconceivable if visited upon the majority of taxpayers who are not dependent on benefits.

Once you take account of income tax and National Insurance contributions, you still lose more than 70p of every additional pound earned. That's a lot more than I, as a relatively high earner, lose when I earn an extra pound. It's a particular problem for second earners in a couple because that withdrawal rate applies from the first pound they earn. Working twenty hours a week at the minimum wage would net such a second earner less than £80. How happy would you be working for an effective wage of less than £4 an hour?

Still, that's better than a withdrawal rate of more than 90p in the pound which faced many under the old system. UC has helped ameliorate this 'poverty trap'. But it can't end the trade-off between reducing poverty and helping people into work. That trade-off is inevitable.

It was demonstrated once more by the decision to cut the withdrawal rate from 63 to 55 per cent, announced in October 2021. That will leave working recipients of UC about £1,000 a year better off on average, and will make earning more, more worthwhile. But it will also pull more than half a million more people into the reach of the UC system, including, remarkably, some higher-rate taxpayers.

Lone parents and single-earner couples with children, paying average sorts of rents, will still be eligible for UC even as their earnings rise above £50,000 a year. This is the point not only at which higher rate tax becomes payable, but at which child benefit itself starts to be withdrawn. These people are judged rich enough to pay 40 per cent tax and not to need child benefit, but poor enough to receive Universal Credit. If you make the system more generous you catch more people within its net.

There are no easy answers. One could decide to make the system more generous. One could increase the basic benefit levels, reduce the rates at which benefits are withdrawn, or increase the amounts that people could earn before benefit withdrawal begins. One could introduce a so-called 'second earner disregard' to get around the problem of second earners losing a large fraction of whatever they earn.

But each one of those policies comes with a cost. There's the simple monetary cost, which would have to be picked up in higher taxation. A system costing over £60 billion means that even relatively small changes in percentage terms cost billions. But making the system more generous also imposes costs on the recipients. The higher the benefit, the longer it takes to taper it away, so the more people are affected by high taper rates and poor work incentives. If you lower the taper rate, you slightly reduce the disincentive effects for recipients but bring many more within the scope of the taper because it inevitably reaches further up the income distribution.

I'll say it again: *there is no way around these trade-offs.* For the second or third time in my professional life, the zombie idea that is a universal basic income is doing the rounds again.

What an attractive idea it is. Give everyone a minimum income, enough to live on. Don't worry about means testing. As simple as pie. No problem of work disincentives, complexity, lack of take-up. It gives everyone a basis on which to build and protects them against the vagaries of economic change in which robots will take all our jobs in any case.

Sadly, there is a reason that no such system exists anywhere in the world. It is moonshine, fool's gold, snake oil. Politicians who pontificate about the need to consider it are charlatans. It doesn't get round any of the trade-offs I've just enumerated. Suppose you wanted to give everyone a basic income of £7,500 a year. That would require an increase in the tax burden, from its current highest level in generations, of somewhere around a third. Doable perhaps, but painful. Of course, a much higher tax burden, with higher tax rates, creates its own economic problems.

And is £7,500 enough to live on? No. Not if you have to pay rent out of it, or if you have extra costs associated with disability, say. It's less than the basic state pension. So even at this level, with the associated and completely implausible tax hike, you would still need a whole host of means tests and top-ups. To quote John Kay:

> The provision of a universal basic income at a level which would provide a serious alternative to low-paid employment is impossibly expensive. Thus, a feasible basic income cannot fulfil the hopes of some of the idea's promoters: it cannot guarantee households a standard of living acceptable in a modern society, it cannot compensate for the possible disappearance of existing low-skilled employment and it cannot eliminate 'bullshit jobs'. Either the level of basic income is unacceptably low, or the cost

of providing it is unacceptably high. And, whatever the appeal of the underlying philosophy, that is essentially the end of the matter.[23]

You can reduce the cost by providing less in respect of children and less perhaps to those on higher earnings. You can provide add-ons for housing costs and for those with disabilities. In so doing you start to recreate something rather similar to what we have. You cannot escape these trade-offs. Am I repeating myself? It bears repeating.

Kay's final warning on the attractions of a basic income is pertinent to the message of this whole book. 'As in other areas of policy, it is simply not the case that there are simple solutions to apparently difficult issues which policymakers have hitherto been too stupid or corrupt to implement.'

Yes, policymakers can be stupid and they can be corrupt. But not all of them, not all of the time, and not everywhere.

So the answer to the problems of UC is not to suggest a UBI. That makes no sense. Nor is it, frankly, to suggest dismantling UC. After more than a decade of work what we have may be far from perfect, but it's a whole lot better than what it replaced. And it works pretty well. It could be more generous, more flexible, more closely reflective of actual rents paid, less swiftly withdrawn. It could embrace more elements reflecting contributions previously paid; we could change the conditionality around searching for work; it could treat the self-employed differently. But abolish it? Replace it with some fantasy system? No. That's not how grown-up policymaking – which actually cares about the actual impact on actual people – actually works.

Tightening the screws

We've seen already that nowadays the benefit system isn't so much about the unemployed as you might expect. In the decade after the financial crisis employment reached record levels, and unemployment got down below 4 per cent. It is still there. Poverty is more than ever before an in-work phenomenon.

Part of the reason for that change is that payment of benefits is now much more conditional than it used to be. You have to be looking for work, and show you've been looking for work, to qualify for unemployment benefits. And staff at Jobcentre Plus will chivvy and help – they might help you upgrade your CV or advise on qualifications. They will probably introduce you to their FindaJob online system. Prodding and pushing, helping and encouraging, reduces the amount of time the unemployed remain unemployed. The lack of such an active role for the benefit system was one, though only one, of the reasons that long-term unemployment levels rose to such high levels in the 1980s.

I got unemployment benefit myself in the summer of 1988, between university and starting my first job. I had the summer off. Nobody chivvied me. I took the money, but it was outrageous that I could. I did nothing for it. I had a job in the bag and had no need of the money. Some tightening of the system was well overdue.

One recent change has been in the way the benefit system treats lone parents – overwhelmingly lone mothers. For decades, if you were single and had a dependent child under the age of sixteen, you could get your benefit paid with no requirement to be looking for paid work. Since 2008, conditionality has gradually been extended so that now only lone parents with children under the age of three are excused the need to search for work.[24]

The impact has been dramatic. As many as 70 per cent of

lone parents with dependent children are now in work.[25] There is even some evidence that this has actually been good for the reported life satisfaction of those affected.[26] This is intriguing, and could be because those affected underestimated the benefits of being in work.

This looks like a great policy success. Imposing job-search conditions on claimants of out-of-work benefits certainly seems effective at getting people to move into work more quickly. But newer evidence suggests that the long-term benefits may be much more limited. While many more single parents have moved into paid work, that work has been entirely part time (less than thirty hours per week) and entirely low-earning (in the bottom third of the overall earnings distribution).

This is precisely the kind of work that tends to bring little or nothing in the way of longer-term benefits for skills, labour market attachment and wages. In combination with the fact that some lone parents have simply begun claims for health-related benefits instead (which come without the same conditions), this has also meant that fiscal savings have been very minor.

It can also go horribly wrong.

Samantha was a single parent who gave evidence to the parliamentary inquiry into benefit sanctions. Until 2013, she was working full time. She was finding it affecting her mental health, struggling to manage and pay for childcare. With support from her doctor, she reluctantly moved to a part-time job. She explained her circumstances to her Jobcentre Plus work coach. They seemed understanding – but she was still sanctioned for three months for voluntarily leaving her job. She had to live on just £300 a month.

After 'paying for food and a small amount of heating, I had quite literally no money,' she said, falling behind with rent and getting food parcels from friends. Two years on, Samantha was still in debt. 'How do you catch up?' she asked MPs. 'You are still getting yourself to work, but the ends are still not being met ... when the sanction [ends], you've still got that backlog. You have still got bills that are outstanding and you are still being chased.'[27]

Jobseeker's Allowance (JSA) at times had a sanction regime so enthusiastic that, between 2010 and 2013, over 16 per cent of claimants at the peak were being referred for sanctions by having their benefits withdrawn, or reduced for failing to comply with requirements to look for work, or failure to attend interviews.[28] Sometimes, they had benefits removed for missing appointments for funerals or hospital visits.

Since then, policy has changed. Sanctioning is now much, much rarer. By November 2020, the proportion of Universal Credit claimants who were sanctioned was down to 0.13 per cent. This makes the most enormous difference to the lives of claimants.

I say policy has changed. Actually, there has been no legislation, no statement to parliament. It's *practice* that has changed. Here, as elsewhere, there is often far too little focus on how policy is delivered and far too much assumption that legislation is the end of the matter.

As we've already seen, active welfare-to-work policy has had other unintended consequences. The numbers of unemployed and the numbers of lone parents out of work and dependent on benefits have fallen. The numbers dependent on incapacity benefits – now known as Employment and Support Allowance – have remained stubbornly high. Indeed, some of the lone parents who moved off Income Support when conditionality was introduced, moved on to incapacity benefits rather than into the workplace.[29] We will look more at incapacity and disability benefits in Chapter 6. Between them they cost well over £30 billion per year. That's a huge sum, and that's just for people under pension age.

What next?

We have rediscovered, in 2022 and 2023, that one aspect of the benefit system is not fit for purpose in the face of high and rising levels of inflation. Benefits rise each April in line with inflation the previous September. This ensures the real level of benefits is generally stable over time. But in September 2021 inflation was only 3.1 per cent. By April 2022 it had hit 9 per cent. The very poorest households therefore experienced a big and unintended cut in their living standards. As inflation rose further through the year that cut only grew. Ad hoc support from government helped, but here as in other aspects of policy we forgot about inflation and how to manage when it is high and volatile. Amazingly, benefit levels are due to remain below their pre-pandemic level right the way through to April 2025 just because of the slow and backdated way in which they are adjusted for inflation.[30] The generosity of Universal Credit, unlike that of older benefits, can actually be adjusted quickly. In such circumstances it should be. Government needs to be much more flexible and nimble in future when this sort of thing happens.

Benefit policy has been in flux over the last twenty years and more. Labour brought in the huge expansion in tax credits, extending provision to millions of low earners. The Conservatives have pared that back and replaced the whole means-tested benefit system with Universal Credit.

There has been an overhaul of the incapacity and disability benefit systems, one which has failed to secure the intended savings. There have been cuts, cuts and more cuts to the generosity of benefits.

The big change has of course been the introduction of Universal Credit. It's been a huge programme, suffering all the usual problems of enormous government programmes of this sort. UC is a long way from being perfect. But the first thing I'd say about the future is that any sane government should, for the next decade or two at least, work with it.

Tweak it? Yes. Make it more generous? Sure. Rebrand it, even. Abolish it? Not if you give a damn for either the lives of the poorest or the intelligent use of government money. Structurally, it is sound. Administratively, it works OK and is getting better. Replacing it would be monumentally disruptive.

As for its generosity, the opportunity to increase it permanently, provided by the temporary £20 a week uplift during the pandemic, should perhaps not have been missed. There are, as I have stressed again and again, trade-offs here. Reasonable people can differ on whether more generous benefits are worth the additional taxes and potential impact on work incentives. But given the extraordinary fact that the real level of out-of-work benefits for some groups has barely risen in half a century, and the even more extraordinary four years of benefit freezes in the late 2010s, the case for some increase is probably now stronger than at any time in recent decades.

It is also worth saying that there may be some *economic* benefit in giving people enough income while they are out of work that they have the time and resources to find a good job, one that fits their skills and experience, rather than just the first job that comes along. That's one reason why many continental benefit systems provide higher levels of earnings replacement in the first few months of unemployment.

Our bloated housing benefit system will remain bloated for as long as large proportions of people are paying high rents in the private sector. Even more than is the case for the rest of the benefit system, housing benefit is there to pick up the pieces when things go wrong. The fundamental problems lie elsewhere. It is no coincidence that it is usually the least well-educated, those who struggled in education and found it difficult to make their way in work, who end up on incapacity and housing benefits.

It is partly that recognition of the limits of welfare policy, partly a simple desire to save money, and partly an increased understanding of how poorly the labour market works and how unjust it can be, that has led recent governments to rely increasingly on minimum wages. The National Living Wage, as it is now known, has risen from nothing to become one of the highest in the world; a remarkable change in thinking over the past quarter century.

It can't, though, be an alternative to the social security system. Minimum wages increase the incomes of individuals on low hourly earnings, while benefits increase the incomes of families with low overall incomes. These are often, indeed generally, not the same people. A lot of minimum wage earners are women with relatively well-paid partners or young people living at home with their parents. On top of that, when people in low-income families get an increase in the minimum wage, they often lose more than half of it in reduced benefit entitlements because of the way the means-testing system works. Benefits and minimum wages do different, but complementary, things. You want both. You can't replace the one with the other.

For all those reasons, I'm not going to propose that we throw the current system up in the air and start again ... *again*. Can you imagine the outcry if the tax system were chopped and changed so regularly and so fundamentally? But higher rates of Universal Credit for those with good contribution records, for example, might be possible. Certainly, we need to have a benefit system that brings the population along with it.

The fact that you can fight a successful election campaign on the basis that you are going to impose swingeing cuts on the benefits received by the poorest, as the Conservatives did in 2015, is evidence enough that our current system fails on one crucial count: public support. At least a third of the population still believe unemployment benefits are too high.[31]

In the end, the benefit system picks up and cleans up the mess that we have made elsewhere. It mops up after unemployment, low wages, chronic illness and high rents. It also risks contributing to each of them. Getting it right is a moral as well as an economic necessity.

Pensions and the Rise of the Baby Boomers

> Total benefits 'directed at pensioners': 2023/24
> £152 billion, of which state pension: £124 billion[1]
>
> Unfunded public service pensions: £53 billion
> (2023/24) with contributions of £45 billion[2]

Pensioners

Let's be cheerful for a minute. During my lifetime, if there is one aspect of British society that has changed beyond recognition, and for the better, it's the position of pensioners.

They are much richer, they are much healthier and they live much longer. I was born in 1967. Back then, 35 per cent of pensioners were living in poverty. Nearly a third of the male population (31 per cent) never even made it to their state pension age of sixty-five. Nearly 90 per cent now make it to that age.[3] And back in the late 1960s those who did make it to sixty-five could expect to live only another twelve and a half years. Nowadays, those who make it to sixty-five can expect to live another twenty-three years.[4] Even by the 1980s pensioners were still far more likely to be in poverty than the rest of the population.

I still remember in the late 1980s, when I was starting work, how researchers and policymakers from other countries would look on aghast at the woeful level of pension provision here in the UK, and at the levels of pensioner poverty. Fast forward to the early 2020s and, after four decades of steadily improving fortunes, pensioners are now less likely to be poor than any other group. In fact, they are easily the wealthiest section of society. Amazingly, once you account for housing costs and the costs of children, their incomes are, on average, higher than those of people below pension age, having overtaken them for the first time in history back in 2011.

That has at least one obvious implication. If pensioners are better off than non-pensioners, and incomes grow over time, then the current generation of pensioners must be better off now than they were when they were working. That is exactly what the overall stats suggest. It's also what you find when you look at individuals' incomes over the course of their lives.[5] We have been too successful, saved too much, transferred more to pensioners than makes any sense.

Today we worry about a different sort of intergenerational inequality. It's the young who are struggling. It's working-age people with children who are most likely to be in poverty. After decades of increases, homeownership rates have collapsed among those in their twenties and thirties to little more than half what they were twenty-five years ago. A combination of the demise of occupational pension schemes and, until recently, rock-bottom interest rates mean that young people have little chance of saving as much for their pensions as their parents did.

Meanwhile, the state pension has enjoyed a rollercoaster ride. The basic pension became increasingly mean between 1980 and 2010, but has got more generous since. Big rises in means-tested benefits helped the poorest pensioners. Many of those retiring in the 2000s got generous earnings-related state pensions. These are no longer available to younger generations. And state pension ages are now set on an inexorably, if belatedly, rising path.

Certainly, none of us can rely on the state for a decent standard of living in retirement. At least none of us who are working in the private sector. The public sector remains the last bastion of generous, earnings-related pension provision.

The current set-up is delivering a comfortable retirement for the current generation of pensioners. But today's thirty- and forty-somethings face a much more perilous time once they eventually stop working. Today's triumphs may be just a prelude to tomorrow's disasters.

And we must have a continual eye on the future. Decisions made today will affect who gets paid what for decades to come. In some cases maybe even for centuries.

Literally as I write this, some remarkable news appears on my Twitter feed. Helen Viola Jackson of Marshfield, Missouri has died at the age of 101.[6] She had married in 1936, at the age of seventeen, a ninety-three-year-old veteran of the American Civil War of 1861 to 1865. As a girl she had been helping to care for him. He had thought, as was not uncommon at the time, to reward her by marrying her and thereby giving her the right to receive his veteran's pension. Having never married since, she could indeed have been receiving that pension until her death in December 2020.

Unfortunately for this story it seems that she never actually applied for it. But earlier in 2020, Irene Triplett, the daughter of a civil war veteran, was recorded as the last person actually in receipt of a civil war pension (of $877.56 a year) to die.[7] There were certainly widows of civil war veterans drawing their pensions well into the 2000s.

Decisions taken on pensions can cast a very, very long shadow.

How it all began

In the early nineteenth century, the impoverished elderly were treated just as any other poor people under the infamous Poor Laws. Relief was normally given in 'workhouses' and no recognition given to the notion of retirement.

Retirement itself is a relatively recent invention. It wasn't until David Lloyd George's Old Age Pension Act of 1908 that legislation was finally introduced. The pension system put in place was funded through general taxation, was means-tested, and available from age seventy to those of 'good character'. 'A scheme for the very old, the very poor and the very respectable,' in the words of historian Pat Thane.[8]

Some debates on the issue from the time still sound remarkably familiar. Of course, there was the question of paying for it. That was in large part what Lloyd George's famous People's Budget of 1909 was all about – raising enough tax to pay for the pensions and other benefits he had promised. He had rather more trouble than most modern chancellors, needing to win two general elections to force it through the Conservative majority in the House of Lords. How to pay for pensions has been a perennial worry ever since.

Also hotly debated was whether the scheme should be

contributory – should entitlement to the pension depend on a record of contributions? After much debate the decision was taken not to go down that route. In words which I would happily echo, *The Times* reported Lloyd George as saying 'that a contributory scheme must be cumbersome, expensive, and, in a country like ours, wholly impracticable ... would be unjust to many people. The vast majority of women would be excluded from its benefits ...'[9]

As we will see, much of the history of the actual state pension over the last forty years or more has been a belated recognition of this fact. The contributory principle has been chipped away so much that it is now close to impossible for anyone who has lived in the UK, with the possible exception of the idle rich, to avoid full entitlement to the state pension. We have all the contributory paraphernalia for no evident purpose.

A limited contributory scheme, predating Beveridge by two decades, was in fact soon put in place. It was swept away after 1945 by William Beveridge's far more comprehensive National Insurance system. Beveridge himself was ideologically wedded to the concept of social insurance – that benefits should be paid because of contributions made. Not only that, but there should be actuarial fairness. If benefits were to be paid at a flat rate, then contributions should also be flat rate. He is lauded as the father of the welfare state, but he was single-minded and unbending in pursuit of a vision which was fundamentally misconceived.

Pensions were paid immediately to those over sixty-five, so of course the contributory basis was broken immediately. No fund could accumulate because current contributions paid for current pensions. Flat-rate contributions proved unsustainable, and inequitable, as costs rose.

The pension was set at subsistence level, so right from the start many pensioners found themselves dependent on means-tested benefits as top-ups. Beveridge thought that the appropriate level for pensions would be fixed, not rise in line with general living standards, making the system increasingly affordable. That was, obviously, an utterly wrongheaded presumption.

Over the decades after that, the level of the pension gradually rose, but it remained very mean. Meanwhile, costs rose, and National Insurance contributions became gradually more related to earnings. A miserly earnings-related top-up to the basic pension – the graduated pension – was added in 1961 followed in 1978 by the vastly, and unsustainably, more generous SERPS (State Earnings Related Pension Scheme). Forgive me for quoting at length from best little book on social security ever written:

The problem is fundamental and recurrent. The provision of pensions through social insurance requires either a very protracted period – fifty years or more – before the scheme reaches maturity; or a rate of contribution which is much in excess of the actual cost of promised benefits; or a large initial subsidy from general taxation. None of these possibilities is ever politically acceptable, and that is why the system is constantly under acute financial pressure. There is an apparent solution to the dilemma. It is to offer ever increasing benefit levels. The advantage is that you can finance current deficits by current contributions which can be justified by reference to benefits which are not now being paid but will be received in the future. The device of meeting yesterday's claims from today's premiums has been familiar to fraudulent and foolish financiers for millennia, and the gaols and workhouses of the world are filled with those private individuals who did not realise that reality breaks through eventually ... This is how the Beveridge scheme was, in the event, paid for – by steadily increasing contribution rates accompanied by corresponding promises of increases in future benefits.[10]

That was written in 1984 by Andrew Dilnot (my predecessor-but-one at the IFS), John Kay (its then director) and Nick Morris. Their warnings still ring loud in my ears whenever I think about pension policy – something which I do on an unhealthily regular basis.

The rise and fall of SERPS

To understand where we are with pensions today we can skip most of what happened in the thirty years after Beveridge, but there is no way we can skip the State Earnings Related Pension Scheme. Nothing that has happened to our pension system in the last forty years is remotely comprehensible without reference to this vast, ingenious and ultimately doomed experiment. It took one act of parliament in 1975 to put in place and forty years of continuous upheaval to eventually put out of its misery.

Introduced by left-wing Labour minister Barbara Castle *with all-party support*, its purpose was to provide something like an occupational pension to those who didn't have access to one through their employer. That cross-party support may have been helped by the unusual friendship that developed across the political divide between Castle's junior pensions minister Brian O'Malley and his Conservative opposite number, Kenneth Clarke. O'Malley was a former band leader. Both loved jazz and some of the details of the bill were hammered out over a beer or two at Ronnie Scott's Soho jazz club.

The system was properly generous, offering a quarter of your average earnings, measured over the best twenty years of your working life, plus a generous widow's pension, on top of the basic state pension. Payments were supposed to relate to contributions; but you've just seen the warning about that.

Its introduction was accelerated so that full benefits would be payable much faster than if it had been genuinely contributory, and it was used as an excuse to increase contributions which were used to pay for current costs. A complex system of 'contracting out' was layered on top. Those with a good occupational pension wouldn't need SERPS too, so they would pay a lower rate of NICs.

In a pretty scandalous, perhaps deliberate, oversight, its long-term costs appear never to have been modelled by the government which introduced it. It took more work from the indefatigable John Kay to demonstrate the massive eventual costs which were set to escalate at an alarming rate into the 2000s. Perhaps because of the speed with which it was developed, perhaps because of the lack of parliamentary scrutiny, that decision back in 1975 has cast a shadow over pension policy ever since. Hence why, to a large extent, the last forty years have been occupied with undoing it.

That was difficult for all sorts of reasons. Taking away something generous is never easy. Though on this occasion public awareness of this enormous benefit was never very high. I recall my own stepfather being astonished when he received his first pension payment at the end of the 1990s to find he was getting something substantially in excess of the basic pension. He had no idea he'd have that extra cushion of income to rely on. In one Gallup Poll in the eighties, only half the population had ever heard of it.

A series of reforms in the 1980s, 1990s and 2000s gradually reduced its generosity before SERPS was finally got rid of in 2016. In its place we now have a single state pension, worth, in 2023, just shy of £204 a week. It is payable, to a first approximation, to everyone who has lived most of their working life and then retired in the UK.

I'm genuinely proud to say that the man responsible for this enormous rationalisation was my old friend and colleague Steve

Webb, pensions minister in the coalition government between 2010 and 2015. When I first met him, I was a new graduate starting at the IFS back in the late 1980s and he was my first line manager. I never guessed at that moment that he would go on to become first an MP and then a minister.

Steve won't mind me saying he was on the nerdy end of the spectrum at the IFS, itself a pretty nerdy place. He liked nothing better than spending weeks sorting out and analysing big and complex datasets. Not the standard training for a minister. We could do with more of the same.

We could also do with more ministers who are not only strikingly clever, highly analytical, and determined to make the world a better place, but also expert. For someone like him who had spent years studying and analysing welfare policy to end up as a minister of state in the Department for Work and Pensions was not just a personal triumph but a huge boon to the country.

At the outset, he said he wanted the words 'single state pension' carved on his tombstone. He knew what he wanted to achieve. He also knew it would be tough, but he persevered. I remember early on in his tenure gossiping with some of his senior officials. They were dismissive of his ambitions. Too complicated. The Treasury would never wear it. I believed them. We were wrong.

Before his reforms, Steve told me, the government was doing 'three things badly rather than one thing well'. The basic pension was lower than in any other advanced country bar Mexico. The pension credit, designed to make sure everyone reached a minimum income above the level of the basic pension, was heavily means-tested and failed to reach many it was intended to help. As for what remained of SERPS, the associated complexity created huge burdens, uncertainty and unfairness.

Steve also took the view that it should not be the state's job to replicate earnings inequality in retirement as SERPS had done. Therein lies a rather fundamental philosophical tension. Beveridge had come out clearly for a flat-rate pension. He didn't think it any business of the state to provide earnings-related benefits.

But Barbara Castle took the opposite view – everyone, not just those fortunate enough to be able to access an occupational pension, should be able to get an earnings-related pension. Most of our Western European neighbours also take that opposite view. Their systems were created in the Bismarckian tradition, named for Otto von Bismarck who introduced a state pension scheme in Germany in the 1880s, a quarter-century before Lloyd-George got his scheme off the ground here in the UK. Steve Webb disagreed.

To bring to life his vision of a single, adequate, flat-rate pension for all, Steve first had to persuade the Treasury. His primary port of call was Rupert Harrison, chief adviser to Chancellor George Osborne and, remarkably, another IFS alumnus.

With Harrison on board, the Treasury could be consulted more formally. The message that came back was oddly phrased – it said that 'HM Treasury is not opposed to this proposal'. And if that sounded a little cold, they also stipulated that no extra money could be spent at all in the early years. Given the context of austerity, the reluctance to spend money was hardly surprising, but it could have scuppered the project. If it had done, the exchequer would still have been on the hook for the costs of the state second pension – all that was left of SERPS. That cost would have been enormous. The Treasury would have sacrificed huge long-term savings if securing them had cost even a small amount up front.

That was, as Webb says, 'dreadful policymaking'. This focus on the short term is, sadly, all too frequent. But those were the constraints within which he had to work. He made the sums add up. He fiddled with the number of years of contributions required to qualify for a full pension. Above all, though, abolishing contracting out – the system which allowed those with good private pensions to opt out of SERPS and hence pay lower National Insurance contributions – earned the Treasury billions. If there is no earnings-related pension, there is nothing for those in occupational schemes to contract out of. What that largely meant in effect was a tax rise for public sector workers – pretty much the last group still in occupational pensions in any number. It also gave the lie once more to the fiction of the contributory system. With the end of SERPS the logic should have been to level *down* the rate of NICs.

Despite these hiccups the package was passed and it even took effect a year earlier than expected, in 2016. Even before that, he says he had come across pension advisors complaining they had been doing work for clients estimating their final pensions – and they were all coming out the same. Which meant that one element at least was working, so far.

Where are we today?

We're sort of back to square one – a single, flat-rate state pension at a level, arguably, just about enough to subsist on. And payable, in principle at least, in return for an adequate record of contributions. You'll have gathered already that that last part is no longer really true.

Time spent ill, or looking after children, or registered unemployed, or caring for someone who is ill, all counts towards the contributory record just as much as being in paid work. And so it should. We are close to having a pension paid in respect of length of residence in the UK and we'd do better just to say so rather than continue to pretend otherwise, because we still create a deal of complexity and unfairness by doing so.

But it isn't just the fact that, in 2023, we have a flat-rate pension of £204 a week that matters. Two other things also matter fundamentally. What age do you qualify to get it, and how fast does it rise over time?

As I write this, the answer to the first question is sixty-six. For women that's six years older than was the case back in 2010. For men, the state pension age has risen by just one year. This is the first time since 1940, when the female pension age was reduced to sixty, that the two sexes have been treated equally in that sense.

Pension ages stayed at sixty-five for men and sixty for women for the next seventy years even as life expectancy rose, and despite the fact that women live considerably longer than men. That pension ages for both men and women should have risen, and be brought into line with one another, seems to me obvious. There is no plausible reason for paying pensions to women at an earlier age than men. And there is no getting around the need to respond to hugely increased longevity. It is more surprising that it took such an extraordinarily long time for either to happen.

The legislation to increase female pension age to sixty-five, aimed at equalising it with men, sailed through parliament in the early 1990s. The target was to start the process of gradually raising their pension age from 2010, with parity reached in 2020. That feels like good policy. It was forward looking, and it gave people plenty of notice. It was also clearly necessary.

The trouble was that it still came as a surprise to many women when they hit sixty and expected to get a pension that then took several years to materialise. It's easy for those of us steeped in this stuff to forget how normal human beings lead their lives, not necessarily focused on every twist and turn in government policy.

A very vocal pressure group, the WASPI women, was born, demanding compensation for those disadvantaged by the policy. WASPI stands for Women Against State Pension Inequality. While recognising their concerns, and the failure of communication involved, it must be right that the policy has gone ahead. It was a high point for their campaign, and perhaps a low point for the

Labour Party, that a late addition to its 2019 manifesto committed a staggering £58 billion to compensating them.[11] Frankly, if governments can't make policy of this sort without offering compensation then they might as well pack up and go home. Whatever the rights and wrongs, if you concede on this then you pretty much accept that you can never change the status quo in a way which makes anyone worse off than they had expected.

Planned longer-term increases in state pension ages for both men and women have a different origin. Faced with the long-term question of what to do about pensions, in light of concerns about costs and about the demise of private occupational provision (of which more later) Blair's Labour government deployed one of its most popular mechanisms for solving, or more often just avoiding, problematic issues.

They commissioned an independent report to analyse the issues and recommend a way forward. The pensions commission, chaired by Adair, now Lord, Turner, was by far the most successful and influential of all the many independent reviews carried out in that period between 1997 and 2010. It set the scene for rises in state pension age. It also changed completely the debate about the indexation of the state pension. And it recommended a revolution in private pension provision – a revolution which has now happened.

The central thrust of the commission's first report was to make it clear that the nation faced an unavoidable choice between four possible options: stick with current policy and allow some pensioners to get poorer relative to the rest of society as the value of the state pension relative to earnings continued on its ever-downward trend; increase the amount of tax revenue devoted to pensions; increase private savings; or raise the average retirement age. Combining analysis of the highest quality with carefully orchestrated public communication, Turner and his team came up with a formula which included long run increases in the pension age.

As they pointed out, life expectancy had shot up in the previous thirty years. In 1971, life expectancy at birth was sixty-nine for men and seventy-five for women. By 2011, that had reached seventy-nine and eighty-three respectively. Life expectancy at sixty-five had risen from twelve and sixteen years for men and women respectively to eighteen and twenty-one years.[12] These were extraordinary changes. A social and human triumph.

At the same time the state pension age had not changed one whit. So this triumph had come at an increasing cost as people were spending more and more time, and a bigger and bigger fraction of their lives, in retirement on the state pension. Paying an adequate state pension from age sixty-five would become increasingly and unsustainably expensive in the face of an ever-growing elderly population.

Turner and his commission did a huge amount to draw the political poison from the idea of a rising pension age. James Purnell, secretary of state for work and pensions at the time the final report was published, reflected:

> Raising the state pension age is one of things which you kind of think 'Oh my God, if you say this everybody is going to go crazy.' But you said it lots and lots of times in a series of controlled explosions and it went from page one of the paper, to page three to page five. And by the end it was 'Oh yeah, everybody knows they're raising the retirement age'.[13]

We now have increases in pension age legislated to sixty-seven by 2028 and to sixty-eight in 2046. The government had indicated that it wanted to bring forward that rise to sixty-eight to 2038. It bottled that decision during 2023, putting off any tough choice until after an election. It will need to get on and legislate if that's what it does want to do.

Turner also had a decisive effect on the other critical parameter which determines the generosity, and cost, of the state pension – the rate at which it should rise each year to compensate for inflation.

In the early 1980s, the Thatcher government had broken the link between the level of the state pension and earnings. Since then, the pension had risen only in line with prices. That was a happy time when earnings tended to rise quite a bit faster than prices. The result was a state pension whose level was falling further and further behind average earnings. It was not enough to live on and not enough to avoid the need to fall back on means-tested benefits.

Turner might have wanted us to wait longer before we became entitled to a pension, but he wanted that pension to be worthwhile, and recommended that it rise over time with earnings. Despite a determined rearguard action from Gordon Brown and the Treasury, this proposal was also implemented.

In fact, since 2010, that proposal has been implemented on speed. The pension doesn't just rise each year in line with earnings, it rises each year in line with the price inflation, average earnings growth or by 2.5 per cent, whichever is the greatest: the so-called triple lock. Given the austerity visited upon pretty much every other aspect of public spending during that decade it has been a remarkable and expensive policy commitment; one reiterated in the manifestos of both main parties ever since.

With my rational and purist policy analyst's hat on, this is a crazy policy. The value of the state pension into the future is a random number. It could be worth a lot more than it is today or just the same depending on the precise level of, and relationship between, price and earnings growth in each year.

You'd think at least that under this rule, if earnings and prices both rose by 20 per cent over a decade, then the pension would rise by 20 per cent. Not a bit of it. If prices rise 20 per cent this year and nothing next year, while earnings rise nothing this year and 20 per cent next, each will rise 20 per cent in total while the pension will rise by 40 per cent.

This is not a rational way to make policy. But, oxymoronically, that doesn't make it irrational. My old friend Steve Webb is the epitome of rationality and he thinks it's a great policy. The circle is squared by considering the art of the possible in politics. If you simply think the pension should be more generous than it is today, but you don't think you can get government to agree a higher level to aim at, then this random walk towards greater generosity may be the best you can do. Over the long run it makes a very big difference. It also adds tens of billions of pounds to the bill.

Paying for the public sector

Among the hundreds of billions of pounds the government spent to support the economy through the Covid crisis, you might have missed the odd £17 billion that it was planning to shell out to rectify a major cock-up.

This particular cock-up relates to reforms to the pensions provided to public sector employees. For the state pension from which we will all benefit is not the only big chunk of money the government pays out in pensions every year. It also shells out around £53 billion a year in pensions to former doctors, nurses, civil servants, police officers and other retired public sector workers. That's getting on for half the total cost of the state pension. Quite a lot, when you consider that only a small minority of pensioners benefit.

It had all started so well. Back in June 2010, one of the first actions of the coalition government was to set up a review of public sector pensions, led by the former Labour cabinet minister Lord Hutton of Furness. These schemes had become far more expensive than ever intended, as life expectancy had risen and interest rates fallen. They had also diverged dramatically from what was available in the private sector.

The same trends in life expectancy and interest rates had led most similar pension schemes to close their doors to new members. It was clearly not sensible to avoid reform any longer. Promising to pay generous final-salary-related pensions from age sixty to millions of public sector workers (Labour had increased the pension age to sixty-five, but only for new entrants) into the indefinite future looked too expensive, and unfair on taxpayers. It certainly was that.

Following Lord Hutton's recommendations,[14] government committed to: increasing pension ages for most public sector workers in line with the state pension age; ensuring that increases in costs were shared with the workforce so that employee contributions would rise; and calculating pension entitlements on the basis of average earnings rather than final earnings. They also made important changes to the accrual and indexation of pensions.

This left much undone, as I see every time one of my civil servant friends in their mid-fifties shuffles off into a comfortable, taxpayer-funded retirement. Or as one sees in the impact of higher contributions on the squeezed wages of nurses and teachers. Or, indeed, in the absurd fact that a long-term low earner working in the NHS (say earning in the low £20,000s) will retire on a higher income than they ever had in work, once you add the state pension to their NHS pension. That just makes no sense. We'd be much better paying them more now and having a less absurdly generous pension.

So where we have landed still needs some work. But in broad terms, this looked like good policymaking from the coalition government. Address a long-term issue around funding and equity. Bring the unions and workforce largely with you. Make the system more progressive.

So, where was the cock-up? Well, in an effort to mollify the unions, the government agreed that those within ten years of pension age should not be affected by the reforms. You can see the argument. Those close to retirement have a set of expectations and plans and limited time to adjust to a new set of rules.

Unfortunately, these reforms affected judges, among the rest of the public sector, and judges tend to be quite conversant with the law. They, and the firefighters, took the government to court on the grounds of age discrimination – because younger workers were treated less favourably than older workers. They won. The government was refused leave to appeal, so clear was the legal case.

The cost of complying with the law? A cool £17 billion. That's because the government chose to comply not by reducing generosity to the older workers but by giving younger workers the option, for a period, to accrue benefits under the older, more generous scheme. Given the way the rules work, this will be a straight give-away from taxpayers to the highest paid and most privileged public sector workers.

You might feel that this was all simply a bit unfortunate. Mistakes happen and, after all, there is an argument for treating those near retirement differently from others. But then you might look back at Lord Hutton's original report. He pointed out that his proposals would have limited impact on those in their fifties. Accrued pension rights were, after all, protected – it was only pension rights earned in respect of future service that were to be affected. And then he wrote this: 'Age discrimination legislation also means that it is not possible in practice to provide protection from change for members who are already above a certain age.'[15]

There are some lessons from this, and not all of them are about pensions.

First, the law is an ass. For government to be unable to implement a policy of this sort, for which there is clearly an arguable case, leaves it unnecessarily fettered. There is a case for adjusting the law.

Second, they still should not have tried to implement the protection. This was all of a piece with a huge and ongoing bias in public policy towards protecting the older generation at the expense of the young. And having lost the case, they should have heeded Lord Hutton's advice that the impact on older workers would in any case have been manageable. Rather than extending the protection to all, the government could instead have simply removed it entirely.

Third, this episode demonstrates yet again the importance of competence in politics, something sadly missing for a long time and at great cost to us all. Anthony King and Ivor Crewe published the wonderful and appalling *The Blunders of Our Governments* back in 2013.[16] Since then there has been plenty of material for a second volume. This particular £17 billion blunder would barely make the cut. The competition for inclusion has been fierce.

The whole episode is also an illustration of how hard change can be when it comes to pensions. The costs are in the future, so there's never quite the burning platform there is when it comes to immediate spending. Given the scale of austerity across the rest of public spending, the cuts to public service pensions were pretty small beer.

I was a police officer from 1971 to 2001 and paid 11 per cent of my gross salary into the pension scheme during all those years ... I am no economist but today I am quite (pleasantly) amazed at my financial situation. Two facts stand out. (1) Since April, this year my pension now equates with my final salary from December 2001. (2) My pension over the first eighteen years of retirement was more than I earned in my career.

Also in the spring of 2017 both our state pensions kicked in increasing our joint income by about £1,300 p.m. ... This reinforces Mr Johnson's comments about some schemes being 'absurdly generous'.

A colleague of mine received that email from a retired police officer after an article I wrote during 2022.[17] It illustrates many of the absurdities quite nicely. And note the date of retirement and the date at which his state pension became payable. This gentleman was clearly able to retire from the police force on a very generous pension at the age of fifty.

Public service pensions remain far more valuable than almost anything available in the private sector. Despite some prognostications, paying them is not going to break us – the fraction of national income which we spend on them is likely to fall over time. But it is time to look at them again, and perhaps reset the relationship between pay and pensions for our public service workers.

Whatever happened to private pensions?

The dodgy financier and showman chair of Mirror Group Newspapers, Robert Maxwell, fell off his yacht one dawn in 1991 in the Bay of Biscay, probably while weeing over the stern. He was embroiled in controversy at the time as he desperately tried to shore up the Mirror Group's share price. Mainly – as it turned out – by siphoning off £453 million from the Mirror pension fund.

That was the beginning of the end for pension funds. It created such a collective panic that they were protected into extinction. There was political uproar when the plight of the Mirror pensioners became clear – though most of them received most of their money in the end. Something had to be done to ring-fence pensions, and there was then a political race to protect the increasingly embattled corporate pension schemes in ways that, paradoxically, helped to bring about their demise.

Legislation gave members of schemes absolute rights to what the schemes had hitherto offered on a 'best efforts' basis, thereby dramatically increasing risks, actual and perceived, faced by sponsoring employers. By 2005, as many as 42 per cent of schemes had closed their doors to new staff.[18] Now they have almost completely disappeared.

In truth, these defined benefit schemes have faced bigger problems than over-zealous regulation. Perhaps the biggest has been the fact that the old compound interest machine has run down. Interest rates have been falling for decades and, at least until 2022, have been close to zero since 2010. That makes meeting future promises ever harder, especially as regulation has pushed more and more of these schemes to invest in very safe assets with minuscule returns.

Which is madness. If there is anything that should be looking for the higher returns available in stock markets it is occupational pensions. They are long-lived, company-backed schemes with far more capacity to manage the risks associated with investing in stocks and shares than you or I with our personal pensions and ISAs.

The world has turned upside down: not long ago these schemes were overwhelmingly invested in equities whilst only the richest private citizens had direct exposure to the stock market. Now most of us have our own individual pensions invested in stocks and shares and we directly bear all the risk of the market going down. We have to invest in shares – it's the only chance of getting any return at all. We who are individually least well placed to manage risk have been forced into taking risks. Big funds with decades of life and corporate backing have moved out of the risk-taking business.

If regulation and rock-bottom interest rates were not enough, ever-increasing life expectancy has – until it flattened out recently – only added to this toxic mix. Of course, living longer is a great thing. But if you're a pension fund committed to paying a fixed amount every year from age sixty until death and your members resolutely refuse to die, then you're going to be in trouble.

Someone has to pay for all this. Unlike state pensions and the public sector occupational pensions, the private sector schemes are funded. The pensioners contributed while they were working, as did their employers. But as it turns out they didn't contribute anywhere near enough. Once again, it's the working-age population, and the company shareholders, who are funnelling hundreds of billions towards a retired generation who were promised pensions which have turned out far more generous and expensive than anyone ever intended.

So, we have inadvertently destroyed the old occupational pensions. But not all is gloom. There has been an enormous upsurge in membership of new schemes in the last four or five years – 90 per cent of employees are now putting money into employer-sponsored private pensions, a figure that has more than doubled in a decade.[19]

Adair Turner and his pensions commission can take much of the credit for this remarkable turnaround as well. In the face of the relentless decline in traditional pension schemes, and evidence that people weren't making their own provision, he proposed a completely new model. Employers would have to offer a scheme and employees would be automatically enrolled into it. They would have the choice, they could opt to be unenrolled, but membership would be the default. Apathy has turned out to be the winner. Hardly anyone has made the effort to not contribute. Pension membership has grown by more than even the most optimistic proponents of automatic enrolment had dared predict.

All is well then? Not quite. For one thing contributions to these new pensions are orders of magnitude lower than contributions to old style occupational schemes. Small amounts in will translate into small amounts out. This new settlement also ignores the growing army of the self-employed. At the turn of the century around half of the self-employed were making provision for their retirement through pension saving. That had fallen to less than a fifth by 2020.[20] They have moved away from pensions in droves.

More fundamentally, these are not really even pensions like the old occupational schemes. They are basically just savings pots. There is none of the risk-sharing that was supposed to be the hallmark of the traditional schemes. If your investments go bad, or you live through a period of low returns, tough. It's all on you.

Governments and companies are better placed to bear risk than individuals, but under these schemes all the risk is on the individual. The volatile stock markets that followed on from the pandemic saw the value of savings accumulated over decades gyrating wildly. Global markets lost almost a third of their value in March and April 2020 before recovering strongly only to fall by 20 per cent again in the first half of 2022.

These days, when you retire and want to use your pension pot, you don't have to actually buy a pension. Until 2015, if you saved in one of these 'defined contribution' pensions, you (mostly) had to buy an annuity at the point at which you wanted to access those savings. An annuity provides a guaranteed income for life – like a pension. It's a form of insurance against living so long you'll run out of money.

But my old friend Steve Webb wasn't just responsible for the transformation of the state pension, he also had a hand in the introduction of so-called 'pension freedoms', the end of the requirement that you buy an annuity. The clamour to end that rule had become impossible to ignore as those ever-falling interest rates had made annuities impossibly expensive. At one point half a million quid would buy you an annuity of barely £15,000 a year if you wanted protection against inflation; thirty years ago it would have bought about three times that. By 2023, with interest rates higher, you might have got £25,000 a year from your half million pounds.

The rumour was that this idea came direct from Chancellor George Osborne, and that the Treasury failed even to consult Steve, despite his job as pensions' minister. This was not the case, he told me. 'As a Liberal, I feel that people should have the right to say no – why should they be forced to buy something which, for good reasons, are not good value.' Indeed, he is perhaps most famous for saying that he wouldn't be bothered if people blew their pension pot on a Lamborghini. Very liberal, but rather out of character for someone I can't really see in an Italian sports car.

Since the average pension pot is currently less than £50,000, this may not be a widespread problem. In fact, as he says now, the bigger worry is that people will undermine their own lives, not so much with reckless spending but with 'reckless caution', keeping hold of their savings into late old age and not enjoying what they have. That, in fact, is what you see in the data – pensioners in general don't spend as much of their money as we economists might consider rational.

The future

Financially, our pension system looks a lot more sustainable than that in many other countries. Even the Americans spend a higher fraction of national income on state pensions than we do. They have a form of earnings-related scheme. As of 2017 we spent about 5.6 per cent of national income on benefits for those in old age against 7.1 per cent in the US, 7.7 per cent across the OECD as a whole, 10 per cent in Germany and more than 13 per cent in

France.[21] We won't be spending anything like that sort of amount even as population ageing peaks later in the century.

The flipside is that with private provision diminishing, the high standards of living enjoyed by many of today's pensioners are likely to be less widespread in the future. This reflects not only the collapse of generous occupational pensions but also less generous state pensions for many, low interest rates, and lower rates of homeownership among younger generations.

On the other hand, there will be plenty more pensioners. Today there are about twelve million over-sixty-fives, representing about 18 per cent of the total UK population. The Office for National Statistics projects that there will be eighteen million of them (us, if I'm still alive by then) by 2050, making up a quarter of the population.[22] That's about twice the fraction as when I was born in the mid-1960s.

As we will see in Chapter 5, when we look at health and social care, the numbers of the oldest old, those over eighty and ninety, will grow even faster.

If we ditch the triple lock and raise pension ages to sixty-eight in 2038 as intended, then state pension spending should only increase by about 1 per cent of national income over the next forty years or so. That's about £20 billion in current terms. Biggish but perfectly manageable. If, however, we keep the triple lock and don't increase pension age to sixty-eight until 2046 as currently legislated, then spending will rise by more like 2.5 per cent of national income, more than £50 billion.[23] That's a serious increase requiring some bumper tax rises. Choices matter.

Now, finally, we have the basics in place – a state pension that is simple to understand and will make sure most pensioners are not in poverty. A couple will get about £20,000 a year from the state pension. Not great for those of us used to earning rather more, but not a bad contribution from the state. A platform on which to build, and one that is financially sustainable.

But – but. All is not well.

Partly, where we've got to is plain unfair. The current silver surfers, baby boomers, call them what you will, have scooped the pool and the rest of us are paying for it (I was born just slightly too late to officially count as a boomer, despite what my kids call me). The boomers benefited from tax relief, rising life expectancy, and interest rates which perfectly served their purpose. They might think they paid for their own pensions, but by and large they didn't.

Not only did younger generations have to deal with zero interest rates and the demise of occupational pensions, they are having to pick up the tab for their parents' good fortune. And that's before we start looking at what has been happening in the housing market. We taxpayers are also still paying for some outrageously generous pensions in the public sector.

But, hey, life's unfair. If those were the biggest problems, we could live with them. Yet unfairness begets unfairness, and these unfairnesses will cast a long shadow through history. The forces which have concentrated wealth in one generation as never before have also concentrated wealth within parts of that generation. Much of that wealth will be passed down to their children.

As earnings stagnate and wealth grows then what you inherit, or how much your parents can help you while they're still alive, is becoming more and more important relative to your own efforts. Never has the imprecation to choose your parents wisely been more apposite.

We could do something about some of those unfairnesses. We should certainly look to get more tax from the well-pensioned older generation. Easy for me to say as an unelected nerd, harder I know for those who need pensioners' votes, but justice really does demand it.

That said, the real long-term challenges lie elsewhere.

First, we need to decide what level of state pension we actually want, rather than relying on the random walk along which the triple lock is dragging us. If we want a somewhat higher pension in ten years' time then let's say so now and get there in a steady and transparent manner.

Second, the quid pro quo for that should be the abolition of add-ons like winter heating allowances and free bus passes which hark back to the days when pensioners were actually poor. The fuss over getting rid of free TV licences specifically for the non-poor over seventy-fives – those on means-tested benefits will continue to get them free – illustrates the continued power of the pensioner lobby. But it is time to resist.

Third, there must be an acceleration of the currently legislated increase in state pension age. It should hit sixty-eight in the 2030s, rising again in the 2040s. That needs to go hand in hand with a clear set of communications about why this is happening and why people should expect to work longer than their parents.

Fourth, we need to stop fixating on just supporting those over an arbitrary state pension age. If you are out of work, benefit levels roughly double when you hit state pension age. Perhaps we need to phase in an increase in the generosity of some benefits before state pension age.

Fifth, and most important, we need to recognise that we have completely trashed our private pension system. Defined benefit pensions are gone from the private sector forever, and the triumph of auto-enrolment is actually a triumph of widespread but small-scale saving, not a pension system at all, let alone a replacement for those DB schemes.

At the least we need to increase default contribution rates and extend to the ever-growing army of the self-employed. More fundamentally we need to find ways of increasing the risk sharing that goes on. Perhaps government could subsidise the first few thousand of annuity provision, or only ask you to provide your own annuity to age eighty or eighty-five and then provide more money to see you through to the end of life.

Risk sharing is even trickier in the accumulation phase. Old style defined benefit plans provided it, but actually resulted in too little risk being borne by the pension recipient. All the risk ended up with the sponsoring company. It may be that part of the answer will lie in collective defined contribution schemes. The idea is to come up with a scheme that gives employees more certainty than they get from a personal pension while giving employers more flexibility than allowed in defined benefit schemes.

That's hard to codify and will require give and take, but we can look in a surprising direction for what might be a glimpse of the future. An organisation no less ancient and august than the Royal Mail itself has blazed a trail in this direction. With contributions from employees and employer, the scheme will guarantee a lump sum at retirement and provide a pension, but the pension won't be guaranteed.

Similar arrangements are common in the Netherlands. A collective scheme like this will keep costs down, avoid over-conservative investments and involve risk-sharing both across and within generations. It will also be mighty hard to communicate and you can just imagine the rows that will ensue when pension payments fail to meet members' expectations. As with everything in this book, there are no easy answers.

5

Health

Department of Health and Social Care budget 2023/24: £186 billion, of which NHS England £160 billion[1]

Let me start by making a small confession. I wasn't among those who went outside during the first Covid lockdown to give our NHS staff a clap. That comes partly from a natural contrariness on my part. But it also comes from a growing irritation at our national obsession with the NHS.

Of course, the work it does is important. Of course, I appreciate the sacrifices made by the nurses and doctors who work for it and care for us – and especially those they made during the pandemic.

Thank you to them. Thank you to the NHS for employing my parents. My father was a doctor. My mother spent most of her working life as a secretary in the NHS. That's how they met. The NHS brought them together. I'm more in debt to it than most for bringing me into this world.

Even so, the NHS really isn't special. Yes, it does do well in protecting people against the financial costs of illness, but we are not in the least bit unusual in providing largely free, publicly funded health care to our citizens. Nor, as our worship of it might lead you to suppose, is the NHS especially good by international standards. It's quite good at some things, but really pretty bad at others. It does not keep us any healthier than health services elsewhere, nor does it keep us alive any longer. It's not awful – though in some ways it can be. It's just rather average. Good in some ways, bad in others.

The truth is we are suffering from a sort of collective split personality about the NHS. We love it in the abstract. It's almost like we daren't say anything else – that's what happens when a service becomes almost a national religion. But we don't love it when it comes to the reality of actually using it. A recent survey carried out for Engage Britain, found that while over three quarters (77 per cent) say the NHS makes them proud to be British, one in five people say they have been forced to go private while waiting for NHS treatment, over a quarter report being dismissed or not taken seriously by health and care workers and one in four say waiting for treatment has had a serious impact on their mental health.[2] We all have our own stories of struggling with one aspect or another of the NHS.

Of course, it could be a whole lot worse. For many millions, the health care system in the USA is a catastrophe, and a monstrously expensive catastrophe at that. If that's the standard of comparison, then thank goodness for the NHS. But that would be rather like worshipping the English cricket team for being better than the French, or our football team for overcoming mighty Monaco. As a rule of thumb, when a politician contrasts the NHS with US health care then it's time to turn off the TV or radio. The USA is the outlier among developed western countries. If they start making comparisons with the French, German or Dutch systems, then maybe it's worth staying tuned in.

There's a reason that most rich countries don't leave health care to the market. It's not just because health care is a necessity. So is food, but we are happy to leave its production and sale to the private sector. Delivery of health care is beset by market failures. There are huge information asymmetries: I don't know if I need the expensive drugs and operations my doctor tells me, and nor does my insurance company. There's 'adverse selection' in the insurance market: people who know they are ill are more likely to buy insurance, driving up the cost. There is probably also 'moral hazard': if I know I'm insured I might look after myself less well. Those are among the reasons that the US's private health system is far and away the most expensive, inefficient and unsustainable in the world.

Our obsession with the NHS *is* justified on fiscal grounds, if no other. It is the single most expensive thing government does. The Department of Health and Social Care had a budget of £140 billion in 2019/20. That rose to £190 billion in each of the next two years as it struggled with Covid, and is £186 billion in 2023/24. Just the increase in health spending between 2019 and 2022 would be enough to utterly transform any other public service. The scale of its activity is staggering. NHS hospitals carry out more than 10 million surgical procedures every year. They deal with around 100 million outpatient appointments.[3] There are over 25 million GP appointments every *month*.

Health accounts for around two pounds in every ten that the government spends, and four pounds in every ten spent on public services – in other words, paying for actual goods and services rather than just redistributing them through the welfare and pension systems. Those proportions have risen inexorably. Health spending grew even faster than the average when public spending generally was rising fast in the 2000s. The rate of growth fell dramatically in the 2010s, but at least it grew while most other areas of public spending were cut. Voltaire once quipped that, while some states have an army, the Prussian army has a state. Increasingly our public sphere looks like a health service with a state attached rather than the other way around.

Yet if there's one thing everyone seems to agree on, it is that we should spend even more. They are probably right. Spending will likely have to rise by 3 or 4 per cent a year, over and above economy wide inflation, into the indefinite future. That's broadly the average rate of increase over the last seventy years. That was also the conclusion of work I carried out with colleagues at the IFS and the Health Foundation back in 2018, on the seventieth anniversary of the founding of the NHS. And the conclusion of another group, commissioned by the world-renowned medical journal, the *Lancet*, which reported in 2021. That would mean an *extra* £100 billion a year on health and social care by the early 2030s. If that's even in the right ballpark, it should be immediately clear that nothing matters more for understanding where taxpayer money goes.

You will recall from Chapter 1 that taxes, by and large, haven't gone up much over the period since the NHS was founded. That's quite a trick to pull off – keep increasing spending without raising taxes. We've done it by largely abolishing defence spending, which has fallen from over 7 per cent of national income to barely 2 per cent today. And by ending support for nationalised industries, stopping public sector housebuilding and, over the last decade, imposing dramatic cuts on most things other than health spending. It may just be a failure of imagination on my part, but I don't see much scope for pulling those tricks again. Meeting demand for health care is either going to mean still more taxes or a pretty fundamental change to how we fund the NHS. The former may feel unattractive. I am willing to bet a large amount of money that the latter will not happen in my lifetime.

It wasn't supposed to be like this. If you've read through Chapters 3 and 4, you will know that another national treasure I have little time for is Sir William Beveridge. Not only did he get pensions and welfare wrong, he got health wrong too. In his famous report, he forecast that spending on health would stabilise or even fall over time as a comprehensive health service made us all healthier. Perhaps it's unfair to criticise with the benefit of hindsight, but he could hardly have been more wrong. It might have just been a clever trick to get the whole idea past the Treasury. Beveridge and Aneurin Bevan, the political founder of the NHS, managed to get an NHS agreed in part because it was generally accepted that you could 'diminish disease by prevention and cure'.[4] Here is Beveridge explaining his estimate of the costs over the following generation:

> No change is made in this figure as from 1945 to 1965, it being assumed that there will actually be some development of the service, and as a consequence of this development a reduction in the number of cases requiring it.[5]

That is, of course, not what happened anywhere. This is not a problem confined to the UK. Perhaps of all the giants that Beveridge set out to slay – Ignorance, Want, Squalor, Disease, Idleness – disease is the one which will be always with us and ever more expensive to keep in check.

That should have been obvious. For one thing, free supply uncovered far more demand than had been expected. Unlike most things, getting better at providing health care doesn't necessarily make it any cheaper. Cure someone once and they have a horrible tendency to get ill again and come back for more, and potentially with something much more expensive to treat. Fail to cure them and no more health spending. Health care developed far more quickly in the decades after 1948 than over any previous period in history. It continues to develop.

Even if the productivity of the system doesn't improve, we will have to keep raising the wages of health care workers in line with wages in the economy as a whole, or we won't be able to recruit any doctors or nurses. That's an effect known to economists as Baumol's cost disease, named for the eminent American economist William Baumol. He observed that it takes just as many musicians to play a Beethoven string quartet today as it took in the mid-nineteenth century (you're right – not much gets past us economists). So the productivity of classical musicians had not increased. Yet their wages had risen along with everyone else's. However much they may love their art we might struggle to find many professional musicians if we paid them a nineteenth-century wage – and the same goes for many public services which need rather more than a quartet to keep delivering.

'Cost increases are in the nature of the health care beast,' he wrote in an essay in the *New York Times* in 1993. 'Efforts to alter this nature will be fruitless or harmful. The real danger is that the nation, mistakenly thinking it must rein in runaway costs, will curtail valuable health services and render them inaccessible for the less affluent. Well-meaning reformers may take the same misstep in education, law enforcement and other handicraft services.'[6]

The NHS alone employs something like 1.8 million people. The health and care system as a whole employs perhaps one in eight of the entire British workforce. Whether or not our nurses and doctors (and teachers and police officers) get any better at their jobs, we have to make sure that, by and large, their earnings rise with the economy wide average.

Health spending did continue to rise even through the years of austerity. It grew much more slowly than usual, but compared with most other public services, the NHS was protected, which is why spending on health just kept on rising as a fraction of the total. Not that it felt like that in the health service; the spending increases barely kept up with the growing size and age of the population, let alone ever rising costs and demand. Since about 2018 though, spending has started rising again. By the middle of the 2020s, health spending will be more than 40 per cent above its 2010 level. Compare that with education spending which will be no more than 3 per cent higher.

As I write, during 2022, waiting lists and waiting times for operations are lengthening, as are waits for ambulances and waits in A&E departments. The NHS is going through one of its regular crises. Despite tens of billions of additional funding it is actually carrying out fewer procedures than it was in 2019. Waiting time targets, targets for time spent in A&E, and targets for times for ambulances to get to emergencies are all being missed, and by wide margins. As of May 2022 average 'Category 2'[7] ambulance waits were forty minutes versus a target of eighteen minutes. Twenty-seven per cent of people were spending more than four hours waiting in A&E versus a 5 per cent target.[8] Even before the pandemic, waiting time targets were regularly being missed. For example, 92 per cent of patients were supposed to be seen by a specialist within eighteen weeks of being referred by a GP. Only around 86 per cent were in fact being seen that fast.

Compare that though with the 1990s. On the eve of the pandemic fewer than 2,000 people had been waiting more than a year between referral and being seen by a specialist. More than 50,000 people had been in that position in the late 1990s. Back then, targets set out in John Major's Citizen's Charter were about avoiding waits of more than eighteen *months*. Things *have* got better.

And so they should have done. Spending on the NHS doubled in real terms between 2003 and the onset of the pandemic. It rose again hugely to deal with the pandemic. Even so, then health secretary Sajid Javid was moved to warn that, with millions missing treatment during 2020 and 2021, and capacity constrained by the ongoing effects of Covid, waiting lists could easily reach a staggering 13 million. And so they could, depending on how many of the millions who missed out on treatment in 2020 and 2021 come back, and depending on how quickly capacity can be expanded. By the closing months of 2023 waiting lists were approaching 8 million – disastrously long, but also mysteriously short. Few of those who missed out on treatment over the pandemic appear to have come back into the system.

Where the money ends up

There are all sorts of ways of looking at where the money goes in the health service. If you ask what sorts of things the money goes on, then the big component is wages. About 40 per cent of the total budget goes on staff costs. In January 2022, there were over 128,000 (non GP) doctors, 344,000 nurses, health visitors and midwives, and well over 750,000 others including scientific, therapeutic and technical staff, infrastructure support and ambulance staff.[9] That makes the NHS one of the world's biggest employers.

Even before the pandemic more than one in ten nursing posts were vacant. We are short of 2,500 GPs – a number which could triple by the decade's end if current trends continue. And it's not all about pay. The 2019 NHS staff survey found one in eight staff experienced discrimination at work and a staggering two in five reported that work related stress had made them unwell. That was *before* the pandemic. Of those leaving the NHS three times more cite problems with work/life balance as the reason for leaving than was the case a decade ago: 28 per cent of nurses and health visitors leave the NHS within the first three years of their service. The fact that we have cut the pay of nurses by 7 per cent over the last decade won't be helping.[10]

You can tell a lot about what is going on in the NHS more generally by looking at staffing and staff numbers. The number of nurses overall didn't change much between 2009 and 2019, but the number of community health nurses fell by 14 per cent and the number of mental health nurses by 10 per cent. While the number of hospital consultants has near enough doubled over the last couple of decades, the number of GPs has grown not at all. Despite all the rhetoric the NHS is becoming less focused on primary care and preventative care, and more focused on hospitals.

The NHS also reflects wider changes. Brexit has had more effect here than on any other public service. Around 15 per cent of nurses in the UK were trained abroad. That's twice as many as the average for developed countries. Since Brexit the proportion of new nurses coming from EU countries has plummeted from 15 per cent of all new nurses to just 2 per cent. The fraction coming from the rest of the world has risen from 5 to 13 per cent. We swapped European nurses for those trained in developing countries, particularly India, the Philippines and Nigeria.

All the problems faced by the workforce have been exacerbated by the pressures imposed by Covid. If there is one area where the health service *must* get better, it is in managing, supporting, rewarding, and providing leadership to its staff. 'Yet,' to quote the King's Fund, a highly respected and independent health think tank, 'the response so far has been piecemeal and accountability for improving the situation remains unclear.'[11] Health Education England, the body responsible for planning, recruiting, educating and training the health workforce had its budget cut by a quarter between 2013 and 2019. Failures of workforce planning are at the heart of many of the problems the health service faces today. And they know it. 'It is unacceptable that a quarter of staff experienced harassment, bullying or abuse from other staff in the last twelve months.' 'Many of those leaving the NHS would remain if they were offered improved development opportunities and more control over their working lives.' Direct quotes from the NHS long-term plan of 2019.[12]

It was only in 2023 that, for the first time in its history, a proper workforce plan for the NHS was published. 75 years late, but better late than never I suppose. But what a plan. It may not have got a huge amount of attention outside of the health world, but this was one of the biggest announcements ever by a government. Just consider some of the numbers. The plan aims to increase the number of staff employed by the English NHS from around 1.5 million in 2021–22 to between 2.3 and 2.4 million in 2036–37.[13] That would mean half of all public sector workers and one in eleven of all workers would be employed by the NHS. By itself this would imply spending another 2 per cent of national income, or about £50 billion, on the health service. These are just staggering numbers.

Another area of health spending that has been cut – by more than a third between 2009 and 2016 – was the capital budget. Despite subsequent increases it was still nearly 10 per cent below its 2009 level in 2019. That's a cut to spending on medical equipment of the kind that has high up-front costs but which will have benefits that last for years. Failure to invest in such equipment thus creates costs which last for years. A health service which saw day to day spending rise by over 20 per cent and capital spending fall by 10 per cent over a decade is not likely to be a sustainable one. In terms of total health spending, the UK's 10 per cent of national income is almost exactly the average of other rich countries. But health capital spending, at just 0.3 per cent of national income is about half as much as the typical high-income country.

Estimates of the scale of the maintenance backlog have doubled since 2010. The size of the 'high risk' backlog defined as where 'repairs/replacement must be addressed with urgent priority in order to prevent catastrophic failure, major disruption to clinical services or deficiencies in safety liable to cause serious injury and/ or prosecution' stood at £1.5 billion in 2019/20 compared with less than £0.4 billion in 2010/11.

Other major expenditure items include spending on health care that is bought in from non-NHS providers. That comes to around 10 per cent of the total. Most of this goes to independent sector providers (ISPs), private sector or voluntary enterprises that carry out a range of services across community health, diagnostics and acute care. The NHS has always bought in some services from the private sector, though the role of the private sector in providing routine community, diagnostics and elective (non-emergency) care was formalised and expanded in the 2000s. A further 9 per cent or so goes on primary care including general practice and dentistry.

On top of the workforce numbers quoted above, there are around 30,000 full time equivalent GPs included in these costs. They are counted separately because they have historically not been NHS employees. Fearful of becoming mere state functionaries GPs argued successfully to remain as self-employed contractors, only coming on board with the idea of a National Health Service at the eleventh hour, even after hospital consultants had acquiesced. History continues to cast its long shadow.

The drugs bill meanwhile accounts for about one pound in seven of spending, roughly evenly split between GP prescribing and drugs and medicines used in hospitals. Prescription charges raise a tiny amount – less than £600 million out of the NHS's £160 billion budget; ironic perhaps given how hotly contested their introduction was, leading to the resignation from the cabinet of Aneurin Bevan in 1951. One reason they raise so little, despite setting me back over £9 a time whenever I need one, is that about 90 per cent are free.[14] We exempt the over sixties, the poor, children, and those with long term repeated needs for drugs. So, charges remain less important than in some other countries which are, like the NHS, broadly universal and free at the point of use. New Zealand, for example, charges around £10 for GP appointments. Germany caps charges on hospital stays at 2 per cent of annual household income.[15]

You could imagine getting more money from charges, and there are ways to ameliorate the side effects of charging. Vulnerable groups – children, older people – could be excluded from having to pay. But if, like prescriptions, about 90 per cent of GP visits were free, this would cut the income from charges to a similarly tiny amount of money.[16] Here's a prediction. We are not going to change the way we fund the NHS in my lifetime. Back in 2007 nearly a thousand doctors were asked whether they believed the NHS would still be free in ten years' time: 61 per cent said they thought not.[17] Doctors seem to be determinedly gloomy. Doctor did not know best.

That's all one way of describing where the money goes – on people and drugs and equipment. Another is to look at where *in the system* the money goes. The answer is hospitals. One way or another something like £90 billion a year flows into the trusts and foundation trusts that run hospitals.

Hospitals are doing more and more. The number of 'inpatient episodes' rose from less than 13 million to more than 20 million between 2000 and 2015 – with big increases for pretty much every reason. There were around a million extra for each of cancer, digestive and genito-urinary diagnoses, and even bigger proportionate increases of over 100 per cent for others including infectious diseases and blood-related, metabolic and musculoskeletal conditions. Overall there are more than twice as many admissions for the over forty-fives than there were two decades ago.

All these costs are likely to rise. People suffering from multiple chronic conditions and mental health problems are pushing up NHS spending. The population is ageing. The number of people over the age of sixty-five is going to grow by more than four million over the next fifteen years, and the number over eighty-five by well over a million. The number of working age will grow much more slowly. Health spending per person over the age of sixty-five is more than three times spending on the under sixty-fives, and it rises fast at older ages.

Then there's the cost of drugs. Both the quantity of drugs prescribed and their average price have been on an ever upward path as we treat more older people, and more with chronic conditions, and become able to treat more conditions in total. Far more new medicines are launched each year now than even a decade ago. New medicines, of course, tend to be more expensive than old familiar ones, reflecting the cost of research and development. Costs will continue to rise.

Our demand for health care is all but insatiable. We are living longer, and longer with multiple chronic conditions. The cost of employing doctors and nurses will continue to rise, as will the drugs bill. We have a backlog of equipment to catch up on. We may currently be spending vast amounts, but those amounts will only go one way. Up.

Not that we are in any way unusual in that. The same is true across the world. International comparisons are notoriously tricky, even when it comes to looking at how much we spend on health. At around 10 per cent of national income in total, the OECD reckon we spend about an average amount – a bit more than the EU15 average, a bit less than the G7 average. Sadly, our dreadful performance on economic growth over the last fifteen years or so means that that is less in pounds terms than in some of those other countries. Economic growth matters. Without it we have less to spend on public services including health care.

Within what is a perfectly respectable amount of spending, though, we seem to manage to have less of most things: fewer doctors and nurses per head than the average, and right at the bottom of the league tables when it comes to hospital beds and equipment like MRI and CT scanners. While noting that we perform well on access and equity, on health care *outcomes* the Commonwealth Fund rates the UK ninth out of eleven major countries with only Canada and the USA behind.[18]

Organising the NHS

Given that, one way or another, the health service now accounts for
getting on for a tenth of our entire economy, it is hardly surprising
that it is a complex beast. If you think of it as a single organisation
and try to manage it as such you'll come unstuck, something which
successive secretaries of state have discovered to their cost and, more
pertinently, ours. Writing in 2016 Mark Britnell, one of the country's
leading health experts, and plausible contender for chief executive
of the NHS had he put himself forward for the role, had this to say:

> If health reorganisation was an Olympic sport, the NHS would
> take the gold medal. Repeated government instigated reor-
> ganisations over the last forty years expose an unfavourable
> consequence of politicised medicine ... Depending on how
> one counts significant national policy initiatives and laws,
> the NHS has (conservatively) witnessed twelve in the last
> twenty-six years ... This gives an average policy gestation and
> birthing period of about two years ... more energy is spent
> producing national policies than ever implementing them ...
> Organisational upheaval cannot produce sustainable clinical
> change and the repeated modifications to commissioning are a
> serious distraction.[19]

As I write everything is once again in a state of flux. A new health
and care act has been passed, yet again reorganising everything.
Or in the words of the late, great health economist Alan Maynard,
re-*disorganising* it. In the usual guff which marks a government
policy document this particular re-disorganisation will apparently
'remove the barriers that stop the system being truly integrated',
'remove transactional bureaucracy' and 'ensure the system is more

accountable'. It will also apparently help to deliver 50,000 more nurses and forty new hospitals, and allow the NHS to 'use technology in a modern way'. Quite why these things are made impossible by the status quo is not explained. But 'this is a unique moment when we must continue to build on the audacious legacy that makes the NHS the very best of Britain. We must seize it.'[20]

God preserve us from this nonsense. What's worse, the claim that forty new hospitals will be delivered is simply untrue, just a parroting of a line from the Conservative manifesto. Having to live in a world dominated by this sort of garbage was one of the reasons I left the civil service.

It is notable how little notice any of this appears to take of the actual patients. They barely get a mention. This is perhaps a trite point, but an important one. The actual priorities of actual patients play remarkably little role in the byzantine world of health policy and delivery. Speak to actual patients and you soon discover that, much though they profess to love the NHS, they soon start complaining about (what in management speak would be) the lack of patient focus, and in particular how un-joined-up the whole system appears to be as they get handed over from one set of clinicians to another. That Engage Britain survey mentioned at the start of the chapter found that: 'About a third (31 per cent) of people have recently needed health treatment for themselves or a loved one but struggled to know where to go to seek help. And for disabled people, this rises to nearly one in two (46 per cent).'[21] Ambulance staff reported spending a lot of their time not taking people to hospital, but helping them navigate the system, and older people with multiple and chronic conditions found getting continuity of care increasingly hard.

The legislation ignores all that. Remarkably it is mostly about making what was already happening actually legal. The huge reforms put in place by David Cameron's first health secretary, Andrew Lansley, in 2012 proved so impossible to work with, so badly thought through and so impracticable, that the NHS spent the subsequent decade developing effectively extra-legal structures and ways of working such as to render them all but irrelevant. Which is a brilliant example of the British capacity to muddle through and effectively ignore the law. But an awful shame given the cost and scale of changes that were initially implemented and the scale of the political row that accompanied them. Then NHS chief executive David Nicholson described the 2012 reforms as 'so big you can see them from space'.[22] Well, you might struggle to see them from earth nowadays.

That 2012 legislation was designed to increase the forces of competition within the system. It reflected concerns over not just the structure but the performance of the NHS. When Nick Timmins, the former *Financial Times* writer and now a roving one-man public services think tank, asked former Labour health minister Norman Warner what previous ministers would have said about the health of the NHS, he said:

> We would have got ... a powerful feeling that the service, when viewed from Whitehall and Westminster, was very unresponsive; both to what patients wanted and to the goals set for it by ministers.[23]

That was more than compounded by the catastrophe that was the mid-Staffs scandal. Up to 1,200 patients might have died as a result of poor care at Stafford hospital, a small district general hospital in Staffordshire, between 2005 and 2009. The Channel 4 drama *The Cure* dramatises the abuse, neglect, and medical and bureaucratic arse covering that characterised that scandal – a pattern repeated in too many similar episodes in the recent history of our health service. It is amazing what we can forget as we worship at the shrine of the NHS.

In September 2007 Julie Bailey's mother Bella went to Stafford

Hospital, run by the NHS mid-Staffs trust, for a non-life-threatening hernia operation, something seen as routine. Two months later she died on the ward from a heart problem developed in the hospital. At one point she was dropped on the floor by an orderly and at another was left without oxygen for twenty-four hours. She entered the hospital as a relatively healthy eighty-six-year-old and deteriorated rapidly over the course of her stay. Her treatment was not unique. A 2009 inquiry by the Health Care Commission found widespread evidence of poor care and medical malpractice. The regulator condemned the 'appalling standards' found at the hospital including receptionists being used to assess medical needs at the accident and emergency department. A public inquiry stated that patients had been left 'sobbing and humiliated' by seemingly uncaring staff. The problems ran deep. Poorly trained health care assistants were bringing meals to patients without helping them feed themselves, elderly men left to wander the ward in a confused state, vulnerable patients left hungry, dirty and often in pain. Some patients were so thirsty they were reduced to drinking from the flower vases scattered around the ward.[24]

The case for something to be done was unanswerable. The Lansley reforms were not a direct response to this disaster, but perhaps it gave them some cover. 'I think the chances now of the architecture of the NHS becoming stable are much higher,' said Lansley after his bill became law.[25]

Fat chance. Under the stewardship of chief executive Sir Simon Stevens – the former Blair adviser, now elevated to the House of Lords – NHS England gradually set about creating new structures designed to circumvent and bypass the legislation. New bodies, with no basis in legislation, emerged to facilitate the sort of co-operation and integration that Lansley had wanted to replace with competition. It's both a tribute to the NHS, and a warning to over-zealous legislators, that such fudging was possible. This has now all been put on a more secure legislative footing.

Broadly speaking the old purchaser-provider split is being ended in favour of managing local health systems collaboratively. Forty-two Integrated Care Systems now plan and coordinate health care in a local area. In truth, this isn't so far off a return to the structures of thirty and more years ago.

'I want clarity on the direction of travel,' said Labour MP Charlotte Atkins in a Commons debate in 2005. 'Have the government put the brakes on? Are they going backwards, or are they going round in circles?' These remain rather good questions today.[26]

In an action uncharacteristic of a minister, Andrew Lansley had also substantially reduced ministerial control over the NHS, devolving much of it to the arm's-length body, NHS England, of which Simon Stevens became the first boss, and hence the most powerful and influential person in the development of health policy from his appointment in 2014 until 2021. Maybe it was recognition of that fact which prompted the second change in the 2021 legislation which returned a lot of the control to the then secretary of state Matt Hancock. Not that secretaries of state have ever really felt able to let go. Jeremy Hunt, health secretary between 2012 and 2018, would regularly bypass formal structures by calling hospital CEOs directly if they missed A&E targets. Aneurin Bevan's famous claim that the noise of a bedpan dropped in Tredegar would reverberate around the Palace of Westminster has always had more than a hint of truth to it.

That central control is once again being formalised. Secretaries of state will be able to change the mandate and objectives of NHS England as they see fit. They will be able to 'intervene in local service reconfiguration changes'.[27] I think that means a general power from Whitehall to determine what happens to any local hospital 'informed' by the lobbying of the local MP or the size of their majority.

This is just the latest chapter in a never-ending saga of NHS reform and counter reform. Centralisation of power causes too many political problems so power is, at least in principle, devolved.

Secretaries of state get itchy and decide, to coin a phrase, they need to take back control, so decision making is recentralised. Not that central control is ever really ceded. Baroness Onora O'Neill observed in her 2002 Reith Lecture that 'central planning in the Soviet Union may have failed but it is well and alive in the NHS'.[28] That remains true to this day. 'The urge to reach for the long screwdriver remains the modus operandi in Whitehall,' says Axel Heitmueller, a former member of the Tony Blair Strategy Unit who now runs Imperial College Health partners.[29] The forty-two Integrated Care Systems were supposed to pave the way for more local autonomy 'and yet the newly appointed CEOs of the ICSs have been met with hundreds of pages of detailed guidance on how to do their jobs'.

That idea of control, though, is illusory. The biggest transformation in the NHS in recent decades happened in the 2000s not because of the actions of any secretary of state but because of the colossal sums of money made available by the Treasury following Tony Blair's promise on *Breakfast with Frost* to bring spending on UK health care up to the European average – a promise which roused Gordon Brown to yell at Blair 'you've stolen my fucking budget'.[30] Stolen or not, Brown was happy enough to take the credit when he did make huge amounts of cash available to the NHS.

That cash, not Lansley's vast legislative programme, was the biggest transformative moment in the recent history of the NHS. The waiting times for elective surgery fell from eighteen months in the year 2000 to around eighteen weeks by the late 2010s. More than 50 per cent of patients had to wait more than six weeks for a diagnostic test, following a GP referral in the early 2000s, compared to under 5 per cent by 2019.

Former health minister Sir Keith Joseph used to complain that, having waited his whole life to get his hands on the levers of power, he found they weren't connected to anything. This isn't quite accurate – the levers from Whitehall are connected, they are just rather floppy. Careful pulling will eventually result in change but only after a long period, and not necessarily the change they intended. Ministers require what few of them have: time, patience, and tolerance of uncertainty. The NHS is too big, too dispersed, and too complex to bend to the will of a minister. One day, probably in a decade or two, another secretary of state will be so burnt by the experience of attempting to achieve the impossible that another re-disorganisation will be visited upon a system still doing its best to deliver that health care to us all.

Then came the Covid hurricane

The NHS was at the epicentre of the Covid storm. By January 2021 – the height of the third UK-wide lockdown, 33,000 people were being treated in hospitals. The worst hit, the Whittington NHS Trust, in north London, saw 63 per cent of beds occupied by Covid cases.[31] Whittington hospital is less than a mile from where I sit right now. At the time of writing there have been over 150,000 deaths attributed to Covid in the UK.

With fewer doctors, nurses, hospital beds, and intensive care beds per head of population than almost all other advanced countries, and working at over 95 per cent of capacity in normal times, the health service was not well set to deal with the pandemic. We were urged into lockdown 'to protect the NHS', a revealing slogan if ever there was one.

As far as the NHS is concerned Covid will be with us for a long time to come. There are ongoing Covid cases, of course, as well as treating long Covid, new rounds of vaccinations, and the costs of infection control and PPE. The bigger effect is likely to come from catching up on missed treatment. Delays in cancer referrals during the first wave of the pandemic are estimated to have undone two, six and eight years of improvements in five-year survival rates from lung, breast and colorectal cancer.[32] By April 2021, the *Lancet* was reporting:

> The UK's NHS currently has more than 4.6 million people on waiting lists for surgery and 300 000 people have been on hold for more than twelve months – a wait time that is 100-times higher than before the pandemic. A large proportion of these delays are for patients with cancer, and the Royal College of Surgeons is particularly concerned . . .[33]

By mid-2023 there were some seven and a half million people on NHS waiting lists, about 3.5 million more than pre-pandemic. That's a big increase, and a big challenge. But it's also an astonishingly small increase. It's astonishingly small because in total, some 7.6 million fewer people joined a waiting list for NHS care in England between March 2020 and September 2021 than we would have expected based on pre-pandemic data. This suggests that there are millions of 'missing' patients: people who, in the absence of a pandemic, would have sought and received NHS hospital care but, in the event, did not.[34]

Between March and December 2020, there were 2.9 million (34 per cent) fewer elective (planned) inpatient admissions, 1.2 million (21 per cent) fewer non-Covid emergency inpatient admissions, and 17.1 million (22 per cent) fewer outpatient appointments compared with the same period in 2019. There were also 57 per cent (332,000) fewer trauma and orthopaedic elective admissions.[35]

They haven't been returning. Throughout 2022 waiting lists were increasing not because more people were joining them. In fact, *fewer* were joining waiting lists than before the pandemic. Waiting lists were growing because treatment volumes were still below prepandemic levels, despite a massive increase in funding.

What has happened to these patients? Some, it is true, will have died. But not in numbers anywhere near big enough to explain even a small fraction of the puzzle. Others will have gone private. This has been boom time for private medical care. There was a 35 per cent increase between 2019 and 2023 in the number of people opting to self-fund private treatment[36], while a recent YouGov poll showed that 22 per cent of people say the pandemic has made them more likely to consider using private health care. But again, the numbers are simply too small to account for more than about 5 per cent of the 'missing' patients.

The truth is we don't know where these patients have gone, and that is rather scary. What happens to those missing millions will define the next few years for the NHS. If they come back then waiting lists will burst through the 13 million mark that health secretary Sajid Javid warned about in summer 2021. The NHS will be under unbearable pressure. But what if they don't come back? There is already evidence that patients are turning up in Accident & Emergency with more advanced and serious health issues as a result of delayed or missed treatment earlier in the pandemic.[37] Either way, the human costs are incalculable.

Spending has been increasing. But despite the huge additional pressures faced by the NHS it is increasing no faster than at the average rate at which spending has risen for decades. In any case, it takes up to ten years to train a GP or fourteen years to produce a surgeon. You can't magic up extra doctors and nurses and hospital beds overnight. Even if the money is there, the NHS, we, will be facing the costs of Covid for some time to come.

Is the NHS special?

On a range of measures where medical intervention is the determinant of outcomes the NHS is I'm afraid nothing special. Five-year survival rates in Britain for colon, breast, lung and prostate cancer are below G7 and EU15 averages, while thirty-day mortality rates after hospital admission for heart attacks and strokes are above international averages. 'The NHS ranks among the worst countries specifically in terms of health outcomes – for strokes and heart attacks the NHS has the worst survival rates. Across five different types of cancer we come sixteenth out of eighteen comparable countries.'[38] The NHS is very good at ensuring nobody loses out because they don't have enough money. It is good at some things like rates of vaccination, and is catching up in some of those areas where it has fallen behind. But, and I'm sorry to keep repeating this, on international comparisons the NHS is nothing special. It is particularly bad at keeping us alive.

In early 2021, a Lancet Commission on the future of the NHS, co-authored by an array of the great and the good in health policy, plus me, said this:

> The response to Covid-19 brings to attention some of the chronic weaknesses and strengths of the UK's health and care systems and real challenges in society to health. Failures in leadership, an absence of transparency, poor integration between the NHS and social care, chronic underfunding of social care, a fragmented and disempowered public health service, ongoing staffing short-falls, and challenges in getting data to flow in real time were all important barriers to coordinating a comprehensive and effective response to the pandemic. More positively, the high amount of financial protection that was provided by the NHS and an allocation of resources that explicitly accounted for differing geographical needs have, to some extent, mitigated the already substantial effect of the pandemic on health inequalities.[39]

There is a reason for banging on about this lack of specialness. Our worship of the NHS is positively damaging. Reflecting on the failings and scandals surrounding such great national institutions as the NHS, the BBC, Oxfam, and the Catholic Church, Matthew Syed has linked the conviction of moral rectitude at the highest levels of those organisations to their failings. The more we treat the NHS as a national religion, the more likely it is to fail, and indeed kill, people.[40]

The Kirkup report into another tragedy in the NHS, attributed the deaths of twelve babies and one mother at Furness General Hospital to a 'lethal mix' of 'serious and shocking' failings. [41] Syed goes on:

> midwives were so convinced of their high standards that they wouldn't change in response to manifold tragedies. As for managers, they had so thoroughly absorbed the theology of the NHS that they felt it was more important to defend its reputation than to shine a light on what was going wrong. We can't have criticism of the NHS! The world might end! We might call this 'organisational narcissism', the way that the interests of sanctified institutions can become superior to the people they are designed to serve.[42]

It is easy, of course, to be cynical of what politicians may write, but one of the most powerful accounts of some of the failures of the NHS comes in a book by former health secretary, and at the time of writing, chancellor, Jeremy Hunt. The book is called *Zero*. It is about eliminating unnecessary deaths. In it is devastating story after devastating story of failures of care, of culture, of treatment, of communication, which left patients dead, disabled or in the most awful pain. According to Hunt, blame culture, short staffing and lack of money are among the causes. Targets, hierarchies, fear of litigation and groupthink among the cultural challenges. He takes his own share of the blame. He offers, at least broad brush, solutions too, including greater transparency, more continuity of care, more use of homecare, greater focus on prevention and better use of technology.

But above all it is a story of human suffering inflicted despite the hard work and best intentions of nearly all of those involved.

Based on his experience rescuing King's College Hospital back in 2017, Ian Smith, who had taken over and turned round that particular trust, concluded that the NHS faced four fundamental problems: poverty of leadership, clinician disengagement, low levels of capital investment, and poor and deteriorating out of hospital care.[43]

Poverty of leadership was down to low management competence exacerbated by under-resourcing, rapid management turnover, and lack of leadership support and training. 'The NHS must empower leaders to lead, encouraging them to celebrate their successes and learn from their mistakes,' wrote Ron Kerr, chair of NHS Providers, in 2018. 'In reality, a culture of blame and negativity continues to pervade the NHS. Despite best efforts, it is a fact of life that mistakes are made and error is unavoidable. The NHS needs to get much better at learning from both successes and failures, moving to a more open learning culture which encourages transparency and honesty.[44]

Clinician disengagement, he put down in part to poor management and in part to dysfunctional clinician behaviour. One certainly doesn't have to go far in the health service to find examples of lack of engagement between the doctors and the managers. And despite the popular clamour against 'wasting' money on NHS managers, the NHS is almost certainly under managed. It spends about half the OECD average on administration and planning.[45]

The NHS is a hugely complex organisation. Perhaps it is not surprising then that the NHS Confederation reports that 'efficiency, quality, and patient satisfaction improve with an increase in management to staff ratios'.[46] The populist call to reduce management numbers is self-defeating.

Low levels of capital investment we have already looked at. They are even lower than they should be as capital budgets are frequently raided to shore up short-term deficits. Poor and deteriorating out-of-hospital care is failing many of the most vulnerable and, in turn, is putting intense pressure on acute hospitals. Our lack of investment in public health, primary care and social care is a false economy.

Some prerequisites for a more effective health care system should be obvious by now. One is to start treating it like any other public service, acknowledge it for what it actually is, and tackle the problems that actually exist rather than sweep them under the carpet, and massively improve its management. Acknowledge the fact of private sector involvement and use it effectively, where it can add value. The self-declared defenders of the NHS who vociferously complain about 'privatisation' or 'the end of free health care' every time a private sector organisation is involved are, potentially fatally, damaging that which they claim to cherish.

Second, acknowledge that it will need a lot more funding over the coming years. It would make life easier for everyone involved if we could just agree that its budget will rise by, say, 3 per cent per year each year for the next decade. That way the managers and clinicians will actually be able to plan with a degree of certainty. We would move away from the cycle of boom and bust in funding which has characterised its whole existence, and which has created such uncertainty and inefficiency, as well as bouts of inflation in pay and costs, followed by painful retrenchment.

Third, focus more of that funding on primary and out of hospital care on the one hand, and investment in capital equipment on the other. Actually start to match the words on the importance of primary care with the reality of funding for it. Lack of effective out of hospital care, including social care, is one of the health service's greatest handicaps. Another is the lack of equipment, CT scanners and so on resulting from inadequate investment and a continued raiding of capital budgets just to keep the show on the road.

Fourth, stop the top-down re-disorganisations. Where we have landed may well be far from perfect in principle, but in practice the various actors will find a way to make it work. The last thing they need is for it all to be thrown up in the air yet again. Make incremental changes. Focus on improving management, procurement and systems. Don't pretend it can all be managed from Whitehall.

Fifth, follow up on that long overdue workforce strategy and make sure it is developed, funded and implemented properly and consistently. Treat the staff properly. It beggars belief that it even needs saying. To quote the King's Fund again:

> High quality leadership is essential to develop cultures that support staff and improve care for patients. There are countless examples of compassionate leadership across the NHS, however recent reports have highlighted the prevalence of bullying and harassment, demonstrating how this coupled with challenging working conditions and long hours contribute to staff burnout. To improve retention and make the NHS a better place to work, there is a need to develop collective, compassionate and inclusive leadership and supportive team-working that values staff'.[47]

Sixth, design and run the system with the patient in mind.

We *will* spend more and more on the NHS. As we get richer and older, we will demand more health care and we will have to get used to paying more for it. But we should not put up with the system we have. It needs to be improved and while that improvement will need money, it will need a lot more besides.

The Costs of Getting Sicker and Older

Spending on adult social care: £22 billion (England only) in 2021/22[1]

Benefit expenditure to support disabled people and those with health conditions 2022–23:

On children: £3 billion

On working age adults: £54 billion

On pensioners: £12 billion

The north of Lambeth which rests against the south bank of the Thames in London is home to one of those ethnic minorities who live in many ways below the radar. As many as one in six who live there speak Portuguese – some of them *only* speak Portuguese.

One of those is an older man called Luiz, who came to London originally from Brazil. Luiz lives alone and speaks little English. But he also lives with no less than three chronic conditions – he has a heart condition, Type 2 diabetes and anaemia.[4]

He told researchers from the Lambeth Portuguese Wellbeing

Programme that he felt stressed by debt and having to rely on family for help. He felt very isolated and talked about how his only social interactions were seeing his family infrequently, going to medical appointments and talking with his landlord in very basic English when he comes to collect the rent once a month.

He told them that he spent his days between the TV and the computer. He also felt that he had not been eating enough because he doesn't like eating alone. All these things have affected his health.

Luiz isn't alone. Over the last seventy years the number of people with chronic conditions has been growing faster than population growth, even after accounting for ageing. Medical advances, public health interventions and changing lifestyle patterns mean that the greatest burden of disease now arises from long-term chronic health conditions, rather than the accidents and infectious diseases that predominated in the infancy of the NHS.

This is a burden not just on health care but on the welfare system and on social care too. In this chapter we will move from examining those health problems to look at the costs of incapacity and disability benefits, and then at social care.

Why we die

The NHS was designed in a very different world. And not a more cheerful one. Sir William Jameson, the chief medical officer, started his annual report in 1947, the year before the founding of the NHS, thus:

The eighth year of austerity, 1947, was a testing year. Its first three months formed a winter of exceptional severity, which had to be endured by a people who in addition to rationing of food were faced with an unprecedented scarcity of fuel. These three months of snow and bitter cold were followed by the heaviest floods for fifty-three years, which did great damage, killed thousands of sheep and lambs, delayed spring sowing and threatened the prospect of a good harvest which was so urgently needed. Immediately after these four months of disastrous weather there followed a period of economic crisis with an ever-increasing dollar crisis. So acute was the crisis that restrictions more rigorous than any in the war years became necessary. Bread had to be rationed for the first time late in 1946; in September 1947, the meat ration was reduced; in October the bacon ration was halved; and in November potatoes were rationed. A steep rise in the prices of foodstuffs and cattle food followed disappointing harvests in many European countries, due to the hard winter and hot dry summer, and in certain crops, notably corn for animal food, in America. Affairs abroad were as depressing as conditions at home.[5]

Apparently, it was traditional to start such reports with a reflection on the weather.

He could instead have started with infectious disease, still a major killer. Hundreds of young children died every year from measles, whooping cough, diphtheria and tuberculosis. Far fewer of the very youngest die from any cause today and almost none from those diseases. Along with smallpox, polio, tetanus, mumps and rubella, these were all but wiped out during the second half of the twentieth century, after childhood immunisation was introduced. My father, hospitalised with polio in the 1940s, walked with a limp to the end of his days.

These days, taken together, the various sorts of cancers are our biggest killers. About 180,000 of us died that way in 2017.

Cardiovascular diseases came only just behind. Over 60,000 of us died from dementia.[6] Things change fast too. Less than thirty years earlier, in 1990, cardiovascular disease was much the biggest killer, accounting for nearly 300,000 of us, almost twice as many as died from cancer. Dementia killed just 34,000. Better lifestyles and better treatments, along with drugs such as statins, explain the falling prevalence of heart disease, and indeed have been key to increased life expectancy. But if that's not what carries us off, something else will, and that something else is increasingly cancer and dementia.

When the historians Peter Razzell and Christine Spence studied bills of mortality and other sources in London for the three centuries before Dr John Snow removed the handle of the public water pump in Broad Street in Soho to stop the 1854 cholera epidemic, they found there was no difference across the social classes in death statistics for babies, children or adults.[7]

And to remind us that progress is not inevitable they also found that infant and child mortality more than doubled between the sixteenth and the middle of the eighteenth centuries – for rich and poor alike. In the middle of the eighteenth century two thirds of children, rich and poor, died before the age of five.

Those days, thankfully, are well behind us. But with better health and longer lives have come big divisions between rich and poor.

Life expectancies went up from forty years for men born in 1841 and forty-two for women, to fifty-five years (men) and fifty-nine years (women) for those born in the 1920s. For men, life expectancy at birth had hit sixty-six by 1951, crawled up to seventy over next thirty years to 1981, and then shot up by a further nine years in the three decades to 2011.

Despite a sharp slowdown in improvements since then, by 2019 life expectancy had reached 79.9 years (men) and 83.6 (women).[8] The health service has played its part in all this, not least through those life-saving vaccinations. But lifestyle changes, including a dramatic reduction in smoking, have also been important. Not that governments have always been keen to get the prevalence of smoking down.

When the health minister Robert Turton presented evidence to Cabinet in 1956 that smoking was harmful and suggested the public be warned, then chancellor Harold Macmillan called it a 'very serious issue'.[9] Not perhaps for the reason you might expect. He was concerned that revenue from taxing tobacco was equivalent to 3/6d on income tax and would be hard to replace. The Treasury apparently (really) believed that getting the additional revenue in was more important than worrying about any impact of smoking on health.

There is clearly scope for further improvement in life expectancy. Men in the wealthiest tenth of areas of England (places like Kensington in London) can expect to live to be nearly eighty-four, almost a decade longer than men in the 10 per cent of most deprived areas (like Kensington in Liverpool). For women equivalent life expectancies are eighty-six and seventy-nine. Heart and respiratory diseases and lung cancer are behind much of these differences.

The gap in *healthy* life expectancy is even bigger – almost two decades.[10] Those living in the most deprived areas spend nearly a third of their lives in poor health, compared with about a sixth for those in the least deprived areas. Not only do the poor have the shortest life spans, they also live more years in poor health. These inequalities are growing. Men and women in wealthier areas enjoyed significant increases in life expectancies during the 2010s. Those in the poorest areas did not.

Michael Marmot, the world's leading authority on health inequalities, concluded in his 2008 review commissioned by the then Labour government, that 'inequalities in health arise because of inequalities in society – in the conditions in which people are born, grow, live, work, and age'. Or as he also put it 'catch the Jubilee line east from Westminster and life expectancy drops one year for each station (for about six stops).'[11]

He's right. Our health is the ultimate outcome of all our life experiences. The poorer we are, the more stress we suffer and less control we feel, the more likely we are to become ill and to die before our time. Health inequalities in the UK are perhaps the single greatest indictment of the way we live, the way we organise our society, and the failure of government. They are not essentially a failure of the NHS. It is there to pick up the pieces left behind by the poor housing, unemployment, low wages, insecure work and inequalities which create poor health.

In different contexts I am often asked how I would measure success in 'Levelling Up'. I always give the same answer. Look at the health and mortality figures. We'll know the country is Levelling Up when there is a 'Levelling Up' in healthy life expectancy.

There has also been a rise in the prevalence of people, like Luiz, living with multiple chronic conditions. While the number of people living with a single chronic condition has grown by 4 per cent a year – outpacing population growth – the number living with multiple chronic conditions grew by 8 per cent a year in the decade up to 2016.

In 2006/07, one in ten patients admitted to hospital as an emergency were recorded as having five or more conditions. In 2015/16, the figure was one in three.[12] Patients with multiple conditions are more costly to treat, stay longer in hospital and are more likely to be readmitted when they are finally discharged. One long-term condition costs the NHS around £1,000 a year. But if you have two, it costs around £3,000 a year, and three costs around £8,000 a year.[13]

Lifestyles play a big role. In recent years, smoking rates have fallen but obesity levels have increased. After seventy years of technological progress and access to health care, people are much more likely to survive with a chronic condition as medical advances improve survival rates. So the proportion of patients with multiple chronic conditions is likely to carry on growing. That will be costly, not least because of increases in the number of older people living with multiple conditions. Over a fifteen-year horizon, it could lead to spending on this group increasing by around £30 billion, an average annual growth rate of 6 per cent.

People with long-term conditions now account for about 50 per cent of all GP appointments, 64 per cent of all outpatient appointments and over 70 per cent of all inpatient bed days. Their treatment and care is estimated to take up around £7 in every £10 of total health and social care expenditure.[14]

Luiz's story reminds us of one of the main reasons why Beveridge got the long-term costs of a health service so wrong – because people's health issues change. And all this also helps explain why new improved health technologies don't tend to produce a lower cost base as they do in most sectors. Instead they often bake in the need for increased expenditure as people live longer.

It starts early. Many people born very prematurely who are alive today and owe their lives to the NHS, have lived to give their parents and friends joy, but may be under medical care their whole lives.

The prevalence of mental health problems has also been growing, by about 0.6 per cent a year pre-pandemic. About one in six of the adult population has a common mental health disorder. Of those, less than half received treatment. Costs will rise, especially if we are to have any success in extending care to more of those who need it. Mental and physical conditions also go increasingly hand in hand.

'Heart disease patients may have depression,' says Martin Prince, professor of epidemiological psychiatry at King's College London. 'People with dementia may develop other physical illnesses. There were links between depression and heart attacks. People with depression were more likely to smoke – or not give up smoking – and more likely to become obese'.[15]

All of that pushes up the cost of health care. It has also been pushing up the costs of benefits for the sick and disabled.

Incapacity and disability benefits

Among people without a disability, more than 80 per cent are now in work, probably the highest rate in history. Yet only half of those with a disability are in paid work, dropping to only one in three of those with mental health problems. The sheer numbers of people with recorded disabilities make this economically significant.

About a fifth of people of working age say that they have some form of disability and more than four million of them are out of work.[16] These are numbers worth remembering. For those of us fortunate enough not to have a disability, it is easy to forget how many of our fellow citizens do.

Who those people are, where they live and the reasons for their disability all tell us rather a lot about the country we live in. Twenty years ago, they were overwhelmingly older men, often living in former industrial and mining areas. Almost unbelievably, in the mid-1990s a quarter of all men aged between fifty-five and sixty-four were receiving incapacity benefits.[17] In parts of south Wales, northern England and the west of Scotland, rates were much higher than that. This was the human consequence of the closure of much of the traditional heavy industry: long-term illness and long years spent out of the labour market and relying on benefits.

The pit and factory closures of the 1980s and 1990s still cast a long shadow, but it is beginning to recede. Numbers of people on incapacity benefits have been falling in many of the affected areas. There is a new shadow, though, over places such as Blackpool and Hastings, Tendring and Thanet, where the numbers receiving incapacity benefits have risen.

As the geography of disability-related unemployment has

changed, so has its demography. There is now a much more democratic spread by age and gender. Older men are no longer hogging
the illness and the benefits that go with it. Women have pretty
much caught up. The gap between older and younger men has also
closed to an astonishing degree.

Life on incapacity benefits is increasingly the preserve of the
poorly educated, irrespective of age. Twenty years ago, highly educated older men were more than twice as likely as poorly educated
younger men to be receiving incapacity benefits. That has now been
reversed. If you are a man in your twenties or thirties who left school
at sixteen, you are now twice as likely to be out of work and on incapacity benefits than is a man with a degree in his fifties or sixties.[18]

Therein lies a great shift in the economy. It is no longer the old
who are left behind in the labour market – it is the low-skilled
and the poorly educated of whatever age, especially those living in
more peripheral areas. That so many are already consigned to long
periods out of work and on incapacity benefits is a tragedy. Nearly
four in five of those receiving incapacity benefits have been doing
so for more than two years. That compares with fewer than one in
five recipients of Jobseeker's Allowance. The reason for increased
reliance on these benefits is also a tragedy. Growing rates of both
recorded disability and of benefits receipt among younger people
are driven by a growing prevalence of reported mental illness.

Financial Times journalist Sarah O'Connor went to Blackpool
to find the real lives behind the statistics. The piece inspired, she
tells me, by IFS research showing how the demography and geography of benefit receipt had changed, won her the Orwell Prize for
2018. In Blackpool she found countless examples of people who
had moved there for the cheap accommodation and had remained
there, out of work, lonely, depressed.[19]

O'Connor was writing about how the UK welfare system
is changing – and failing. It is doing precisely what successive
governments have tried to prevent: it is maintaining people in

poverty and misery, despite all the nudging and hassle it puts them through. Half of those who start claiming incapacity benefits now have a diagnosed mental health problem (most commonly depression, stress or anxiety) as their main health condition, up from less than a third at the turn of the century.[20]

She described a woman whose doctor has put her on an array of anti-depressants and tranquillisers. She says the health care professional doing her assessment had asked her:

'If you're depressed, why have you got your nails done?'

The woman looks down at her glittery gold and red nails. 'I've not had false nails off my hands for ten years,' she says. 'I did these at three o'clock the other morning because I couldn't sleep ... Even when I took an overdose [and] sat on the railings in the park in the rain, I still had my nails on. D'you know what I mean?'[21]

Back in 2010 a British GP, a columnist for the doctors' magazine *Pulse*, briefly wrote his own blog under the name 'GPforhire', called Random Mutterings of a Doctor Up North. Writing about patients with, as he called it, 'shit life syndrome', he mused:

About five minutes into their history your mind will start to wander ... Several minutes later your mind will wander back to the patient who will still be telling you about all the terrible things that are going on in their life. There isn't really much you can do, you ponder that if your life was going as shit as theirs you'd feel pretty depressed too. What about counselling? 'Nah, tried that before doc and it was rubbish' (Waiting list is vast anyway). OK then, what about antidepressants? Won't change a thing but will make the drug companies happy. I know! Exercise, going for nice walks, going out with your friends? Gym's too expensive, have you seen where I live doctor, and I've not got money to go out – the three rapid replies. This patient has 'SLS': nothing you can do for them other than listen. Maybe sign the odd 'fit-note' so they can get a bit of extra cash ... [22]

Phil Cumberlidge, a GP from Liverpool, trained and worked in the Vauxhall Primary Health Care practice for ten years, before he also wrote about Shit Life Syndrome for the *Mirror* newspaper:

Imagine being a single parent after finally getting away from your abusive alcoholic boyfriend. Your baby is unwell and frequently in hospital. You have no family support. No money. Your flat is surrounded by drug users and alcoholics. Or how about being middle aged, losing your job, your partner and your house within six months? Sounds shit? Try living it. So when she comes to see you, distressed, unhappy and not wanting to get out of bed you can hardly blame her ... [23]

Much of the benefits bill, and of the bill for health spending, is rooted in economic and social failure. Benefits, and the NHS, are where you end up when life has just got too much. But in the end, there is a limit to what they can do to help.

All of which helps explain why continued efforts to reduce spending on incapacity benefits – designed to support people who are out of work and too sick to work – have not worked in recent years. There are well over two million individuals claiming these benefits. The last Labour government set in train major changes, replacing the old Incapacity Benefit with the new Employment and Support allowance (ESA). The clue to the intention is in the change of name. More claimants were to be encouraged and supported into work. Despite well publicised cases of very sick people being deemed able to work, intended savings largely failed to materialise. Projections from 2012 suggested spending would fall by more than a quarter between 2010 and 2017. In fact, spending rose.

ESA is now one of those benefits being rolled into Universal

Credit. It is both means-tested and based on an assessment of a person's incapacity for work – known as the 'work capability assessment'. In order to be eligible, you must be part of a family with low income (the means test) and also judged unable to work or to carry out work-related activity. If these criteria are met then in 2023 you get an extra £390 per month added to your universal credit entitlement.

These *incapacity* benefits are paid to people who are out of work and judged to be too sick to work. There is another whole superstructure in the benefit system: *disability* benefits designed to help with the living costs of those who have a disability, irrespective of whether they are in work or not, and on an entirely non-means-tested basis. Claimants for these disability benefits, currently known as Personal Independent Payments (PIP) are entitled to between £117 and £749 per month, with the precise amount depending on the severity of their disability.

Many people receive both. While you do not need to be out of work to receive disability benefits, most recipients are out of work. Rather than being assessed on capability to work, eligibility to PIP is determined by assessed capability to do certain tasks such as moving around or dressing yourself. At the time of writing, in 2023, government is consulting on moving to a single assessment, based on the current PIP system. The idea is that if you are entitled to a higher rate of Universal Credit *because* you have shown you can't work then you are rather incentivised to keep showing you really can't work. As we will see below there are risks to this approach. Numbers claiming and receiving PIP have been rising very rapidly.

As with much else in the benefit system spending on disability benefits is big money – around £20 billion a year or around 1 per cent of national income. About £15 billion of that goes to those of working age. The share of working-age adults reporting a disability, and the fraction of working-age adults in receipt of disability benefits, have both been rising steadily over the last three decades. In the early 2020s there were around 2.2 million working-age people receiving such benefits, compared with 1.9 million in 2012/13 and fewer than 600,000 in 1992/93. The number of working-age people reporting a disability (a long-standing and limiting condition or illness) stood at 7.4 million in 2020/21, up from 6 million in 2012/13.

The reform of the disability benefits system, replacing what was the disability living allowance (DLA) with the personal independence payment (PIP) began in 2013 with the aim of reducing government spending by 20 per cent while targeting support to those with the highest medical need. It has failed in that aim.

Since the PIP rollout started, spending has instead increased – and indeed has been growing at a faster rate than before.[24] Four fifths of the growth in numbers over the last two decades is accounted for by increasing numbers with mental health problems and learning disabilities claiming the benefits.

Growth has really taken off since 2020. Prior to the pandemic around 19,000 people started a new working age disability benefit claim each month. By the start of 2023 that number had, astonishingly, roughly doubled. As of spring 2023 the OBR was forecasting further huge increases in spending. They reckoned that over the five years to 2027–28 total spending on benefits to support disabled people and those with health conditions would increase by £19 billion to over £73 billion a year. Simply staggering numbers. This is yet further evidence of a very big, very severe problem in our population, and also in the operation of our welfare state. It is a problem which is felt far more by the economically disadvantaged and poorly educated. 30-year-olds with no qualifications are more likely to be disabled than are 60-year-old graduates. By the time they are in their 50s, fully half of the least well educated report being disabled compared to fewer than one in five graduates.[25]

Adult social care

It is beyond the reach of a health service to close the gaps in our life experiences which result in the huge gaps in life expectancy. It is beyond its reach to deal with Shit Life Syndrome. It is also beyond its reach to deliver social care.

The need for the latter is, though, growing for many of the same reasons we have just discussed. The chronic health problems suffered by people like Luiz, by those who have survived through childhood with lifelong conditions such as Down's syndrome, and by older people with needs associated with dementia or other health problems, all require social care.

The social care system matters for the health system. The pressure on NHS beds is overwhelming, yet on any given day more than 10,000 beds are occupied by people suitable for discharge. Many are held in NHS beds because of difficulties finding and providing appropriate social care.

While the dividing line between health care and social care is inevitably blurred we can think of the latter as supporting people of all ages with certain physical, cognitive or age-related conditions in carrying out personal care or domestic routines. That support can be in their own home or in a residential setting. It can help them to sustain employment in paid or unpaid work, or in education, learning, and leisure, supporting them to participate as fully as possible in society.[26]

If you think that's a slightly woolly definition, you're right. Therein lies one of the problems. Who needs social care, who should provide it, and who should fund it, are not questions with straightforward answers.

What we can say with certainty is that it matters to an awful lot of people. With a workforce of around 1.5 million, the social care sector employs a similar number to the NHS. Around 840,000 people were receiving publicly funded long-term care in 2020/21, with more than 200,000 in receipt of short-term, time limited care.

Of the 840,000 in receipt of long-term care nearly 300,000 are actually under the age of sixty-five – this is emphatically not just about caring for the elderly. Indeed, the under-sixty-fives account for around half the annual budget. And all the pressures are upward – not just more older people, but also a continuing rise in numbers of younger adults in need of care: one of the consequences of a health care system that keeps more children alive into adulthood, but with severe needs.

All that care is the main business of our local authorities, accounting for well over half their expenditure. A figure that is growing. It is administered and funded through them and largely separately from the NHS. Means-tested, heavily rationed, run through local government, the current system is a product of history, a history that can be traced back to the infamous Poor Laws, with their stringent needs and means testing, via the National Assistance Act of 1946 which kept social care within the ambit of local government and the means test. This was never designed with current needs in mind, nor for a world in which dementia is one of the biggest killers, and in which thousands with dementia are looked after in the social care system.

Failure to fund social care properly, and failure to reform it for more than thirty years, must rank as one of the great policy failures of the past generation, by governments of all hues. It has been a failure with awful human consequences which became all too apparent during the pandemic.

The means-tested nature of the system can lead to frail elderly people having to use their lifetime's accumulated savings, and sell their home, in order to pay for their care. Also awful has been the lack of funding. Even those who are poor enough to qualify for free social care, are increasingly judged not needy enough. Smaller budgets have meant more stringent criteria.

Of those requesting help in 2019/20, only around four in ten got some form of service, three in ten got some advice about where they might get help, and a further three in ten got nothing at all.[27] The gap between expectations and reality is huge.

Cuts since 2010 led to an astonishing 30 per cent fall in numbers receiving care in their own homes between 2009/10 and 2013/14 despite increases in the number of older people.[28]

Other impacts include the now notorious fifteen-minute visits for those receiving care at home, which may allow for only one basic task (such as help with showering, the toilet, cooking, getting changed or anything else) when several may be needed, and which can leave those with dementia utterly bewildered. Then there is low pay, zero-hours contracts . . . and council fees for the homes which are often below what it would cost to stay at a cheap hotel chain.[29]

Despite a number of emergency top-ups to local authority budgets after 2017, as the Treasury belatedly realised the consequences of the excessive squeeze, total spending had only just returned to 2010 levels by 2020 despite ever-increasing demand.

That lack of funding has had inevitable consequences for the quality of care, and for the pay of those employed in the sector, many of whom are on minimum wage. So cash-strapped are local authorities that care homes, mostly privately owned, can't survive on their fees. They therefore charge much more to those who have to pay for themselves – 40 per cent more, on average.

Not only are many older people not supported by the state in their hour of need, they literally end up subsidising the government by paying over the odds for their care so that the state can pay less than the cost of supporting those who do qualify for help.

The fact that most care homes are now in the private sector is also an accident of history. Back in 1946 there were far fewer older people. The rich could afford private care homes, there was some charitable provision, and councils maintained a few residential places, many literally in old workhouses. Councils were also the main employers of home helps. A lot of long-term care, though, took place in the geriatric wards of hospitals. Even as late as the 1980s, the NHS still had 50,000 'long stay' beds.

Councils built more care homes from the 1950s on. But in one of those accidents of policy design, during the 1980s councils and the NHS realised that they could escape the cost of care if they handed it over to private providers, where the social security system would pick up the tab.

As Nick Timmins puts it:

> The bill for that rocketed from £10 million in 1979 to £2.5 billion by 1992. By then, a quarter of a million residents were having their care paid for by social security. All the incentives were for people to go into care homes, whether or not they would have preferred to be cared for at home, and indeed would have been better supported there. The bill, and the buck passing, was becoming unsustainable.[30]

Another perfect example of poor policy design and the effects of the operation of different incentives on different parts of the public sector, with a wholly unintended long-term consequence: the effective privatisation of social care provision.

That privatisation was entrenched following the Griffiths Report of 1988 which led to the social security cash being transferred to local government, but on the condition that much of it was used to commission services from outside providers, rather than provide them directly.

One result has been no public capital investment. Another has been a lack of a single voice for social care and an astonishing lack of consistent data and information on the system which,

while it has a few large-scale providers, is still made up of thousands of small-scale operations, many of them running just a
single care home.

We have a system that is fragmented, complex, and next to
impossible for the user to navigate. Engage Britain found that
fully *half* of unpaid carers say they have had to 'fight' to get
care and one in six of all adults have struggled to arrange care
for an elderly relative.[31] Among those the researchers spoke to
were Celine:

> It's knowing where to go and getting into the system. When
> my dad got dementia and he couldn't be at home because my
> stepmother just couldn't cope with him, to get him in a care
> home and to get him fully funded was a complete nightmare.
> You're dealing with so many agencies . . .

And Liz:

> With regards to continuing health care assessments, I can
> only describe ours as having been traumatic. The buck passing
> between social services and health, the lack of accountability.

With 152 local authorities buying care from 18,000 organisations with 34,000 establishments, this confusion is hardly
surprising. Especially when set alongside the lack of coordination
with health services and the uncertainties about even whether it
is the NHS or the local council's care services that you need to be
trying to access.

One of the most moving programmes I have watched in recent
years has been *Caring for Derek*. TV presenter Kate Garraway
shares her experience of taking care of her husband, Derek Draper,
after he is rendered permanently disabled by Covid. For me it is all
the more moving because I knew Derek very slightly many years

ago when he was a somewhat hyperactive young political adviser. The contrast between the man I remember and what we see of him today could not be starker or more distressing. In the programme, after he has been discharged from hospital, we see Garraway wrestling with the care system:

> Trying to understand the social care system ... and navigate a way through is ... just unbelievable and overwhelming. And it's life-or-death care still ... you find yourself in a system where you haven't got access to come of the things you need. Some of the things are funded by one pot, some of the things are funded by another, some of the things you have to fund yourself. It is not in any way understandable what does which.[32]

And that's the experience of someone who comes across as about as competent, positive and energetic as it's possible to be.

Boris Johnson had already promised, on becoming prime minister, that he would finally 'sort out' social care.

After thirty years of failed promises, a royal commission, at least a dozen white and green papers, and an extensive report by Sir Andrew Dilnot, such a sorting out was certainly long overdue. As was an ending of the disgraceful party politics played over previous reform proposals. Labour's perfectly sensible proposals in 2010 dubbed a 'death tax' by the Conservatives. The Tories' equally sensible 2017 proposals decried as a 'dementia tax' by Labour.

Johnson's proposals were slow to arrive. Very slow. We had been promised proposals on a regular basis since at least 2017. The proposals though, and all the debate about them for years, have had nothing to do either with the fragmentation and complexity that surrounds social care, nor the level of funding. They have been all about the question of who pays, and in particular how those who need it can avoid the catastrophic costs of long-term care that can, for an unlucky few, reach hundreds of thousands of pounds and result in them having to use up a lifetime's savings and sell their home in order to pay for their care. Currently (as of 2023), anyone with assets of more than just £23,250 has to pay for all their own care. Entirely free help only kicks in when your assets are down to £14,250.

It's easy to write this off as the complaints of the entitled off-spring of the current older generation wanting to inherit the parental wealth and home. And it is true, the main financial ben-eficiaries of limiting the amount that people pay for their social care will be the children who will inherit more. On a distributional calculus such changes do look regressive. They are of no benefit to those with the least assets because they don't pay anyway.

But that does not make the current system right, and nor does it make proposals to limit what is paid, wrong. We don't regard the NHS as an aberration because it treats the rich as well as the poor. If we consider it problematic that the children of the rich inherit a lot, we do not in general suggest that a way around that would be to insist that better-off elderly people pay for their cancer operations, heart drugs and arthritis treatment so that they have less to leave to the next generation. If we want a fairer distribution of inheritances then we should look to the tax system to deal with that.

The case for the state – the taxpayer – to take on the costs of social care, at least once it exceeds a certain level, is simple enough. It is the case for social insurance that underlies much of our welfare state. 'The magic of averages to the rescue of millions' as Winston Churchill had it. Indeed, this is arguably the strongest case in any area of public policy. Very high costs of long-term care hit a minority of people.

Back in 2011, Andrew Dilnot estimated that about one in ten

people aged sixty-five could face care costs of more than £100,000 over the rest of their lives.[33] More recent analysis suggests that fraction has grown. It makes no sense to save hundreds of thousands on the off chance you might need those sums to pay for your care. This is a typical insurance risk. Yet it is essentially uninsurable on the private market. This, according to the Dilnot report, is why:

> The problem is that there is currently too much uncertainty involved for the private sector to take on the full risk. There is uncertainty over how long people will live, uncertainty over changing care and support needs, uncertainty over costs, and uncertainty over wider changes that could affect care (such as medical advances or changes to the economy). These uncertainties have meant that the sector has struggled to design affordable and attractive products that people want to buy. No country in the world relies solely on private insurance for funding the whole cost of social care.[34]

Some are well ahead of us in developing a much clearer role for the state. The Nordic countries, for example, largely provide free care funded through general taxation, while the likes of Germany, Japan and the Netherlands have developed social insurance schemes with compulsory contributions funding provision.

If the private sector can't do it, then that's where *social* insurance comes in. The state can provide the insurance. But if that kicks in from the first pound of need then it risks becoming hugely expensive, with the likely consequence that the quality and eligibility will be cut in the face of fiscal pressure. It might also risk moving huge amounts of care that is currently provided within families into the domain of state action.

This is one of the aspects of much social care which is different from health care. We rely on millions of husbands and wives, daughters and sons, mothers and fathers, to provide care for their loved ones. Some might argue that it would be desirable to hand all of that over to the state, that relying on them is a form of exploitation. But as ever, a balance is needed. A world in which this familial care is completely squeezed out by state provision does not feel like an attractive or desirable one.

All of which led Dilnot to propose a system whereby the initial costs of care would be paid by the individual, but once those costs exceeded a certain amount – around £35,000 in his view, in 2011 – then the state should step in and pay the rest.

That wouldn't mean they would live for free in a care home. He also suggested that while the care element of residential care should be free once those conditions were met, people should be expected to meet their normal living costs – of up to £10,000 a year – from any income or assets they did have.

We actually got as far as a law based on these proposals reaching the statute book as long ago as 2015. But it was never enacted. The Treasury was, as ever, worried about costs. Instead we got a series of White Papers promised but never delivered, as a seemingly never-ending string of ministers and civil servants in the Department of Health, Number 10 and the Treasury wrangled over options.

A different set of policy proposals may in fact have cost the Conservatives their parliamentary majority in 2017. In spectacularly poorly judged fashion, they sprung an entirely new policy idea on an unsuspecting world in their manifesto.

The idea itself was perfectly defensible. They proposed lifting the £23,250 asset threshold mentioned above to £100,000. That would simply have made the current system considerably more generous. The problem arose because they proposed paying for this by aligning the way the means test worked for people getting care in their own home with the way it worked for those needing residential care. They wanted to do that by including housing wealth in the measure of assets considered when assessing eligibility for support for home care.

As things stand, the value of your home only comes into play if you need residential care. Not surprisingly in the context of a general election this was leaped on by opposition parties, dubbed a 'dementia tax' and was one of the contributory factors in the Conservatives' poor showing at the polls. Quite plausibly, failure to sort out social care policy had the direct effect of creating a state of parliamentary deadlock which led to the particular form of 'hard Brexit' with which we have ended up.

Finally, in September 2021, we did get an announcement of what I, perhaps naively, believed were reforms that would be implemented. The reforms meant that council-funded adult social care services in England would still be subject to an initial means test, but one that is substantially more generous: the upper asset threshold was to be increased to £100,000 (from £23,250) from October 2023, meaning those with assets up to that level would be entitled to some support with their care costs if their incomes are insufficient. The threshold to be potentially eligible for full support was set to increase to £20,000 (from £14,250).

The big structural change, in line with the Dilnot proposals, was that a lifetime cap of £86,000 was to be put on the amount anyone has to pay for personal care (as long as that care is deemed to be 'necessary' as part of a council care needs assessment). Once eligible costs exceed £86,000, the council would pay in full for any further personal care costs they consider necessary, no matter what your assets or income.

All of that was to be in place in autumn 2023. It was legislated. Families were planning on that basis. Yet with less than a year to go the plans were delayed again, for two years, supposedly to save some money, though the amount saved through delay will be small indeed. This is a disgraceful way of making policy. I now fear these reforms may never come into effect.

I'm not suggesting the proposals were perfect. Far from it. They were far less generous than Dilnot originally proposed. Eighty-six thousand pounds might not look like a catastrophic payment to those of us owning houses in London and the south-east worth multiples of that, but there are plenty of parts of the country where payments of that amount could still eat up most of the assets even of homeowners. The average house price in Hartlepool in 2022 was less than £130,000.

Worse, in direct contrast to Andrew Dilnot's recommendations, the government has said that only people's own out-of-pocket payments would count towards the cap. No payment made by the council because you are entitled to some means-tested support was to count. The effect of this was to make the proposed system only marginally more generous than what currently exists for those with modest levels of assets.

If your total assets are around the £100,000 mark, you could still end up using up 70 per cent of them under this system. If you have half a million, by contrast, you end up losing less than 20 per cent of your wealth. Doing it this way makes it cheaper, but it doesn't look terribly fair. It also results in a geographical hit which doesn't look entirely consistent with a desire to 'level up'. People in the north-east, Yorkshire and Humber, and the Midlands will see the biggest erosion of their protection against high social care costs.[35]

And then there's paying for it. The government allocated just £1.8 billion a year over three years, not only to roll out these reforms but also: to improve training for social care staff; provide more advice, support and respite services for informal carers; and give private payers the ability to ask their council to organise their care at the same price the council is paying, among much else. There is no chance that this will prove adequate.

Instead of making the funding adequate the government again chose delay, procrastination, uncertainty, stasis, and disaster for those affected. This really is government failure writ large. It is unforgivable.

Looking to the future

None of this does anything to undo a decade of cuts to social care funding. Restoring access to 2010 levels would require something like an additional £10 billion a year of spending. That is, I would hazard, not going to happen.

But providing adult social care is only going to get more expensive. That's partly because the population is ageing, but also because of growing numbers of working age adults, most with learning difficulties, in need of care. Spending on both working age and older adults is likely to need to grow at up to 4 per cent a year over the next decade simply to keep services at their current, barely adequate levels.

Once you take account of the impact of recently announced reforms, let alone further improvements to access and quality, that could easily lead to a doubling in spending by the late 2030s.

We will need to pay for that, of course, just as we will need to pay for the extra spending on health and pensions that looks all but inevitable. For social care, though, another complexity is layered on top – the fact that it happens through local councils. Not that that seems to bother national politicians as they make policy.

It was telling that when, in September 2021, the prime minister announced a major shake-up in the provision and funding of social care, he did not even deign to mention that it would be local authorities who would have the responsibility for carrying out his wishes.

In fact, so big are their social care responsibilities that local authorities are becoming organisations devoted almost entirely to providing social care – for both adults and children. It already accounts for more than half of their budgets, a proportion which grows inexorably, just as the share of the NHS in the national budget is on a seemingly ever upward path. As we will see in Chapter 9, government ambitions to make councils more self-sufficient, funded by council tax and business rates with little or no central grant, cannot be realised in the face of this reality.

It is already the case that standards for social care are set centrally. The new means-testing regime and cap on costs which local authorities will need to administer will add to the complexity. Meanwhile, there is no correlation between what councils can raise from their own resources and what they have to spend on social care.

Indeed, it is often poorer coastal communities like Blackpool where needs are greatest. To return to the theme of the first part of this chapter, needs not just for social care but for health, welfare, jobs, and housing vary enormously between different places and for different people. Whether it's Luiz in Lambeth or Kate Garraway trying to navigate her way through the system, what we have at the moment succeeds neither in closing those gaps nor in providing adequate insurance for those – from whatever background – who need it.

7

Schools

Spending on schools: £57.3 billion in 2022/23[1]

Jim Coupe is a teacher, with a commitment to the children in his school and a driving need to 'make a difference'. Brought up in Weston-Super-Mare, the seaside resort near Bristol, he now lives in what was once, but is no longer, a somewhat rundown area by the sea in Sussex.

His rise to become principal of Shoreham Academy, managing the academic lives of around 1,800 pupils, has coincided with the toughest financial climate for schools in a generation. The school he presides over also happens to be the one which I attended until I took my A Levels in 1985. And, as if in confirmation, there is my photo grinning inanely over the main door of the school, alongside some other more recent and probably more famous alumni, mainly models and sports personalities rather than economists.

I didn't have any great sense of returning to my roots though. Rather unnervingly the buildings that had made up my school when it was called King's Manor, an institution which started life as a girls' secondary modern, had disappeared completely. They were where the football pitch now is. It is as if they were never there at all.

Jim uses the word 'leaky' to describe the old buildings. That's certainly one of my main memories – of buckets filling with rainwater all over the floor. It's remarkable that we allowed our schools to reach that level of decay. The (state) schools which my children attended are palaces by comparison, in large part as a result of the huge sums spent by the last Labour government under the 'building schools for the future' programme. The programme was axed by Michael Gove in one of his first acts as education secretary back in 2010. An act he now says he regrets.[2]

Jim's predecessor in my day was a tall and cadaverous individual glorying in the name of Aubrey Whitehead. He left just before I did. Never an academic powerhouse, to put it kindly, the school seems to have declined in the subsequent two decades. By 2007, only 23 per cent of its pupils were getting five GCSEs at grade C including English and maths, half the national average.[3] It was identified as a failing school by then secretary of state Ed Balls, coincidentally my old Oxford tutorial partner. It was shut and reopened as an academy with a new name and under new management. It was typical of the first wave of academy schools opened by the Labour government, explicitly designed to provide a fresh start, an injection of funding, and a new way of managing hitherto failing institutions.

In the case of Shoreham Academy this seems to have worked. By 2019, 71 per cent of students were achieving five good GCSE passes, including English and maths. Even given broader improvements in grades, that's a phenomenal change. It has moved from leaky sink school with falling rolls to oversubscribed school of choice for the local community. Jim Coupe can take appropriate credit. Leadership matters. That academy policy and some extra money also helped – as did the 'gentrification' of Shoreham which saw an influx of commuters, graduates and young families pushed along the coast from Brighton and out of London by rising housing costs.

Running a school like Shoreham Academy is a big job. Jim is managing a multi-million-pound operation, including human resources, finance and buildings, as well as looking after the education and welfare of 1,800 children. 'As part of a multi-school academy trust, I get the most fantastic support,' says Jim. 'But nothing quite readies you for that responsibility.'

His job is not made easier by constant changes to government policy and funding. As a teacher since 1996, Jim has seen periods of both feast and famine. He has also seen several cycles of policy changes. 'You have to adapt in order to achieve your goals for your students,' he says, 'according to what you have available to you. The goal you are seeking to achieve is to provide a deep and rich education to underpin their future plans and careers. That doesn't change according to how much money you have at the start of the year.'

Jim tells the story of the schools' careers service. In 2000, Labour had reformed the old careers services creating a new national organisation called Connexions to provide information, advice and guidance to thirteen- to eighteen-year-olds. That Labour government created a lot of new institutions. Connexions is far from the only one not to have stood the test of time. It was wound up soon after 2010. This institutional merry-go-round, particularly affecting post-sixteen and vocational education, is one of our pervading failures. It's a merry-go-round that Jim and others actually trying to deliver education need to manage around. The clear signal in the early 2010s was that careers advice was not a priority. It became 'non-statutory' – voluntary in other words. Schools inevitably concentrated their dwindling resources on other things.

That has changed. Careers advice is now 'statutory'. There are targets that have to be met. Yet, much of the expertise that was there has now gone. It will be, it already is, expensive and disruptive to build it up again, to find local companies prepared to provide work experience and so on.

As an academy trust – part of United Learning – Shoreham Academy gets its money from ESFA, the Education and Skills Funding Agency, in effect directly from central government. This is a piece of government machinery that didn't exist twenty years ago but now employs 1,800 staff. It's half as big as the entire education department, and represents a remarkable centralisation of decision-making over school and college funding. A slice of that money per pupil gets passed on to the academy trust to pay for the support services they provide. That works the other way around for local authorities, through which funding for schools which aren't academies still flows, which take a slice per pupil – much smaller than it used to be – before passing it down to the school.

Both types of school use the same local school funding formula, set by the local authority for each area. Shoreham Academy gets its funding based on the West Sussex formula, plus the various other subsidies they get for the number of pupils on free school meals (pupil premium), or with educational health care needs. More important than the details are the fact that schools were affected by austerity along with most of the rest of the public sector. Funding per pupil is about the same today, in 2023, as it was in 2010. It's hard to convey quite how extraordinary a fact that is. No increase in 13 years. In fact it was only in 2023 that funding recovered its

former level, having been below its 2010 level for the entire intervening period. The sixth form and further education sector, which
of course get far less coverage, have done considerably worse.

Not that any of this is always obvious to those of us outside
the sector. There were headlines about schools not getting
enough funding in the mid-2000s even as the money was flooding in. Indeed, such stories were enough to persuade the then
Labour government to make what was actually a significant
constitutional change, dramatically constraining local authority
freedoms over school spending. Continued academisation, and
planned complete centralisation of funding formulae, will soon
complete the journey to the virtual ending of any role for local
authorities in school funding.

Stasis, or worse, in funding since 2010 means, at the very least,
that our increasing expectations have not been met. We saw in
Chapter 5 that health has been taking an ever-growing fraction
of national income. The same has not been true of education. The
government spent 4-5 per cent of national income on education
back in the 1980s. That's roughly where it still sits today.[4] Given
growing expectations and the growing importance of education
that is a real surprise, and not a very welcome one. Especially
unwelcome to teachers, perhaps, whose real wages have fallen,
and fallen substantially, over the last decade.

I have followed all this for a long time. I was chief economist at
the Department for Education back in the early 2000s. Actually,
I joined the Department for Education and Employment. It
soon lost its responsibilities for employment and became the
Department for Education and Skills. By the time Ed Balls took it
over, it was the Department for Children, Schools and Families,
before becoming the Department for Education in 2010. It didn't
change its name in 2016, but it did change remit to take on the
responsibility for higher and further education which it had lost in
the 2000s. Since I started there in 2000, there have been fourteen

secretaries of state. That's an average tenure of less than two years. I leave you to draw your own conclusions about the seriousness and long-term consistency with which our leaders treat education.

With their beautiful, airy building, from where you can see the South Downs, Shoreham Academy has been relatively lucky. But like other schools it has had to cope with cuts which have put teachers, and perhaps especially headteachers, under strain. 'When you've managed to make all the possible efficiency savings you can, then all you can do is to persuade your staff to reach inside themselves and put even more energy into their jobs,' says Jim.

On the upside, these cuts came off the back of very big spending increases during the 2000s. Schools may be struggling, but they are in a much better position than they were back in the 1980s and 1990s. As we'll see in the next chapter, that is unfortunately not true of our neglected system of further and vocational education.

School spending

Schools remain the big beasts of education spending. There are a lot of them educating a lot of children. In England we spend around £57 billion a year on nearly 9 million pupils in 17,000 primary schools and 3,500 secondary schools. As Jim Coupe couldn't fail to notice, there has been a long squeeze on school funding. Spending per pupil in England fell by around 9 per cent in the decade to 2019/20, the biggest cut in more than forty years.[5]

One set of schools has not seen any squeeze on resources. Whilst core school spending per pupil in state schools in England fell in real terms between 2009/10 and 2019/20, private school fees rose by 23 per cent above inflation. In 2009/10, the gap between total state school spending per pupil and private school fees was about £3,100 or nearly 40 per cent. By 2020/21, this had more than doubled to a difference of £6,500 or over 90 per cent.[6]

A large part of the burden of the spending squeeze has been borne by teachers. Experienced teachers – that's the majority of the profession – had experienced a 13 per cent fall in the real value of their pay between 2010 and 2022.[7] It isn't surprising that a recent report of the review body charged with advising the government on teachers' pay concluded: 'There is a broad consensus ... that action on teachers' pay ... is necessary to urgently improve teacher recruitment and retention ... there are severe and persistent problems with teacher supply.'[8] The 6.5 per cent award for teachers for September 2023 will do nothing to undo any of that fall. There has to be a limit beyond which this continued reduction in what we pay our teachers – a reduction both in absolute terms and relative to pay for similar jobs – cannot go.

What's more, because pay varies little according to where the teacher lives or what subject they teach, recruitment and retention problems are greatest in the most expensive areas, in the least desirable areas, in more challenging schools and in subjects where external options are the most attractive. The pattern of recruitment difficulties has changed over time. As London has boomed, and despite high living costs, recruitment problems have been relatively muted in recent years. It's in more deprived areas away from London that recruitment, especially in subjects like maths, physics and computing, has been most difficult. For example, while around 80 per cent of GCSE teachers of music, art, biology and general science have relevant qualifications, this falls to around 50 per cent of teachers of modern languages, maths and physics. And these teachers are not evenly distributed across schools; pupils in more disadvantaged schools are less likely to have teachers with relevant degrees, especially if they attend school outside London.

Ofsted also assesses teacher quality. They find nearly a quarter of schools in the most disadvantaged tenth fail to meet the standard for 'Good' teaching. In the least disadvantaged tenth, over 95 per cent of schools meet the standard (and more than four in ten have 'Outstanding' teaching).[9] We end up with the most vacancies, and the least well-qualified and least effective teachers in the most economically valuable subjects, and in schools where pupils have the greatest needs.

Not that spending more is a guarantee of achieving more. In contrast with England, spending per pupil rose somewhat in Scotland during the 2010s, not least because teacher pay has become relatively more generous north of the border. That's a choice the Scottish government was able to make within the generous confines of the Barnett formula (see Chapter 9). But results in Scotland, have not improved any more than those in England. Recent work from the Education Policy Institute even suggests the reverse may be true.[10]

That said, there is increasingly clear evidence that resources do matter. If you're surprised that I even need to say that then just consider how hard it might be to prove that relationship. Within state schools those with poorer intakes get more money but get less good results. Resources change over time, but so does just about everything else that might have an impact on outcomes. Think about my old school. Has it got better because it has new buildings, more money, because it's become an academy, because of the quality of its leadership, or just because Shoreham has gentrified? Recent studies which have tried to get around these problems do find that more money helps. One found that an extra £1,000 per primary pupil per year raised attainment by about four to five months of educational progress.[11] Extra money also seems to deliver the largest benefits for schools that have a more disadvantaged student body.[12]

Of course, it matters what you spend the money on. Reducing class sizes is a popular option. A 2019 poll of English teachers, for example, found that this was the top priority for around a third of teachers[13] and this issue regularly polls at or near the top of parents' priorities for education.[14] Making classes *much* smaller can indeed have substantial benefits. One American study found that children in very small classes (with thirteen to seventeen pupils) had test scores around four percentage points higher than those in classes with twenty-two to twenty-five pupils.[15] But research that looks at smaller changes in class size – which are arguably more realistic in a context of constrained resources and problems with teacher recruitment – tends to find much smaller benefits from smaller classes, if any impact at all.[16] In that context the fall in average class sizes of about two pupils over the last fifteen years in England are likely to have had only very small impacts on attainment.

Delivering larger reductions in class sizes would be very expensive. For example, according to Department for Education statistics, the average primary school class in England had just over twenty-seven pupils in 2019.[17] Cutting class sizes to seventeen pupils – as in the study mentioned above – would mean creating around 60 per cent more classes. With 4.7 million primary school pupils in England, that equates to around 100,000 new teachers and a salary cost of close to £4 billion – before factoring in costs like additional classrooms or teaching assistants.

One thing that does make a difference for sure is having more effective teachers. They make a big difference to exam results and also to future earnings, and even general wellbeing.[18] But how to identify and recruit good teachers? It turns out that their educational record or success in teacher training are often poor predictors of future effectiveness. Effectiveness does increase as teachers gain more experience, though unfortunately there is some evidence that more effective teachers leave the profession more quickly.[19] In the end the only way to know an effective teacher is to measure their effectiveness. As we've seen, so far as we can measure these things, the most effective teachers are not teaching in the most needy areas.

We do know that it is harder and costs more to educate more disadvantaged pupils. If you remember two things about the role of the Liberal Democrats in the 2010 to 2015 coalition government's education policy, then the second (after HE tuition fees) is likely to be the 'pupil premium' – an additional payment to schools in respect of pupils in receipt of free school meals. You qualify for free school meals if your parents are out of work and receiving means-tested benefits.

Despite the branding and fanfare, this wasn't really a new policy. Schools have always received more in respect of poor pupils and those with other needs. During the boom spending years of the 2000s, the funding received by the most deprived schools rose from about 25 per cent above the amount received by the least deprived to about 35 per cent above. Despite the introduction of the pupil premium, that difference had actually shrunk back to around 25 per cent by 2018. That's partly a reflection of an incredibly complex and opaque funding system, and one that responds slowly if at all to socioeconomic change in the local area. There is a serious gap between government rhetoric and reality – deprived secondary schools outside London have seen the fastest falls in spending per pupil (13 per cent) since 2010.[20] So much for using school funding to 'level up' poorer regions.

In the long run, the new National Funding Formula (NFF) should make sure the funding system is more responsive. You might be surprised to learn that a true national funding formula for schools is a recent innovation, only partially introduced in 2018. It calculates a notional funding allocation for every school in England based on the number and characteristics of their pupils. This amount is then summed across each school in a local authority to determine the local authority's budget. Local authorities can use these NFF allocations or implement their own local funding formulae, so actual funding allocations to schools currently still to some extent reflect local authority choices.

One immediate consequence, though, of the NFF has been another redistribution away from the most deprived schools and local authorities. It introduced something that sounds rather good – a statutory minimum level of funding per pupil for every school. Who could be against that? Well, maybe it's right, but the least well-funded schools are those in the most affluent areas, so they are the only ones who will gain from the policy. With a fixed budget this statutory minimum means less for the most deprived.

We are currently at a sort of halfway house. The NFF is calculated at a school level but local authorities can deviate from it when they make allocations. The government says that it intends to move to a 'hard' national funding formula in the future, where funding to individual schools directly reflects NFF allocations, but is yet to set a date. The obvious reason for delay is that, when resources are tight, there will be losers as well as winners – never popular.

With hindsight, but not just with hindsight, we should rue the opportunity missed during the feast years of the 2000s. Fixing things when there is money about is a whole lot easier than fixing them when money is tight. Then again, I suppose when you've got plenty of cash you feel you can live with an illogical and downright perverse funding system even if it means very similar schools getting very different levels of funding.

Inequalities

One thing is for sure, disadvantaged pupils do much less well than their better off peers. There are so many ways of seeing that, so many statistics that demonstrate it. In 2019, at the end of primary school, 47 per cent of pupils who were eligible for free school meals – broadly speaking the poorest fifth of pupils, about two million in all – reached the expected level in reading, writing and maths, compared with 68 per cent of other pupils. Sixty-nine per cent of students not eligible for free school meals obtained at least a grade 4 in both English and maths GCSEs, against only 41 per cent of pupils eligible for free school meals. By age nineteen, just 35 per cent of those who were FSM-eligible at age sixteen obtained Level 3 (A Level or equivalent) qualifications compared to 60 per cent of all other pupils.

In fact, right across the income distribution, the richer your parents the better you do at school. This is not just a difference between the poor and the rest. Each step up the income distribution matters, and in fact the biggest gap, even within the state system, is between those from the most advantaged families and the rest. Of those born in 2000 and 2001, more than 70 per cent of pupils from the richest 10 per cent of households got five good GCSEs including English and maths, something achieved by just a quarter of the poorest tenth. More than a third of the richest got at least one A or A*. Fewer than one in twenty of the poorest tenth did so. Among those taking GCSEs in 2006, more than half of young people from the poorest fifth of families had not got as far as A level standard by the age of twenty-six compared with fewer than 20 per cent of those from the richest fifth.[21] Fewer than a fifth of the poorest pupils at state schools go on to university against half of the richest. Over 70 per cent of private school students go on to higher education.

I could bombard you with ever more statistics, but you get the idea. There are plenty of other inequalities. Girls do much better at school than boys, for example. At the end of primary school, 60 per cent of boys reach the expected level in reading, writing and maths, while 70 per cent of girls meet the threshold. There is also a clear gender gap in GCSE results; the share of girls achieving at least a grade 4 in both English and maths GCSEs is eight percentage points higher. While 51 per cent of young men achieve A Level (or equivalent) qualifications by the age of nineteen, 63 per cent of young women do so. In 2019 58 per cent of those completing an undergraduate degree in England were women.

There are also big differences in achievement between different ethnic minorities.[22] Overall, most ethnic groups do better than white British in the education system. For some groups this a relatively recent phenomenon. Chinese and Indian students have been doing better for a long time. In more recent years students from Bangladeshi, Pakistani and Black African backgrounds have caught up in terms of GCSE achievement. By age twenty-six, white British are less likely than any other ethnic group to have a degree and more likely to have no qualification beyond GCSE. By international standards this is most unusual. Most ethnic minority groups underperform the majority in most of Western Europe and in the USA.

One big difference between these ethnic and gender inequalities on the one hand, and socio-economic differences on the other. The advantage enjoyed by girls and some minorities in the education system does *not* translate into the labour market. Women earn less than men, and most ethnic minorities earn less than whites. Those from better off backgrounds not only earn more than those from poorer families, they *gain more* from the qualifications they do achieve.

We all have our own experiences of the education system. Despite going to a rather unsuccessful school, I did well out of it. Exams, A levels, university suited me down to the ground, rather as it suited nearly our entire political class. It's not the same for everyone. Here is Sir Steve McQueen, of *12 Years a Slave* fame. I was fortunate enough to meet him in my role as a member of the *Times* education commission. He attended a secondary school in West London in the 1980s:

It was awful. School was painful because I just think that loads of people, so many beautiful people, didn't achieve what they could achieve because no one believed in them, or gave them a chance, or invested any time in them. A lot of beautiful boys, talented people, were put by the wayside. School was scary for me because no one cared. At thirteen years old, you are marked, you are dead, that's your future.[23]

Children still face a system that narrowly rewards particular academic skills, sets them up for failure and then puts barriers in their way, rather than showing them the best routes into rewarding work.

Inequalities matter at every level. Those who don't make the expected grade at age eleven in their Key Stage 2 tests have almost literally no chance of getting the benchmark five 'good' GCSEs at age sixteen. Yet that is the only measure of success we have. They are set up for failure from age eleven, and they know it. Then, just missing a grade C in GCSE English by one solitary mark dramatically reduces your chances of getting further qualifications and going on to well-paid work. As Sandra McNally and co-authors from the London School of Economics found:

Narrowly missing the C grade in English language decreases the probability of enrolling in a higher-level qualification by at least 9 percentage points. There is a similarly large effect on the probability of achieving a higher academic or vocational qualification by age nineteen – which is a pre-requisite for university or getting a job with good wage prospects. There is also an effect on the probability of entering tertiary or higher education ... Narrowly missing a grade C increases the probability of dropping out of education at age eighteen by about 4 percentage points (in a context where the national average is 12 per cent). It increases the probability of becoming 'not in education, training or employment' by about two percentage points. Those entering employment at this age (and without a grade C in English) are unlikely to be in jobs with good progression possibilities. If they are 'not in education, employment or training', this puts them at a high risk of wage scarring effects and crime participation resulting from youth unemployment in the longer term.[24]

To be clear, this isn't the difference between getting a C and a D. This is a comparison between those who just squeak a C by a single mark and those who just miss by a single mark. They will be very similar in their capabilities. Instead of providing opportunities and ladders up, our system too often slams doors shut. It slams them shut in part because it has become increasingly focused on just one route, via university.

Disadvantage is deeply rooted. Take for example the 415 schools which were judged below standard in 2019, many of them for the past thirteen years. According to reports immediately before the lockdown, many have become 'dumping grounds' for problem children. Many of the same schools also reported low levels of literacy and employment among parents. Ofsted found that some children were 'sent to school hungry'. Others even try to get excluded so they can go home 'because they are concerned that their parents are victims of domestic abuse'.

And that was before Covid, which has compounded the differences between schools and places. 'Covid has brutally revealed the health inequalities in our society, so too it illustrates the educational ones that have arisen for similar reasons,' wrote professors Simon Burgess and Anna Vignoles in 2020.[25] 'Perhaps this unprecedented crisis is a time to rethink how we go about reducing deeper economic inequalities that underpin these problems.'

In my view this is likely to be the biggest long-term effect of

Covid lockdowns. The loss of learning by poorer children was enormous. Poorer pupils were less likely to have access to computers and the internet, and schools with poorer intakes were less likely to make use of online teaching. Some had more difficult home environments in which to study. Worse, you can see the effects in the cognitive and socio-emotional development of two-year-olds.[26]

I have had the privilege of meeting Frank Cottrell-Boyce, the children's author, screenwriter, and the man responsible for much of the 2012 Olympics opening ceremony. In visiting schools and talking to children he sees up close what my colleagues and I see in the data.

> I've been to dozens of schools, talked to thousands of kids and one big thought is EVERYTHING has changed for children. The relationship between school and home, between themselves and their screens ... in a reversal of the natural order of things, during the pandemic we asked our children to sacrifice friendship, education and fresh air to protect the old. Where is the recognition? Where is the payback?[27]

The effects are big, persistent and worrying. Results in Key Stage 2, the national assessments at age 11, are well down on pre-pandemic attainment levels. These tests are much more objective and comparable over time than GCSEs and A levels where results have essentially been 'fixed' so as not to show any decline. The fraction of 11-year-olds meeting the expected standard in reading, writing and maths in 2023 stood at 59 per cent, well down on the 65 per cent pre-pandemic level. That's years of progress lost.

Even more worrying are figures showing big increases in absences. In autumn term 2022 very nearly one in four pupils were defined as 'persistently absent', that is they missed at least 10 per cent of school days. That was almost double the pre-pandemic rate of persistent absence, and the highest on record. 'Two groups stand out as being worst affected since 2019: disadvantaged pupils and children with special educational needs. As these groups also entered the pandemic with some of the highest levels of absence, it appears that absence is widening educational inequalities.' So wrote Emily Hunt of the Education Policy Institute.[28]

It is hard to disagree with the evidence given to the Covid-19 inquiry by former children's commissioner Anne Longfield. While the pandemic had been a big challenge for most children it had been a 'disaster' for the most disadvantaged. It had heightened existing vulnerabilities and laid the foundation for long term problems. She warned that the long shadow of Covid was likely to be felt by those children for the next two decades.[29]

The scale of the problem is potentially huge. Suppose children lost half a year of progress from Covid. Well, we spend £50 billion a year on schools in England, so we could effectively have lost £25 billion worth of investment in our children. But the impact on future earnings of the children affected is likely to be many times bigger than that.[30] In that context, the government's announcement in spring 2021 of just £1.4 billion in additional funding for schools – an announcement which led to the resignation of their own education recovery commissioner, Sir Kevan Collins – looks worse than merely inadequate. It looks short-sighted.

What's more, we have been here before. The UK abandoned plans to create proper secondary schools after the First World War because of concerns about affordability. An increase in the school leaving age to sixteen was delayed from the late 1940s to 1973 for the same reason. We know now that the economic benefits of acting earlier would have far outweighed the initial costs that so concerned the Treasury. Let's hope we are not making the same mistake all over again. We can hope, but the chances are that is exactly what we are doing.

But then, look how far we've come

In October 1976, Jim Callaghan made a speech at Ruskin College, Oxford – one of his first as prime minister – launching a 'Great Debate' on education. He urged a new openness by the teaching profession and warned against anyone who preferred to keep the curtains drawn and the shutters closed. 'It is almost as though some people would wish that the subject matter and purpose of education should not have public attention focused on it,' he said. 'Nor that profane hands should be allowed to touch it.'[31]

That may sound like a slightly abstruse reference at this distance in time. But it was a big moment in the history of schools policy. It reflected a frustration at the lack of public engagement in, and accountability of, the school system and teaching profession. Since then O levels have been replaced by GCSEs; many additional national tests, notably at age eleven, have been introduced; league tables are now part of the furniture; we are used to the idea of 'choice' – being able at least to express a preference over where our children should be educated; Ofsted is responsible for inspecting schools; we have a national curriculum; local authorities have lost almost all their responsibilities over education; and the vast majority of secondary schools are now academies. I could go on.

Some of this additional central control has worked much better than it really should have done. When I joined the Department for Education and Employment back in 2000, I had presumed that the role of government in schools should be to set structures, incentives, accountabilities, and let the school leaders and professionals deliver within a broad framework. I was amazed to find the department saw its role quite differently – a lot of micromanagement and a focus effectively on telling teachers how to teach.

I was even more amazed to discover that it worked, at least up to a point. If there is one intervention that we know was really effective, it was the national literacy and numeracy strategy, overseen by educationalist-turned-targetologist and management guru, Michael Barber. This was a set of instructions to primary school teachers on exactly how to improve the literacy and numeracy of their charges. Serious evaluation by Steve Machin and Sandra McNally at the LSE showed big positive effects. 'Whichever way one looks at it ... the benefits seem to be large and the costs small' was their robust conclusion.[32]

You can only take that level of direction so far, though. Michael Barber would be the first to admit that central direction like this can get you over a hump, but it can't be a long-term solution and way of working. Or to put it in his own words 'you can mandate adequacy, but you cannot mandate greatness'. Ministers have been searching in vain for similar impacts ever since, creating academies and free schools, tweaking the curriculum, changing exam structures, berating teachers, the list of interventions goes on, and on. The number of missives received from DfE HQ by headteachers like Jim Coupe is endless. None of this activity has had as much impact as that simple intervention back in the late 1990s. And much of it still misses the point. The most important input into effective learning is good teaching. A decade of pay cuts for teachers is not going to help.

All that said, there can be no doubt that we offer our children a far better education than we did back in the 1970s when Callaghan made that historic intervention. Yes, there has been some grade inflation, but that definitely isn't the only reason why we have so many more young people getting the opportunity to go to university – nor why we have moved from a quarter of the cohort getting five O levels at C or above to nearly 60 per cent getting at least five good GCSEs, including English and maths, today.

Not that all is well. We are at best middling in international league tables of attainment, and below middling when it comes to the wellbeing of our children. There are big and persistent gaps in how well children from different socioeconomic backgrounds do in our schools.

Before school

One additional achievement about which I could, and perhaps should, have a written an entire chapter. In the 1990s and before, there was no right to any state funded childcare or early years education. There is now a huge and complex set of rights and associated funding. This represents a major extension in the scope and role of the welfare state.

All three- and four-year-olds have a right to fifteen hours a week of free childcare, with another fifteen hours a week for those with working parents. Over 140,000 disadvantaged two-year-olds also get free places. The government spends £4 billion a year on these programmes. There is in addition an array of benefit entitlements to help poorer families pay for childcare from which around 300,000 families benefit via the tax credit and Universal Credit systems. Over 400,000 benefit from tax free childcare. Total spending runs into the billions, and parties now regularly compete with each other at elections to promise more.

Indeed, one of the most eye-catching announcements of recent years was the commitment made by chancellor Jeremy Hunt in 2023 to 30 hours of funded childcare a week for all children in working families from nine months old. He also announced an increase in spending on current provision. This is all due to be in place from September 2025, at an annual cost of £5 billion a year. That will more than double current spending on the free entitlement. Quite an announcement at a time of severe fiscal constraint.

Yet the system is not delivering for millions of families. For those who need to use formal childcare for hours in excess of those provided for free, costs are high. As with the situation in social care that is in part because they end up subsidising the free places for which government funding is often inadequate. Funding per hour has barely changed since the early 2000s even as wages, which account for 70 per cent of providers' costs, have risen, not least driven by big increases in the minimum wage, on which too many childcare workers subsist.[33]

In terms of what people actually pay this is, in some ways, a smaller problem than is often portrayed. More than half of families with pre-school children pay nothing towards formal childcare – often because they make use of grandparents or other friends and relatives. The role of the state again butts up against the role of family. Nevertheless, about a fifth of middle earners with pre-school children say that they struggle to manage childcare costs. Ten per cent of childcare users in London spend more than £350 a week on it.[34]

The policy landscape is complex. Some providers are owned by local authorities, some are voluntary, and others profit making. The range of government funding streams is large and ever changing. More fundamentally, governments have swung to and fro as to whether the main purpose of pre-school provision is to provide good quality learning for young children, and especially a leg up for the most disadvantaged, or to help working parents.

Overall the direction of change has been away from targeted provision for the most needy and towards universal care to help working parents. That most recent, costly, announcement of free provision for all *working* families with children over nine months

explicitly involves no money for the poorest. Perhaps that is inevitable when that latter path helps more voters, but it's not where
the original impetus for this leg of the welfare state arose from.
In the 2000s the overwhelming evidence that high quality early
years provision was vital for giving poorer children a leg up so as
to start at school more on a par with their better off peers, as well
as to help them later in life, led to a system much more focused
on poorer children than the one that currently exists. Funding
is much less targeted than it used to be.

That's even before we consider Sure Start. First introduced in
1999 and accounting for a third of early years spending by its
peak in 2010, Sure Start offers a 'one-stop shop' for childcare and
early education, health services, parenting support, information
about health and child development, and employment advice. It
was introduced off the back of the international evidence on the
effectiveness of such programmes. Recent evaluations by my colleagues have shown that it was indeed highly effective, not least
in improving the long-term health of children. Spending on Sure
Start has been cut by 60 per cent since 2010.[35]

Where to from here?

Sixteenth of June, 2004. That's the date on the memo I sent to
colleagues in the then Department for Education and Skills as I
got ready to leave to take up a new role at the Treasury. Entitled
'Departing Thoughts', it contained a summary of some of what
I thought I had learned during my previous four years as chief
economist.

Remarkably for an internal civil service memo, this one from

2004 still exists to be wheeled out occasionally. For the sad truth is that nineteen years and fifteen secretaries of state later, most of what I put down on paper back then still rings horribly true. I made only five points in that memo. They're not quite the same as the five I'd choose today, but they would still make it into my top ten. So here they are.

First, policies that have an impact on students consistently and over a period of time are more effective and deliver better value for money than one-off policies. That's actually the strong conclusion of recent research. Success builds on success, intervention on intervention. There's little point, for example, improving outcomes for eleven-year-olds if you don't follow up and ensure that those improvements are maintained. We also have a system that we know doesn't work for some. Among those pupils who don't make it to the expected level at age eleven, almost none go on to reach the benchmark achievements at GCSE level.

Second, the school system puts too little focus on 'non-cognitive' outcomes. Call them 'soft skills' or social skills or whatever you want, the things that really matter in life and in work – communication, teamwork, motivation, empathy – are too easily sidelined in an education system focused on exam results.

The evidence that this is important, and increasingly so, is overwhelming. These aren't merely nice to have. They matter in the labour market as well as in life. Happily, the evidence that these skills can be taught is also strong. The problem is that a system that only measures exam passes is never likely to put enough focus where it really matters.

Third, inequality in educational outcomes is pervasive. The better off you are, the more likely you are to progress successfully. That isn't merely a difference between the poor and the rest, although that is a big gap that matters. It's true at every point up the income or social class distribution. In fact, the biggest gaps are often between the very best off and those just below. The privately educated do best. The richest pupils at state schools also do much better than their slightly less well-off peers.

Gaps in attainment start young and widen. Top performers from poor backgrounds tend to fall behind as they get older. Where gaps between groups have closed over time – for example, in proportions reaching expected levels at age eleven, or getting five good GCSEs, or going to university – they tend to balloon out further up the system.

Getting five good GCSEs is no longer enough; the competition is to get the top grades. Getting to university isn't enough; getting into a selective institution or going on to do postgraduate study is used as a way of marking yourself out from the crowd. So that's how the better off keep their position. Education, after all, is a positional good.

Fourth, we have an education system in which girls do far better than boys. Back in 2004, this was a gap that was already big and was a trend that had been emerging for a couple of decades. The gap remains. Girls outperform boys at every stage. They are about 30 per cent more likely than boys to progress onto higher education.[36]

There is, rightly, a lot of focus on those areas of maths, computing and engineering where girls are still underrepresented and there is definitely a problem of girls often picking less lucrative options post-sixteen. However, the bigger story is of boys, and especially white working-class boys, being left behind. While we know that these educational inequalities are not reflected in the labour market, it surely should give us pause for thought that boys and girls do quite so differently at school.

Finally, I asked plaintively, what is going on between the ages of sixteen and twenty-one? We had then, and we still have, a weak and inconsistent offering for those not looking to go to university. Our lack of strong technical and vocational routes holds back both students and the economy. Uniquely in the world, our sixteen- to eighteen-year-olds specialise in only three subjects. The basic literacy and numeracy of our sixteen- to twenty-four-year-olds are shocking. We live in just about the only country where this age group has worse basic skills than do older generations. More on that in the next chapter.

That is not a comprehensive list. It misses, for example, the role of teachers, the importance of leadership, the design of the curriculum, and the entire apparatus of GCSE exams – we are very rare in the world in having exams of this type at age sixteen, followed by such extreme specialisation – to name but a few.

It is true that we often expect too much of the education system. Unequal outcomes reflect much more than what happens in schools and colleges. Schools cannot fix all our social problems. They cannot fully compensate for the hugely different home experiences of rich and poor children growing up a in a very unequal country. But government can and should do better. Tackling many of these problems requires consistency of purpose across time and across government. It is an abiding failure of our system of governance that, with an average time in the job of less than two years, secretaries of state barely have time to understand the problems, let alone to be part of the solution. Unbelievably there have been six of them in the last four years. They can too often end up being part of the problem.

Education After School

Public spending on:
Further education and sixth form colleges (16-19):
£4.5bn in 2022/23
Apprenticeships across all ages: £2.3bn in 2021/22
Adult education: £1.5bn in 2021/22
Total tuition fee loans for English domiciled under-
graduates in 2021/22: £10.3 billion[1]

School leavers

I have four sons. One of them has finished university and is in a
graduate job. Two are at university. The middle one (the last two
are twins), now in his early twenties, didn't go to university at all.

While doing his A levels at a sixth form college he did apply to
various universities and received several offers. After failing by

a wide margin to get the grades supposedly required by his first choice he was still offered a place. After all, he came with £27,000 of funding attached, so why not let him in? Thank goodness he didn't go. While Coventry University would have benefited financially, it would have been a waste of his time, and of my money, his money, and taxpayer money.

Thankfully he had also applied for a string of apprenticeships. Some years ago, he and I spent a large part of the Christmas holidays, and subsequent months, making applications. This was a vastly more complex and time-consuming job than applying to university. If you're not following the well-trodden route from A levels into higher education even finding the right opportunities can be fearsomely hard. UCAS gives you access to the whole university system.

Many apprenticeship applications meanwhile appear to be barely edited versions of the graduate process – hardly encouraging, or suitable, for the average seventeen-year-old. Each one takes many hours. In 2020 just 16,000 young people under the age of twenty-four started a higher-level apprenticeship[2] – that is above A-level standard but below degree level. Around thirty times that number started a degree. More eighteen-year-olds won places at Oxbridge that autumn than embarked on a higher-level apprenticeship. Absurd. And deeply damaging.

In our system, everything points to university as the default. It may cost a lot in the long run, but that's the long run, and today it's so much easier than the alternatives. Our education system almost seems designed to make life hard for anyone who doesn't fit the traditional academic mould. For them the routes are opaque and complex.

'The current situation is financially unsustainable,' wrote Professor Alison Wolf, both an adviser to the government and the country's leading authority on post compulsory education, in her report Heading for the Precipice:

It is deeply inegalitarian in its allocation of resources. It is also inefficient and bad for the 'human capital development', which increasingly drives and justifies education policy. In post-nineteen education, we are producing vanishingly small numbers of higher technician level qualifications, while massively increasing the output of generalist bachelor's degrees and low-level vocational qualifications. We are doing so because of the financial incentives and administrative structures that governments themselves have created, not because of labour market demand, and the imbalance looks set to worsen yet further.[3]

This is mirrored in a public debate that focuses relentlessly on universities, their funding, their students, or the pay of their vice-chancellors. That is not where the fundamental problems lie. It is our failure to get enough young people into high-quality, job-based training at eighteen that creates our skills shortages, low wages and productivity problems.

The good news is son number two has made a huge success of his apprenticeship. Work we have done at the IFS shows why. For the few who do these qualifications at levels between A levels and degrees, particularly in technical subjects, they do well, often earning more than their graduate contemporaries well into their twenties. Yet the opportunities are limited.

Looking back at the cohort who were taking A levels in the mid-2000s, more than two thirds went on to do a full university degree. Just 4 per cent went on to study or training which got them a qualification at a grade between A level and degree, often exactly the sorts of qualifications in technical and vocational subjects that are in short supply.

Other European countries offer far more opportunities at these intermediate levels. Indeed, we used to. Many of my contemporaries from school (I left in 1985) went on to successful careers after gaining technical qualifications at below degree level. But now it's all about university.

The skill gaps

Even before it comes to university entry, things have changed enormously in one respect since I was a sixth former back in the mid-1980s. Back then, only about 40 per cent of sixteen- and seventeen-year-olds were in full time education. Today it's about 85 per cent, nearly all of whom are following traditional classroom-based courses.

The numbers in work-based or employer funded training are disappearingly small. The figures for 2020 were distorted by the pandemic, but in that year just 3 per cent of sixteen- and seventeen-year-olds were doing apprenticeships and 2 per cent were in employer funded training. The numbers in normal years are not much different.

As numbers in post-sixteen education have risen, so funding per student has fallen. Further education colleges and sixth forms have seen the biggest falls in per-pupil funding (about 12 per cent) of any part of the education system since 2010/11. For FE colleges, which did not share in the boom years that preceded 2010, this has been especially hard to cope with. Funding per student is little different to its level thirty years ago, and a third less than the amount allocated to educate students at university. Yet FE colleges are where more expensive vocational courses are taught and where a large fraction of students are from disadvantaged backgrounds.

Even so, this neglected part of our education system is rather big and important. There are something like 1.4 million adults and 670,000 sixteen- to eighteen-year-olds studying at 240 colleges in England – about 190 FE colleges and fifty sixth forms. They get a bit over £5 billion a year of public funding.

Numbers will rise further. One of the challenges faced by schools and colleges is that demographics change. There are remarkably big differences in the number of children born across different years, and those changes differ by location. This creates a serious headache for planning the need for buildings, teachers and capacity.

Colleges had to deal with more students than usual studying for A levels and BTECs in 2020 and 2021 following the abandonment of GCSE exams, and the considerable grade inflation that accompanied teacher-awarded grades. The number of sixteen- to eighteen-year-olds is projected to rise by 18 per cent between 2021 and 2030, which would make for 200,000 extra students by 2030.

There have been some signs in recent spending reviews that government is beginning to recognise the need for change, but recent settlements don't undo even half the cuts of the previous decade. Indeed, growing student numbers will mean that funding per student will barely change.[4] There certainly won't be enough money available to raise salaries in FE colleges even to the level of teachers' salaries. Oddly enough, finding high quality teaching staff in economically valuable skills is not easy when you pay just £25,000 for a qualified lecturer.[5]

Meanwhile, despite the rhetoric, on-the-job apprenticeships are not filling the gap. Only about 77,000 young people under the age of nineteen started an apprenticeship of any kind in financial year 2021/22. Compare that to over a quarter of a million eighteen-year-olds heading off to university.

In fact, most apprenticeships nowadays are undertaken by older workers, over 40 per cent by those over the age of twenty-five.

That reflects the way that employers respond to incentives in the system. There is money available, not least through the apprenticeship levy – a levy of 0.5 per cent of pay on employers with payrolls of more than £3 million. If they don't use the money, they lose it. So long as they can fit it within the rules they use it on things they want, for example, training their current employees, often senior ones, rather than necessarily what government had intended.

The history of adult skills policy is littered with similar examples. There's another lesson here in the stories of firms using this apprenticeship money to provide executive education, MBAs and the like. Left to their own devices, private sector organisations are much more likely to pay for training of people who are already well educated. Not just within the education system, but right through working life, education begets education, skills beget skills, to those that have shall be given.

There are good reasons for that. The already well educated are often easier to train. The returns to an employer from spending money on someone they already know, and who may be more likely to stay on afterwards, may be considerably more than the returns from training a youngster straight out of school, who might well decide to head off to another company as soon as they have the relevant qualification. That's precisely why government needs to be involved in supporting this kind of training. Left to itself the market will provide too little.

Perhaps when you imagine an apprentice you not only have a young person in mind – an often false impression as we've seen – but also maybe an engineer, or someone learning a craft skill. About one in six apprenticeships in England are indeed linked to engineering. But half are in just two other sectors: business, administration and law; and health, public services and care.[6]

The overall weakness of our further education, apprenticeship, technical and vocational sector isn't just an issue for the young people themselves. The whole economy suffers when there are skills shortages. In the summer of 2019, the relatively newly formed, but now disbanded, Industrial Strategy Council, chaired by Andy Haldane, then Bank of England deputy governor, and the government's adviser on boosting the productivity and competitiveness of the economy, published a report setting out how skill shortages were holding back growth.[7]

According to Haldane, in some sectors, such as construction and parts of manufacturing, a shortage of qualified staff was a major bar to firms expanding and bidding for new work. Even before Covid, about 60 per cent of UK companies were finding it tough filling vacancies. Not only did a large majority of employers say that lack of access to the right skills was a big threat to UK competitiveness, it was also clear that England had a major problem with basic literacy and numeracy skills. Digital skills are in short supply. He found that 40 per cent of workers had a skills mismatch with their job, 28 per cent were underqualified and 12 per cent overly so. Just bringing that skills mismatch in line with the OECD average would increase productivity by 5 per cent. You can quibble with the specifics, but overall the story is clear and consistent across numerous analyses. We have too many people without even the basic skills they need to perform effectively in the workplace.

There is a striking mismatch between this indisputable fact and the apparent success of our school system. GCSE pass rates have soared. Far more young people are going to university than in the past, to the extent that we may have just about met the old New Labour target of getting 50 per cent of young people into university. Our workforce is more educated than ever before.

Or is it?

Low basic skills in numeracy or literacy, roughly speaking defined as below the level required to pass GCSE maths and English, can seriously limit people's capacity to participate in working, civic and personal life.[8] While English fifteen-year-olds have similar literacy levels to their counterparts in countries such as Germany, Denmark and Japan, by the age of twenty to twenty-two their literacy skills fall behind.

The same is true of numeracy.[9] In 2012, one third of sixteen-to-nineteen-year-olds in England had low basic skills, more than nearly all other comparable countries, and three times the proportion found in strong performers such as Finland, the Netherlands, Japan and Korea. This lowest-skilled third of teenagers represents a worryingly large pool of young people facing compromised life chances.

So something is clearly going wrong at that crucial stage between fifteen and twenty. It's not hard to see what. We just stop teaching literacy and numeracy skills to the huge majority of young people at that age. Some go on to a very narrow A-level curriculum, others to a disjointed vocational system of variable quality, and others to very little at all. As the OECD has pointed out, there is, in England, 'an imbalance between an entrant pool with weak skills and a high level of university participation'.

Virtually every review of education in England has recommended a broader curriculum between the ages of sixteen and eighteen as a way to begin to overcome these issues. The most comprehensive study, carried out for the then Labour government by former chief inspector of schools Mike Tomlinson, was published as long ago as 2004. It provided a blueprint for a reformed system, better integration of academic and vocational pathways, and a broader fourteen-to-nineteen curriculum.

It was effectively rejected out of hand in favour of maintaining existing 'gold standard' GCSE and A-level exams. There can be little upon which politicians of all stripes are so united as their extreme conservatism when it comes to maintaining our outdated, ineffective, and yes, positively damaging, system of public examinations.

As of later 2023 it is, as is rather often the case, quite hard to discern where we are likely to go next. The present government effectively got rid of AS levels, which at least allowed a small broadening of learning for some. And it is in the process of replacing BTECs, with new T levels. The latter are yet another attempt to achieve 'parity of esteem' between A levels and a vocational alternative. The latest in a very long line of such attempts.

They will further narrow available choices. It is currently possible to mix and match between BTECs and A levels. That won't be possible with T levels. At sixteen young people will be making an even bigger choice among an even narrower set of options. It's taken a couple of decades for the BTECs, funding for which is to be withdrawn, to find their feet as a recognised and respected part of the qualifications architecture.

Then in October 2023 prime minister Rishi Sunak made a rather remarkable announcement. He said that A levels would be replaced by a new 'advanced British standard' with everyone studying English and maths to eighteen, and a broadening of the curriculum to five subjects rather than the traditional three. Great if it happens. I am not optimistic. Even more remarkably he said that vocational qualifications would be rolled into the same system, effectively announcing the abolition of T levels before they are even half rolled out.

This is all too typical of policy on vocational qualifications. No consistency, no strategy, no idea where we'll go next. Each set of qualifications, each set of institutions, is ripped up and started again, time after time after time. Announcing the abolition of T levels quite so early in their gestation is perhaps a new low.

'With each change at the level of senior policymaking, it seems we have to reinvent the wheel, making our case once again, often defending the sector against either cuts or ill-conceived reforms,' wrote Dame Ruth Silver, president of the Further Education Trust for leadership, and for seventeen years principal of Lewisham College . . .

Too often, I have attended meetings with politicians and their senior advisers where the policy solution up for discussion is one that has been attempted before, often more than once, and has been found not to work after a fair try. Such encounters are wearying and dispiriting. However, the fault is not entirely theirs. No one has inducted them in the history of FE because FE is not held in sufficiently high regard to be considered to have a history that matters ... [10]

If you miss out on the basics, there isn't much support available. There have been huge cuts in spending on adult education for nearly two decades – cut by around a third in real terms since 2003/04. Learner numbers fell from four or five million a year during the 2000s to nearer 1.5 million by the early 2020s.

Spending on apprenticeships has risen somewhat, but total spending on adult education and apprenticeships combined is still about 35 per cent down on 2009/10.[11] Reductions in numbers studying at lower levels, those getting basic qualifications, have been particularly severe – a fall of a half in the numbers doing qualifications at GCSE level or below.[12] The cost of failure at school has risen and risen in recent decades, while the ladders up have been pulled away.

The independent review of post-eighteen education funding led by former banker Philip Augar and published in early 2019 concluded that there was a huge disparity between a university sector 'both cared for and cared about' and an FE sector where, for decades:

Nothing much has happened except for a steep, steady decline in funding. That decline is widespread and protracted. Teachers in FE colleges are paid on average less than their counterparts in schools. Funding levels are inadequate to cover essential maintenance or to provide modern facilities, and funding flows

are complex to navigate. Not surprisingly, the sector is demoral-
ised ... No prior government of any persuasion has considered
further education to be a priority. The consequence has been
decades of neglect and a loss of status and prestige amongst
learners, employers and the public at large.[13]

He came up with a series of recommendations for transforming
funding for post-eighteen education and increasing funding for
adult education.[14] This included proposals to introduce a lifelong
learning loan allowance intended to equalise support for those
taking higher and further education courses, proposals to restore
public funding for Level 2 (GCSE equivalent) and Level 3 (A-level
equivalent) courses for all adults who have no qualifications at that
level, and proposals for relaxing rules so as to allow more people
to gain valuable qualifications even if they have a qualification at
the same or a higher level already.

While the government has broadly responded positively, four
years on from the Augar review there is still plenty to be worked
out. Effectively extending the higher education funding system
to qualifying further education courses is definitely a move
in the right direction. It will redress the arbitrary inequality
between below degree level courses for students in further and
higher education and remove the incentive for students to enrol
on higher education courses merely because they offer better
support for living costs (as well as the incentive for providers
to offer higher education courses in order to be able to charge
higher fees).[15] If it works, this could prove at least one small
step to making available that missing second chance, opening
doors to those who underperformed in their teens, by giving
them access to loans to pay for education over the course of
their lifetime, paying back through payroll taxes, just like university students.

To give one sense of the disparity, in 2022–23 government

lending to those doing advanced FE courses, through the Advanced Learner Loans system, was less than one per cent of the amount lent through Higher Education loans.

As my son has discovered there are parts of our system of technical and vocational education which work well. For all its faults, current apprenticeship policy is getting more money into high quality apprenticeships, and numbers doing more advanced apprenticeships are gradually rising.

But long-term failures of policy which restrict education after age sixteen to an absurdly narrow curriculum, under-resource a struggling FE sector, and create a massively over-complicated set of vocational qualifications continue to deny opportunities to millions and to inflict harm on the economy.

If there is one thing that the next government needs to commit to, it is to build on where we are. Both institutions and qualifications were ripped up and started again in the 1980s, the 1990s, the 2000s and the 2010s. We can't afford to start again, again. We need to build expertise in the institutions and trust in the qualifications. We don't need another set of politicians drunk on their own sense of self-importance throwing it all up in the air and leaving another generation of young people, and another generation of employers, wrestling with yet another new and impenetrable set of qualifications.

The strange world of university finance

My guess is that most of you reading this book will have a somewhat better idea of the university funding system than you do of the FE system. Government provides a loan to each undergraduate to pay annual fees of £9,250. After graduation they pay back a fraction of their earnings over a threshold until either the loan is repaid or they are timed out and the debt is forgiven.

We'll come to the details in a minute, but that is how much universities in England get paid per UK domiciled undergraduate student they enrol, and is the basis on which students are said to incur debt and then pay it back. Universities themselves also earn money from postgraduate courses, overseas students, and for carrying out research. But we'll confine ourselves to the system of undergraduate student finance.

There is a lot to be said for a funding system a bit like this. On the whole the young people who go to university are more privileged than those that don't. More importantly, by going to university they enhance their earnings prospects. One recent study by colleagues at the IFS found that the (discounted) difference in lifetime earnings between graduates and non-graduates was £430,000 for men and £260,000 for women.[16] That is, a male graduate can expect to earn £430,000 more over his lifetime than a non-graduate man, with female graduates earning £260,000 more than their non-graduate counterparts.

Part of that difference reflects the fact that graduates are different from non-graduates; on average they come from better off families, are more academically able and so on. Even once you control for those differences, though, you still find big returns to getting a degree, of £240,000 for men and £140,000 for women. There is a lot of uncertainty over the precise numbers and different studies and different methods of estimation will provide somewhat different estimates, but they consistently show the same broad result.

Going to university, on average, substantially boosts your lifetime earnings. And that boost, in proportionate terms, has remained pretty stable over the last forty years as the number of graduates has doubled and doubled again.

So, going to university makes you better off. But only on average. Not everyone benefits. It also benefits the rest of society if graduates pay more tax and, as much evidence suggests, going to university also does things like reduce propensity to commit crime, increase propensity to volunteer, and lead to better health. A university education is also expensive.

All of which suggests that some sharing of costs between taxpayer and graduate makes sense. High earning graduates should pay for the cost of their degree, whilst those who do less well shouldn't have to pay the full cost. That, in broad terms, is what the current system achieves. But there is an awful lot of devil in the detail, and the details have changed several times since the current system was put in place back in 2012.

When I attended university in the 1980s it was free. There were (means tested) maintenance grants. No loans at all. Of course, it wasn't actually free, someone had to pay, and back then that someone was the taxpayer at large.

With less than 20 per cent of young people attending university that effectively implied a less well off majority paying for the education of an elite, mostly from better off families, who would go on to be the highest earners. This was one of many aspects of the way spending was then targeted which led Julian LeGrand in his seminal early 1980s work *The Strategy of Equality* to conclude that: 'public expenditure on the social services in Britain benefits the better off to a greater extent than the poor', a striking conclusion and one which was especially true of spending on education.[17] The modern welfare state is in fact much more redistributive than it was forty years ago, and one reason for that is the change in the way in which we fund higher education.

Loans to cover maintenance costs were first introduced in 1990 and replaced grants altogether in 1998/99, which was also the first year in which loans to cover part of the cost of tuition were introduced. The 1990s had seen a huge expansion in higher education and a very tight squeeze on university funding which did not anywhere near keep up with the increases in student numbers.

The initial tuition fee loans were set at just £1,000. A jump to £3,000 occurred in 2006 following an epic battle within the New Labour government with prime minister Tony Blair only just carrying the day in parliament; seventy-one of his MPs voted against the second reading of the Bill which introduced the changes, reducing the government's majority to just five. A bitter row, presaging more bitter rows which accompanied the 2012 reforms introducing higher fees. Higher education funding seems to raise emotions more than almost any other aspect of government policy. By comparison, continued cuts to FE funding go almost unnoticed.

Controversial though the £3,000 loans had been, the government wanted further reform. Rather than risk putting anything before the electorate, or even before its own MPs, in 2009 it commissioned former BP boss Lord Browne to advise on the funding of universities. He was explicitly asked not to report until after the 2010 election, with the intention of taking the political sting out of the issue. Fat chance, as the Liberal Democrats will tell you.

His report proposed allowing universities to charge unlimited fees. The key to making that acceptable was a system of income-contingent loans. Graduates would only start to repay those loans at a rate of 9 per cent on earnings over £21,000 a year, rather than the £15,000-a-year starting point for repayments under the old system of £3,000 fees. All debt was to be forgiven thirty years after graduation.

He assumed that universities would compete on price, with market mechanisms leading to differentials between high and low value courses. The government took his recommendations on board, but with a £9,000-a-year cap on fees. They also assumed that there would be price competition. David Willetts, the universities minister, said that he expected fees to be mainly around £6,000.[18]

In the event, virtually every course at every university was very

quickly charging the full £9,000. There was and is no price competition. That isn't surprising. It should not have been surprising
at the time. It is an astonishing failure of a basic understanding of
the incentives built into the system that anyone could ever have
thought otherwise.

One reason was a worry among universities that pricing at less
than the maximum would be an admission of poor quality. More
importantly there was no reason or incentive to price at less than
the maximum. If you provide a low-quality course, after which
the graduates don't earn much, then they get no benefit from you
offering them low fees. The vast majority would never pay off the
loan in any case, and have any debt written off after thirty years, so
a reduction in fees would make no difference to them whatsoever.
It would harm the university, come at no benefit to the graduate,
and benefit only the taxpayer. Universities and their students don't
care too much about taxpayers.

Having gone into the 2010 election promising no increase in
student fees, the Lib Dems paid a high political price after the election for supporting trebling them. They might feel at least a little
miffed about that. The lack of political honesty across all parties
about this subject is disgraceful. The Conservatives were against
Labour's fee increases when in opposition, then trebled them in
government. Labour announced the Browne review knowing full
well what sort of response was likely to be forthcoming, then cam-
paigned against change in opposition.

The reforms were in any case, perhaps counterintuitively,
progressive, overall. They resulted in many low-earning graduates being better off. That's because they raised the point at
which fees began to be repaid. For many lifetime low earners,
especially women who might take time out of the labour market
or work part time, this more than offset the effect of the higher
levels of debt taken on. They simply never get anywhere near
paying it off.

This all smacked of a reasonable compromise. Because a high interest rate on loans was set, at up to Retail Price Index inflation plus 3 per cent, graduates who do well end up more than paying for their education. Those who don't do so well, pay a lot less than the full cost. Getting on for half the cost overall is still being borne by taxpayers and three quarters of graduates are not clearing their debt after thirty years.

In truth, as far as students and graduates are concerned, this system looked little different to the imposition of a thirty-year graduate tax of 9 per cent on earnings over £27,000 (the threshold as of 2022), with a substantial redistribution from high earners to low earners. The main difference was that a minority of high earners would stop paying before the thirty years was up, though the high interest rate ensured even they would still end up paying more than they borrowed.

In 2022, changes were announced which at first glance appear merely nudges to the system. It is still an annual £9,250 loan to cover tuition with repayments at 9 per cent on earnings over a threshold. But three changes mean that we will be moving from something that looks like a thirty-year graduate tax to a forty-year graduate loan.

First, the threshold for repayment is to be cut to £25,000, then frozen until 2025, and then increased in line with prices rather than, as previously stated, in line with earnings. That has the effect of ensuring that over time significantly more of graduate earnings will be subject to the 9 per cent repayment rate.

Second, the repayment period is to be extended from thirty years to forty years. That means that many more graduates will have time to pay off the loan in full. This extension won't affect the highest earners who will pay off within thirty years anyway.

Third, the interest rate on loans is to be cut from up to RPI plus three to just RPI. This will benefit high earners the most and will put paid to the current situation in which they pay back more than they borrow. It will also allow more graduates to clear their debt.

The overall effect, then, of tweaking these three variables will be to move from a system under which the large majority never paid back the loan in full, and high earners paid back more than they borrowed, to one in which the large majority can expect to pay back in full, and high earners will, in inflation adjusted terms, only pay back what they borrowed. So what looked like a graduate tax lasting for thirty years now looks like a loan over a forty year period. The reforms will benefit high-earning graduates and hit low-to-middling earners. It's more honestly now a loan system, which is what it was always sold as.

Except. As we have already seen on several occasions, this isn't a loan system the like of which any private company could get away with. The terms and conditions change at the whim of the government. The most recent reforms will also hit current graduates hard as the repayment threshold they face is also being cut. Mind you it was increased by Theresa May in a doomed attempt to curry favour with students and graduates.

In the face of these uncertainties, all is uncertain. The idea that the currently favoured system will be in place in its current form for the next forty years is for the birds. What will be happening to inflation, interest rates, graduate earnings and non-graduate earnings in the 2060s, we have not a clue. We have equally little idea what governments will do over the next forty years. The Labour party went into the 2019 election with a pledge to get rid of student loans altogether and perhaps write off existing graduate debts entirely.

One thing that is clear is that over the last decade to too great an extent policy has been driven by arcane, and often borderline insane, public sector accounting rules. If we had something called a 'graduate tax' then the full annual spending of over £20 billion a year on undergraduate education would count against public borrowing. Under the rules in place when it was introduced, the almost identical student loans system added precisely nothing to borrowing, despite the fact that only about half was ever expected to be repaid.

An even more absurd bit of the rules meant that selling off the loan book to the private sector, even though it reduced public sector income in the long run, reduced measured borrowing immediately and never led to it rising in the future. Policy followed the accounting rules rather than the economic reality. This is, self-evidently, a bad way of making policy.

More recently, the accounting treatment of loans has been tidied up. About half the cost of loans now counts as borrowing, reflecting the amount likely not to be paid back. Yet absurdities remain. Cutting the interest rate on loans reduces the amount that will be paid back. It costs the government money. Yet it appears as a boost to the finances because the lower interest rate means a higher fraction of what is owed will be repaid.

There has been one other big change which we mustn't ignore. In 2015, the cap on the number of students that could be recruited by universities was abolished. Altogether there are nearly 2.4 million students in UK universities, of whom about 1.8 million are undergraduates. Getting on for half of young people get some experience of higher education. When Lionel Robbins wrote his famous report back in 1963, the report which led to the initial expansion of the university system in the 1960s, only about one in twenty went to university. What a change in my lifetime.

It's a change which will be partly paid for by graduates, but which comes at a very big up-front cost to the government. For universities, the introduction of the £9,000 fees led to a big uptick in income per student, but the fact that the cap on fees has been raised only once, to £9,250, and looks unlikely to be raised again in the foreseeable future means that, in inflation adjusted terms, the resources they have to teach undergraduates are being squeezed over time. Mind you, they still get a lot more per student for a lot less personal attention than either FE or sixth form colleges.

As we've seen a degree is still normally worth doing from a financial point of view. Even after accounting for higher taxes and student loan repayments, graduates will be more than £100,000 better off over their lives if they choose to go to university.[19]

Still, not everyone will do that well. It used to be the case that the government would provide more money for high-cost subjects like science and engineering than cheaper to deliver arts and humanities courses. With a few exceptions, that differential has now gone. We effectively subsidise arts and humanities studies more than scientific ones. The former are both cheaper to provide and their graduates earn, and therefore pay back, less. Indeed, our work suggests that many students studying subjects like creative arts will actually end up earning less than they would have done had they not gone to university at all.[20] The Augar review concluded that:

> A twenty-year market in lightly regulated higher education has greatly expanded the number of skilled graduates bringing considerable social and economic benefits and wider participation for students from lower socioeconomic groups. However, for a small but significant minority of degree students doing certain courses at certain institutions, the university experience leads to disappointment ... Generous and undirected funding has led to an over-supply of some courses at great cost to the taxpayer and a corresponding undersupply of graduates in strategically important sectors.[21]

From there it was a short step to proposing that state support for many courses should be limited, with extra available for 'high value' – generally science and vocationally related – subjects. And therein lies one of the great debates about the role and value of education generally and higher education in particular. There can be great value in allowing students to study arts and humanities subjects, value for themselves and for society, which does not necessarily show up in higher earnings. But, with limited resources, how much of that should be funded by the taxpayer?

The issue is particularly acute when we know that skills gaps exist, and when large numbers of graduates end up being disappointed when they are able to access only jobs which don't require a degree, where earnings are low, and where many degrees confer skills and knowledge that are only peripherally valuable in the labour market. Remember that one in ten students don't even have basic literacy and numeracy skills.

Perhaps the biggest indictment of the way we run our system of higher education is the way it rewards and rewards and rewards those who are already advantaged. We know that the better off are much more likely to go to university in the first place, and especially to one of the more prestigious ones.

What has shocked, though perhaps not surprised, from our own research is that that is far from the end of the story. Those who struggle from a poorer background to get to the same university, to study the same course, and get the same degree as their richer brethren still end up earning a lot less. You'd hope the reverse would be true. They must on average be brighter, have more grit and determination, and have overcome more obstacles to get there. Employers still look for and value skills and attributes which universities do too little to instil in their charges.

With vast numbers doing degree courses unrelated to any job, and with virtually nobody nowadays being awarded less than an upper second-class degree, the fact of an applicant having a 'good' degree is almost useless to an employer in deciding whom to employ. So increasingly they have to rely on A-level results, or the reputation of the university, or their own tests of intelligence and competence. The greatest beneficiaries of this unregulated mass of high degree classifications? Graduates of Oxford and Cambridge, and those who can afford to go on and do postgraduate degrees in the never-ending qualifications arms race.

The future of higher education

Unlike most of the other institutions featured in this book, universities are in fact private entities. Any one of them could at any point decide to stop playing ball with the government, charge much higher fees, and try to rely on private income to survive. For some research focused and internationally facing institutions, UK government financed undergraduate provision is already only a relatively small part of their total income.

The LSE, for example, would almost certainly be able to thrive without government support for British undergraduates. Income from research grants, endowments, alumni donations, student accommodation and postgraduate provision all contribute to university finances, especially the more prestigious ones. Some, like University College London, just round the corner from the IFS, turn over well over a billion pounds a year.

Postgraduate provision is increasingly big business. In 2020 there were over 700,000 postgraduate students at UK universities, nearly 300,000 of whom were from outside the UK. Measured by their research output, their rankings in international league tables, and their popularity with foreign students, our universities are a huge success story. They compete successfully in a global marketplace. To do that they need to attract the top talent, and in some subjects that means paying very large salaries. It's not so different from football's Premier League. Successful clubs are only successful if they have the best players. Revenues from global audiences are huge. The players have the bargaining power and they get most of the financial rewards. In some subjects universities work in much the same way. If your excellence and reputation mean you can land big research grants and, more importantly, can charge large numbers of postgraduate students tens of thousands of pounds a year to study, then it is the talent – the academics – who will reap the rewards.

Big six-figure salaries are therefore commonplace in some subjects. Salaries in some business schools are astronomical. I know of one recent PhD graduate in her late twenties being offered very nearly £200,000 to start as a lecturer at one. Newly minted economics PhDs can command salaries getting on for £100k in top departments. But this a very marketised sector. Salaries vary dramatically by subject and by institution. Many academics spend years in low paid and insecure employment. Those in the arts and humanities working at less prestigious institutions earn just a small fraction of what medics, economists and lawyers earn at the most prestigious places. Perhaps more than any other sector examined in this book, universities are driven by the logic of the market place. That may have its downsides, but there can be no doubt that that freedom and ability to compete internationally has been key to their success. It is why we do still have some of the world's best universities.

Successful as it is, the sector faces challenges. Our top-rated academic research still too rarely translates into business investment and economic success. Too many graduates struggle to find graduate employment. Universities are often notoriously badly run, and academics hard to manage. The long-term freeze on student fees will squeeze resources available for teaching. Our failure to openly acknowledge that Imperial College London and London South Bank University, for example, play entirely different roles in teaching, research and the economy, will continue to hold us back.

To return finally to the split between higher and further education. A senior mandarin summed it up to me recently. On a visit to one of our great cities he had been entertained at the Russell Group university there, where it was explained to him that they had a policy of only serving vegetarian food. Visiting the local FE college the next day he was offered a choice between a sausage bap and a bacon bap.

It's a sausage bap for me.

9

Levelling Up, Local and Devolved Government

English local government 'core spending power'
2023/24: £60 billion[1]
Scottish budget: £60 billion[2]
Welsh budget: £26 billion[3]
Northern Irish budget: £14 billion[4]

From day one, the defining mission of this government has been to level up this country. To take the radical steps needed to make us more prosperous and more united by tackling the regional and local inequalities that unfairly hold back communities.

So begins the former prime minister's foreword to the 2022 Levelling Up White Paper. 'We will usher in a revolution in local democracy,' Boris Johnson goes on to assert.

Long trailed as the most important policy statement of the

Conservative government's period in office, the White Paper is a remarkable document. If followed through it could represent the start of a genuine revolution in the way the country is governed. I'm not being naive. I would put the chances of it genuinely being taken forward at somewhere between nil and a snowball's chance in hell. But bear with me, for while it is aimed at addressing geographical inequalities in economic outcomes, it presents a compelling analysis of one of this country's great peculiarities and abiding problems – the almost unique degree of centralisation, within England, of tax, spending and policymaking powers.

The executive summary contains one of the most radical and exciting statements I have ever seen in a government policy document. Achieving 'Levelling Up' will, it says, require: 'Root and branch reform of government and governance of the UK. It is about putting power in local hands, armed with the right information and embedded in strong civic institutions.'[5]

The great economic inequalities between English regions, and the lack of economic power wielded by any state actor in England beyond Whitehall are linked. Local government has, over decades, had powers and responsibilities stripped from it, and in the last decade has faced huge cuts to its funding. Devolution to Scotland, Wales and Northern Ireland has placed much spending, and limited taxation, powers in the hands of the devolved administrations, but England remains a unitary state.

Geographic inequalities

Spatial inequalities in the UK are profound and persistent. Male life expectancy in the south-east is nearly seven years higher than in the north-east. It is seventy-four in Blackpool and eighty-four in Westminster.[6] In 2019, average wages in London were 60 per cent higher than those in Scarborough and Grimsby. Employment rates ranged from 66 per cent in Skegness and Louth to 90 per cent in Harrogate. In 2018 more than a quarter of births in Sunderland, Blackpool, Middleborough and Liverpool were to single mothers (neither married nor cohabiting) compared to around 7 per cent in Wokingham, Winchester, Mid Sussex and Cambridgeshire.

Around half of working-age adults in London and Brighton had degrees, compared with less than a fifth in places such as Doncaster, Mansfield and Grimsby.[7] That's partly because young people in London, the south-east and other prosperous places are more likely to go to university, and partly because they attract graduates from elsewhere. A quarter of graduates who move from their local area, move to London. Meanwhile, even the relatively small numbers of young people from poorer and peripheral areas who go to university tend to move away, and they are not replaced by others moving from out of area.[8]

Graduates move to where the graduate jobs are, and where they can earn more. Average earnings in the south are higher than those in the north mostly because there are more graduates and fewer people with low-level qualifications in the south rather than because the similarly qualified earn dramatically different amounts according to where they live. To put it another way, it is the availability of jobs which determines living standards.

The problem for levelling up is obvious. To level up you need the best educated and highest skilled to move to, or stay in, poorer areas. That means moving high skilled and well-paid jobs. But at the moment there aren't the people there to do them, and no reason for companies to relocate.

Indeed, there are well established benefits to 'agglomeration' – that is for companies to locate close to other companies doing similar things and using similar skills. That creates a bigger and more viable labour market, and allows ideas and innovations to spread more quickly. That's why so much high tech is focused in Silicon Valley in California, and banking and finance is located in the City of London, rather than being spread out evenly across the country. It's a real chicken-and-egg problem. One firm is unlikely to move if other firms don't move and if there aren't the qualified people to employ. And qualified people aren't going to move if the jobs haven't moved.

That, in a nutshell, is the challenge of levelling up.

Geographical disparities are not specific to the UK. We are not, despite the headlines, the most geographically unequal country in the world. We are pretty typical, just about in the top third among developed countries. This is a problem shared across the western world. Think of the US 'rust belt' or the former mining and industrial areas of northern France. The thing that really distinguishes the UK is the dominance of London and the relative failure of our other major cities.

Manchester, Birmingham, Leeds and Liverpool are much less productive than equivalent 'second tier' cities in France and Germany, for example. Coastal towns, old industrial and mining areas, and rural communities distant from big cities lag behind in most other comparable countries, just as they do here.

Another thing to be clear about. The big differences that are often quoted refer to differences in productivity. These translate into differences in average (mean) earnings, though not one for one. Look at differences in median earnings, and the gaps between regions fall further. Look at differences in living standards, measured by disposable income after housing costs and they narrow further still. So-called 'gross value added per person', a measure of economic productivity, is 80 per cent higher in London than in the country as a whole and 2.5 times higher in London than in the north-east. Median incomes, after housing costs, are bang on the national average in London. On this measure, household incomes range from just 109 per cent of the UK average in the south-east of England to 93 per cent of the average in the north-east of England.[9]

It is also not the case that the poor are concentrated in the north. They are pretty well spread across the country. In fact, London has more than its share of people with very low incomes. There is more inequality within regions than between them, and London is far more unequal than any other part of the country.

The big differences between regions are among the rich. They *do* mostly live in London and the south-east. Around a third of full-time workers in London earn more than £50,000 against just 10 per cent in Yorkshire, the north-east, Wales and Northern Ireland. The top 1 per cent and top 0.1 per cent are hugely geographically concentrated, with very few living outside London and the south-east. Inequality between the regions is not an inequality of misery, it is an inequality of plenty. The misery is well spread out; the plenty is not.

Because highly paid people and profitable companies pay a great deal of tax, and because public spending in poorer areas is higher than in richer ones, government already does a huge amount to spread money around the country. In 2019/20, the year before the pandemic, the national deficit worked out at around £860 per person. Taking account of tax and spending in different regions, Londoners were net contributors to the tune of around £4,000 per person. London ran a big surplus. The south-east also ran a pretty substantial surplus.

Other regions, effectively subsidised by London and the south-east, ran big deficits of around £4,000 per person in the north-east, and £3,000 in the north-west and the West Midlands, for example. Economic activity, profits, high incomes and wealth are unequally spread. It is a right and proper thing for governments to want to spread wealth around the country. And it does a lot of that already. What it does not do is offer much in the way of real power, either over taxation or spending, to local government in England.

Local government

On Armistice Day 2020, Croydon Borough Council issued a Section 114 notice. That's as close as you get in local government to declaring yourself bankrupt. It means that the council can't spend money on things it is not legally required to provide, things like parks and community centres. Any new spending decisions had to be signed off by Croydon's chief financial officer for three weeks.

'Collective corporate blindness to both the seriousness of the financial position and the urgency with which actions needed to be taken,' said the council's auditors, Grant Thornton. 'The council's fragile financial position and weak underlying arrangements have been ruthlessly exposed by the impact of the Covid-19 pandemic.'[10]

Croydon was heading for a loss of £60 million by the end of the financial year. It had spent heavily over the previous five years to acquire property in the hope of making a return. Unfortunately, those investments, most recently in shopping centres, the Colonnades Retail Park (shut in June 2020) and the Croydon Park Hotel (shut in March 2020), had not worked out well.

As the blow fell in Croydon, Kent, Leeds, Manchester and Nottingham were also issuing warnings.[11] Sharp falls in revenue and increasing demand for services like social care had been faced by councils across England for the previous decade, reducing their resilience and capacity to deal with new shocks.

Northamptonshire had effectively declared bankruptcy two years before the pandemic. In 2018, after wandering up and down the corridors of Northamptonshire's brand new £53 million offices, One Angel Square, it became clear to the government inspector Max Caller, that the council had 'lost tight budgetary control and appeared to abandon strong and effective budget setting scrutiny ... Councillors ... did not and could not address the regular budget overspends which were covered by one-off non-recurring funding sources.'[13]

And so it was that in February 2018 this Conservative-run council also came close to bankruptcy. It went bust a second time five months later. Only special permission to sell those same new headquarters – One Angel Square – and to use the money to plug the gap prevented a third Section 114 the following year. In the meantime, the government commissioners were sent in. They closed twenty-one of the thirty-six libraries in Northants.

In September 2023 the council running England's second biggest city, and the largest local authority in Europe, also went bust. Facing huge equal pay claims estimated at an astonishing £760 million, and following a disastrously expensive IT project Birmingham city council issued its own section 114 notice. If that can happen to an authority the size of Birmingham, the fear must be that nowhere is safe.

These are specific stories of individual councils which have had their own idiosyncratic problems. But they are part of a wider picture. English councils suffered some of the deepest spending cuts of any part of government over the 2010s, the decade of austerity. Spending per person fell by nearly a quarter between 2009/10 and 2019/20.[14]

Outside of social care, cuts have been even more dramatic. Councils have cut what they spend on housing, transport, planning, and cultural and leisure services by 40 per cent or more per person. More than half of everything they spend now goes on providing social care for adults and children.

In truth, local government has shown astonishing resilience in the face of these extraordinary cuts, but services have been reduced, facilities closed, and social care itself has been starved of cash, as we saw in Chapter 6. Councils have become more reliant on their own sources of income as government grants have been slashed. Many are shadows of their former selves.

A little back story

County councils were established by the Local Government Act of 1888, taking over responsibility from local magistrates and the quarter sessions. Like much else they were the result of a political row and a series of compromises. Legislation was forced on Lord Salisbury's administration by Joseph Chamberlain's Liberal Unionists as the price for their support after they had broken away from Gladstone's Liberal Party over Irish home rule.

The exhausting passage of the bill through Parliament became an orgy of county creation. By the end of the process Yorkshire and Lincolnshire had been divided into three, and Sussex, Suffolk, Cambridgeshire and Northamptonshire into two, while making the Scilly Isles, Anglesey and the Isle of Wight into separate counties. Eventually, the Scillys became the Scilly Isles Rural District Council; the rural and urban sanitary districts all became district councils. Most cities of over 50,000 people became unitary 'county boroughs' – rather as they are again now. Attempts to make the Staffordshire Potteries into a county council, as well as the Cinque Ports on the south coast, were voted down.[15]

Counties themselves are far older. Some of the ancient county boundaries go back to Anglo-Saxon times. My home county, Sussex, now divided into East and West for administrative purposes, can trace a history back to the fifth century AD, as one of the kingdoms of Anglo-Saxon England. Occasionally, the ancient borders get obliterated. You can still see the line of trees marking the original boundary between Oxfordshire and Berkshire, outside the village of Binsey. The boundary was tidied up and moved south of Abingdon in 1974. Meanwhile, Middlesex County Council has disappeared. The former Middlesex County Hall in Parliament Square now houses the UK Supreme Court.

Currently, thanks to Michael Heseltine's 1992 Local Government Act, we have a rather complicated series of different systems and styles of local council, with some unitary authorities and some two-tier county and district authorities, as well as metropolitan counties (six of these) and boroughs (sixty-nine, including London's).

The 1992 act also abolished some of our least loved counties – Avon, Humberside, Cleveland – and brought back Worcestershire, which had been in suspended animation for a generation. We now have twenty-four counties and 181 districts, plus all the specialist local authorities, the five joint waste authorities, forty-five fire and rescue authorities (some of them inside county councils), ten national parks and so on.[16] The City of London still has its medieval shape, complete with aldermen (abolished everywhere else in 1972).

Councils had limited powers in the early days of the 1890s, extending to the police and local courts (until 1964), maintaining roads and official buildings, building bridges and licensing. They also had responsibilities for asylums and lunatics, plus wild birds, pest control and trading standards. They took over schools in 1902.

At their height they covered schools and polytechnics, health and hospitals, parks, housing, planning and the environment. Then, one by one, over the past eight decades, those responsibilities have tended to dwindle away. They were stripped of most of their powers over the funding of schools by the last Labour government, whilst extensive academisation since then has left them with little power over other aspects of schooling today. By far their most substantive role nowadays is in the provision of social care – the focus not of this chapter but of Chapter 6.

Where does local government get its money?

About half the money received by local authorities comes from council tax. That's up from under a third a decade ago. Years of cuts to central government grants have made councils ever more dependent on their own resources. Nowadays, just over a quarter comes from the element of business rates which they get to keep, and just under a quarter from grants from central government. Because, with the exception of the proceeds from newly developed properties, business rates are shared out according to need, pretty much all that a council can do to increase its income, other than through fees and charges for things like parking, is to raise council tax.

Like much else in our public finances, the origins of council tax lie both in a messy compromise of relatively recent origin, and deep in history. Until 1990, local authorities levied domestic rates on local residents, at a level dependent on the rental value of the property they occupied. The rates, which still exist in Northern Ireland, have a history going back centuries, even before they were universalised by the Poor Relief Act of 1601. They were swept away by the Thatcher government and replaced by the massively unpopular poll tax, officially called the Community Charge, a flat-rate tax payable by all, irrespective of means. Possibly the most unpopular tax in history, in large part responsible for Mrs Thatcher's defenestration, the poll tax was replaced by council tax in 1993.

The latter was something of a compromise between rates and the poll tax. Like the rates it was based on property values. But like the poll tax, it was capped – the council tax payable on all properties that were worth more than £320,000 in 1991 is the same. It is also regressive.

Properties in band H, the top band, are worth at least eight times those in band A, the bottom band, but council tax bills for the top band are only three times those for the bottom. That was never the case for the old domestic rates. The council tax bills for expensive properties in central London, for example, are still lower in cash terms than the rates bills were at the end of the 1980s. It is the only tax I can think of that is designed to be deliberately regressive like this. In another nod to the poll tax, those living by themselves are entitled to a 25 per cent discount on the main rate.

Suboptimal by original design, council tax has, as we saw in Chapter 2, become increasingly absurd with time. Bills are still based on values as at 1991. We seem stuck in an indefinite time warp in which your annual tax bill is determined by an estimate of what your house or flat was worth more than thirty years ago. There has never, in England or Scotland, been any attempt to revalue properties.

All of this matters. It matters, of course, because it's just not fair. It is particularly extraordinary that a government supposedly committed to 'levelling up' is happy to live with it. The over taxing of low-value houses and under taxing of expensive properties was always a boon to London and the south-east and an unwelcome burden on inhabitants of other regions. This imbalance has only grown over time as house prices have risen much faster in London and the south-east than elsewhere.

Politicians of all parties are happy to talk about our housing problems, but refuse to do even the most obvious things within their grasp to begin to tackle them. The taxation of housing, both council tax and stamp duty, is riddled with damaging incentives, complexities, and unfairnesses. What we have designed is a set of taxes which reward people for staying put and punish them for moving. That helps to gum up the housing market. It contributes to the problems of young families not being able to buy places to live and the older generation not being able to unlock the wealth tied up in their homes.

However unpopular it might be, a version of council tax makes sense in principle. There is a good economic case for taxing people on the benefit they derive from living in their home. The problem is that our current system does this in a rather silly way. What you pay bears increasingly little relationship to the actual value of your house. Those living in houses worth a million pounds and more pay much less tax as a fraction of their house's value than do those living in the cheapest houses. It's rather like charging VAT at a lower rate on Bentleys than on Fords.

While about half of the money that councils get comes from council tax, the other half comes from business rates and from central government grants. While councils do now get to keep a portion of any additional business rates income that arises as a result of new development, business rates are set largely centrally and money still effectively flows into a central pot before being redistributed back to councils alongside other government grants.

Business rates themselves have got rather a bad name, blamed in particular for the demise of town centres as internet shopping has taken off. This largely reflects a misunderstanding, though a completely understandable one. Business rates are charged on the occupants of business premises – offices, factories, warehouses, shops. (Though not farms. Farmers enjoy special exemptions across the tax system, it seems.)

In the long run, the level of business rates will be reflected in the rents that occupants pay to their landlords. Remember the discussion back in Chapter 2: he who pays the tax is not necessarily the person on whom the tax is eventually incident. In this case the tenant sees a big tax bill. They do not see that, absent that tax, the landlord would charge a higher rent.

That is unquestionably true in the long run. It's one of those wonderful statements that works both in theory and in practice. There is a problem, though. It is not necessarily true in the short run. Rents adjust only gradually and increases in business rates can be genuinely painful for tenants in the shorter term.

In any case, the structure of business rates is of little concern to us in this chapter since they are effectively a national tax. We may imagine that councils are proud, independent institutions, paid for mainly by local taxes – maybe even presided over by mayors in red robes. In truth they are supplicants, dependent on the whims and funding arrangements set in Whitehall.

There are good reasons for that. It's not just a desire by national politicians and a London-based civil service to retain central control that leads to this picture of dependence. Some councils and regions are much, much richer than others. Without central funding, services in poorer areas would be far worse than those in richer ones. Government explicitly sets out to equalise funding – to make sure that, broadly speaking, councils which have little revenue of their own, or face bigger challenges, or higher costs, can provide similar services to those available in richer areas with more of their own cash and fewer demands on their services.

What happened after 2010, though, was a reduction in this equal-isation. A reduction in central government support of about 40 per cent – a huge cut – which penalised poorer, needier areas more than it penalised better off, leafier ones. In the period up to 2020, spending cuts per person in the most deprived tenth of council areas averaged 31 per cent (£432), compared with 16 per cent (£134) in the least deprived tenth.[17]

That was a direct result of a policy choice by the coalition gov-ernment. These additional cuts to poorer councils have not been undone since. Northern and urban areas, including London, have suffered the most.

Equalisation does still happen, though. Spending per person in the most deprived councils is still 30 per cent higher than in the least deprived. It was 60 per cent higher in 2009/10. More deprived councils also rely on central government funding for more of their revenues than less deprived councils. They raise less in council tax in cash terms (£336 per person in the poorest tenth against £599 in the richest in 2019/20) and as a percentage of their overall revenues (29 per cent against 68 per cent).

How much of this redistribution happens depends on a complex set of formulae, used by what is now called the Department for Levelling Up, Housing and Communities – a rebranding of the Ministry of Housing Communities and Local Government, intended to advertise Boris Johnson's government's commitment to 'levelling up'. The erasure of local government from the title may make those in the front line of local delivery feel even less loved by their lords and masters in Whitehall.

Whatever the name of the department operating it, there is no scientific, objective way of determining exactly how much more funding is required in Liverpool than in Woking, or anywhere else for that matter. Historically, statistical analyses have been carried out to relate actual spending levels to everything from population age and structure to local employment levels and wages. From the statistical relationships which emerge, formulae have been created to allocate funding.

This is far from perfect. For one thing it can bake in historic patterns, whether they are appropriate or not. Because it would be based on current spending patterns, carrying out such an exercise today would allocate less money to poorer and more urban areas than would carrying out the same exercise a decade ago. It would simply confirm the broad pattern of cuts imposed in the 2010s.

That sounds bad enough. What we actually have is far worse. Allocations to councils to pay for social care in 2022, for example, are being made based on a formula last updated in 2013, using population projections based on data from 2011 and 2012, and even using some data from the 2001 census. This is extraordinary. In fact, it is nothing short of scandalous.

Since then, overall and older adult populations have changed in drastically different ways in different council areas. Other factors, such as the health and wealth of residents will also have changed. Allocations to councils are increasingly arbitrary and unrelated to contemporaneous needs. For example, while the overall population of Tower Hamlets is estimated to have increased by 21 per cent between mid-2013 and mid-2020, that of Blackpool is estimated to have fallen by 2 per cent. The change in the number of adults aged 80 or over is estimated to vary between -13 per cent in Barking and Dagenham and +36 per cent in Hart in Hampshire.[18]

To quote my colleagues Kate Ogden and David Phillips: 'England currently lacks a rational basis for allocating funding between councils.' That is not a good place to be. The so-called fair funding review, aimed at coming up with a new and rational basis for allocating funding, was launched as long ago as 2015; remember those long-distant times when David Cameron was still prime minister?

That review was supposed to have been concluded and a new system implemented by April 2019. In the autumn of 2022 the local government minister suggested that implementation was unlikely before 2025. This is quite simply a fundamental failure of governance, a failure which slowly, insidiously undermines any rational basis for funding local government and inevitably leads to disillusion, disempowerment, and disengagement.

What's more, the longer change is delayed the harder it will be. Winners will win big, but losers will lose big, and they will complain. Vociferously. Just as in everyday life, difficult but manageable decisions postponed can fester and become ever more painful over time.

District councils in particular are heavily dependent on other revenues entirely. Pre-pandemic, nearly 30 per cent of the net expenditure of shire district councils came from income from fees for parking, cultural and leisure services, planning, and trade waste schemes. More than one in ten got over half their income from these sources.[19]

These revenues were especially badly hit by the pandemic, to the tune of around £3 billion in 2020/21. One can get a glimpse of the variety and complexity of local government by looking at some of the effects of the pandemic on their revenues. Government had to provide large amounts of special support: to Croydon, which had invested in a struggling property development company; to Redcar and Cleveland, recently subject to a ransomware attack; to Luton which owns Luton Airport; and to Eastbourne, which relies heavily on income from tourism and conferences.

A number of councils have moved into commercial property and enterprises in recent years in an effort to bolster their finances. As we saw in the case of Croydon, with sometimes disastrous consequences. Chorley has bought their local shopping centre.[20] Barking is investing widely in local land and property, hoping that regeneration success will push up land values (hence the council's new slogan: '17 minutes to Fenchurch Street'). Spelthorne, a local authority near London, with a core annual budget of around £11m, borrowed more than £1 billion to build a property portfolio mainly outside its own area.[21] Thurrock in Essex borrowed five times its £220 million budget, much of it then invested in renewable energy projects. Portsmouth even bought a large banana export company.[22] In fact, local authorities spent £6.6 billion on real estate between 2016 and 2019, according to the National Audit Office – fourteen times more than in the previous three-year period.

It's easy to see why they are doing this. They are short of money, they can borrow cheaply, when they invest in their own area they may be doing good for their current and future residents, and as long-lived institutions they should be able to take advantage of returns that these sorts of investments are likely to generate over the long run.

Even so, we would probably look askance if central government started buying up shopping centres and the like. Even the 2019 Labour manifesto wasn't proposing nationalisations on that scale. And with good reason. A free market economy depends on widespread private ownership. And local authorities are taking risks which they know won't end disastrously because they will always be bailed out. It's our old friend moral hazard.

And where does the money go?

There was a time, not so long ago, when much of education was delivered by local government. Even for those schools that are not now academies, the money that comes through local authorities to pay for them is fully ring-fenced, and most of the money they used to get to pay for central services now goes direct to the schools.[23]

This represents a huge diminution in the role and power of local government, a diminution crystallised in a panic by the last Labour government wanting complete control over the amounts paid to schools in the face of negative headlines about spending cuts. This is how our state develops; unplanned, huge, almost constitutional change as a panicked response to soon-forgotten newspaper headlines.

Nor does local government any longer play a role in further or higher education, having lost its last control over the latter in 1992 when the last polytechnics were turned into universities. They lost most of their control over local health back in 1948.

These days their biggest job by far is to deliver social care – for adults and for children – which accounts for about 60 per cent of their total budgets. The street cleaning, rubbish collection, planning, and looking after other local amenities, is all increasingly incidental, at least financially speaking, to this last big social role that our local councils play.

Even outside the social care system, money is increasingly

focused on older people. A quarter of local transport budgets now go on free bus passes.

The long period of austerity faced by local councils has exacerbated this increasing focus on care. They have cut everything else to the bone in order to continue providing social care services. Spending on children's social care has actually risen since 2010. The number of children in care has crept up from 50,000 in 1996 to over 80,000 now.[24] The scandals keep coming, but not for want of financial prioritisation.

By contrast, in 2019 spending per person on planning and development was down by around 60 per cent, on cultural services and housing services down by over 50 per cent and on transport down over 40 per cent. These are staggering numbers. In 2021 Councillor David Renard, transport spokesperson for the Local Government Association, said: 'It would already take £10 billion and more than a decade to clear the current local roads repair backlog.'[25]

That's a lot of potholes. And potholes can be as much a matter of life and death as anything else. In January 2016, Kate Vanloo, a keen amateur athlete, was cycling home from training with Rugby triathlon club. She hit a pothole, was thrown into the path of a car, and died at the scene. The hole had been identified a year earlier but had not been repaired for 'financial reasons'. David Hodge, leader of true-blue Surrey County Council complained in 2016 that 'we cut £450 million already, we squeezed every efficiency and we can do no more.'

It's pretty clear that local government was pushed to the brink by the austerity years. Over the brink, in the case of the Croydons and Northamptonshires. It wasn't always like this. The 2000s were times of plenty. Former chancellor Alistair Darling is said to have realised things were getting out of hand in 2009, when his own local council was advertising for a trampoline development manager. As late as 2012, one senior local government manager confided to me that they had been 'pissing money against the wall' and were capable of managing significant cuts. His was by no means a solitary voice. By 2016, though, most were in agreement with David Hodge. There was no fat left to cut.

In the longer term, something has to give. Growing costs mean that councils are likely to need £10 billion more in 2024/25 than they spent in 2019/20, simply to maintain services at their, much diminished, pre-pandemic levels. Big council tax increases are likely. The problem with that – apart from the obvious – is that, as we have seen, richer places can raise a lot more from this source than poorer places. Poorer local authorities simply can't close these gaps without help from the centre. Belated recognition of that fact is finally becoming evident. The 2022 funding settlement, announced in the dying days of 2021, was intended to ensure that all councils would get some increase in spending power, with more for the less well-off.

It looked at one stage like a combination of cuts, increasing cost pressures, and a government determined to make councils self-sufficient, could break English local government. A series of additional payments to prop up social care, a slightly more generous settlement for 2022, more council tax rises to come, and a move away from the idea that local government can do without central support, means that ministers have stepped back from the brink. For now, it looks like councils will stagger on.

Some may do more than stagger on if they end up benefiting from the devolution of extra responsibilities and funding as part of the government's levelling-up agenda. The last few years have seen a series of devolution deals agreed between Whitehall and councils or new 'combined authorities' (covering groups of councils), largely in urban areas. Just to add to the general confusion around local government, the responsibilities and funding devolved have been agreed on a case-by-case basis and vary between areas. They typically cover adult education, business support, and elements of employment support, transport funding, planning and economic development.

The Greater Manchester Combined Authority, for instance, is also involved in decisions over prison and probation services and has oversight of an integrated health and social care system.

While some real powers really have been pushed back down to some local areas, the inconsistent and patchwork nature of these deals leaves local electorates with little idea of what their specific local authority does and does not have responsibility for, and the rest of us with little sense of a governing strategy. It is in the interests of all of us to overhaul this system, create a layer of government which is genuinely capable of driving local economic transformation, and which has the powers and resources to do so.

That means power at a level below Whitehall, but covering bigger areas and bigger populations than most of our current local authorities. That's the kind of radical change to our system of governance that is implied by the Levelling Up White Paper with which we started this chapter. Absent that, we at least need to put the current system of local government finances on something approaching a more rational and sustainable basis.

Scotland, Wales and Northern Ireland

The last quarter century has involved one grand movement towards devolution – the creation of the Northern Ireland assembly, the Welsh Senedd and the Scottish parliament. They are responsible for most spending on public services in their respective nations. The Scottish and Welsh governments also have some limited powers over tax.

Now, the most important fact to lodge in your mind when

considering the three devolved nations is that Scotland is rich, while Wales and Northern Ireland are not. For the purpose of making economic comparisons, the UK is typically divided into nine English regions plus those three countries. On most measures Scotland is the third or fourth richest of these twelve regions, while Wales and Northern Ireland tend to vie with the north-east of England for bottom place. The challenges each face are, therefore, quite different.

The second thing to get straight is their relative sizes. Northern Ireland is tiny. Its population is almost precisely the same as the population of Kent. At just over three million the Welsh population is just under double that of Northern Ireland. Five and a half million people live in Scotland – the same number as call Yorkshire home.

These bald facts matter for the politics of independence movements. Scotland can perfectly well afford to go independent. As we will see it would still lose a lot of money because it receives substantial transfers from the rest of the UK. But it is a wealthy nation. Wales would struggle. It is poor and it would lose the fiscal support it currently receives from the rest of us.

The question for Northern Ireland, of course, is not about going it alone, but about possible merger with the Republic. Merger would present the Republic of Ireland with a significant economic and fiscal headache. On a per-person basis Ireland is if anything a bit richer than the UK as a whole, but it is only about one tenth the size, so taking on the north, a poor region dependent on fiscal transfers, would be a ten times bigger fiscal burden on Dublin than it is on Westminster.

You might expect from these facts that, because they are poor, Wales and Northern Ireland enjoy significant subsidies from the rest of the UK, just as poorer councils get more central funding than richer ones. And indeed, they do. Spending per head in each is about 20 per cent higher than in England, and tax revenues per head are much lower. That's just what you'd expect. Scotland is the odd man out. It also receives large transfers from the rest of the UK and also enjoys spending levels per head getting on for 20 per cent more than in England, despite being no poorer than England as a whole. If it were treated in the same way as an English region it would get an awful lot less money.

That's because of Barnett. Joel Barnett was the Chief Secretary to the Treasury in the Callaghan government at the end of the 1970s. He gave his name to the formula that has governed the funding of the nations of the UK since 1979. Before that, public spending amounts for Scotland, Wales and Northern Ireland were settled by negotiation on much the same basis as for other government departments. Because such negotiations were often difficult, and because there were referendums on devolution to Scotland and Wales taking place, a more mechanical approach to budget allocation was introduced: hence, the Barnett formula.

Not that this was the first time a formula had been used. Back in 1888, the then chancellor, George Goschen, used one to allocate probate duties to each nation of the UK in proportion to their respective populations. This 'Goschen formula' came to be used to allocate further areas of public spending over time. But it assumed that the populations would remain constant relative to each other. In fact, Scotland's fell relative to that in England and Wales. By the 1960s, when the formula stopped being used, Scotland got a great deal more than its population-based share of UK government spending. And that is what has remained baked-in ever since. Oddities in the way money gets spent have a long and murky history.

Barnett started with this status quo of higher spending in Scotland, but his formula did have a built-in mechanism for narrowing the gap in spending per head *if* the populations of England and Scotland grew at the same rate. But that hasn't happened. Scottish population growth has continued to lag behind. Which is why spending in Scotland is still so much higher per head than it is in England.

Barnett himself was made a life peer when his parliamentary seat in Manchester disappeared with boundary changes in 1983. He used to joke about the unexpected sense of immortality the formula had given him (it has outlived him too; he died in 2014). But he wasn't happy about it. After devolution in 1998 he said his formula was now clearly unfair to England, something he repeated just before his death and before the 2014 referendum on Scottish independence. The formula which still bears his name had become an embarrassment.[26] Embarrassment or not, more than forty years on it is still in use, looking as permanent as anything in the whole of our public spending architecture. And ensuring that the Scottish advantage is still baked in.

Education spending per person in Scotland is a remarkable 28 per cent higher than in England.[27] That gap has grown a great deal since devolution, indicating that education has been a big priority for the Scots. Spending per pupil aged three to nineteen is £1,000 higher than in England and there are no university tuition fees. Yet international comparisons suggest fifteen-year-olds in Scotland lag behind their English counterparts, and HE participation has grown more slowly.

It takes more than money to achieve results. The Scottish advantage in spending on many smaller programmes is higher still: spending per person on transport, environmental protection, culture, and housing and community development is between 40 per cent and 100 per cent higher than in England.

Where education has been a priority, health has not. At the turn of the century health spending per person was more than 20 per cent higher in Scotland than in England. Twenty years later it was just 3 per cent higher. Health outcomes are far worse, with a life expectancy differential of more than two years and worse outcomes for most serious conditions including cardiovascular disease and cancer. The death rate from drugs in Scotland is more than three times higher than in any other European country.[28]

This deficit long predates devolution. Scotland, long dubbed the 'sick man of Europe', has had lower gains in life expectancy than most of western Europe since 1950 for reasons that are not fully understood,[29] and certainly can't be explained by the usual measures of income, poverty or health services which are so important to explaining mortality rates across the developed world.

More recently the Scots have also been increasing welfare provision. While they don't have anything like full control of the social security system – which remains largely reserved to Westminster – they have been able to make changes and additions, all aimed at increased generosity, in particular for disability related benefits and families with children. As of 2023 a Scottish Child Payment of £25 per child (up to age sixteen) per week is available to any family receiving means-tested benefits.

The laws of fiscal arithmetic are not suspended north of the border, though. None of the devolved nations escaped austerity. Their budgets largely fell in line with those in England under the Cameron governments.

Right from the start of devolution in 1999 the Scots had the power to vary the standard rate of income tax by up to three pence in the pound. They never used that power.

But they have used powers conferred in 2016 which gave them the right to set rates and thresholds and to introduce new rates and bands above the UK-wide personal allowance. Scotland now has a five-band structure for income tax, with a 19p starter rate and a 21p intermediate rate. From April 2023, the higher rates in Scotland are 42p and 47p respectively. Most importantly the point at which higher rate tax becomes payable is now much lower in Scotland than in the rest of the UK, at £43,662 in 2023/24 as opposed to £50,270 elsewhere.

That's a big difference and means that higher earners in Scotland pay a lot more income tax than their English, Welsh and Northern Irish peers. Someone in England earning £60,000 would be paying just over £11,400 a year in income tax. If they moved to Scotland on the same salary their income tax bill would rise to more than £13,000.

Unfortunately, Scottish income tax revenues have not risen with these increased tax rates. That's not because higher taxes themselves have stymied growth, rather that the Scottish economy in general in recent years has been doing even less well than that in the rest of the UK. That has hit tax revenues. Devolution brings additional power, but it also brings additional risks. It looks like the Scots are on course for a double whammy of higher tax rates but lower revenue than if income tax had not been devolved.

So, to return to that point about the laws of fiscal arithmetic. Transfers from England are still big enough to fund much higher spending in Scotland than in England, but that doesn't mean there is no budget constraint. And as of 2022 that budget constraint started binding.

Announcing the Scottish spending review, Finance Minister Kate Forbes presented a far-reaching programme of spending cuts with the axe due to fall on virtually all Scottish public services including justice, police, universities and local government, with only minuscule increases in the health budget. Additional spending in England could, via Barnett, result in more money flowing from the UK exchequer to offset some of these cuts, but planned cuts there are. That's the choice the Scottish government has made – more for welfare, less for public services. And that after all is the point of devolution, to be able to make different choices.

We've focused more on Scotland than Wales and Northern Ireland mostly because there is more to say. Tax devolution to Wales is more limited and they've made no use of the power they have to vary income tax rates, while tax devolution to Northern Ireland is non-existent. Both governments have control over most public service spending and while, like Scotland, they have quite a lot more to play with than we do in England, the reasons are much clearer – they are considerably poorer, and of course face additional challenges in the case of Northern Ireland. Like Scotland both spend relatively more on some of the smaller elements of public services.

As I pointed out as chair of the Independent Fiscal Commission for Northern Ireland, spending there on things like agriculture, housing and culture is more than twice per head what it is in England.[30] Like Scotland, the Northern Ireland Executive has also chosen to be more generous than England on issues like tuition fees, social care and some aspects of welfare. Not charging any water rates costs an especially large amount.

As I also concluded there is plenty more scope for tax devolution should Westminster and the devolved administrations want to go in that direction. We have seen that substantial devolution of income tax is possible in Scotland. There is no reason in principle why that couldn't be extended to Wales and Northern Ireland, though the Welsh have explicitly opted for more limited powers. Smaller taxes like stamp duty land tax have also been successfully devolved to Scotland and Wales. It is possible to go further, and there may well be benefits to be had from doing so especially in ensuring greater accountability of the devolved governments to their own electorates. In our current halfway house, the temptation always to blame Westminster is hard to resist.

Going forward

We English easily forget that among the most far-reaching changes implemented by our government over the last twenty-five years has been the devolution of powers to elected assemblies in the other constituent nations of the UK. That is a journey which has a distance to run.

England itself remains among the most centralised states in the developed world. Despite the rhetoric of governments of all stripes, the direction of travel has been towards more centralisation of powers and fewer resources for local authorities. The most recent big take into central control has been the school and school funding systems, started by the last Labour government and largely completed by coalition and Conservative governments. Our local authorities have suffered bigger funding cuts since 2010 than almost any other part of the public sector.

Where to next? Do recent devolution deals to combined authorities like Manchester and the gradual spread of mayors with their personal mandates augur more substantive change? Was the Levelling Up White Paper so much hot air, or will it usher in the radical changes to the governance of our country that it promised?

As a nation we face multiple difficulties and economic challenges over the coming decades. We are reluctant to learn from the experience of others. But I at least am persuaded that it is worth taking a punt on *not* assuming that those challenges are best dealt with by a single source of power, situated in Whitehall, and setting policies for the whole country.

Nor can it be the case that our current patchwork of local government institutions can be equal to the task. I am with Michael Gove on this. *Radical* change to the country's governance is needed, and not just for levelling up, but to improve economic performance and the delivery of public services throughout the country.

10

Where to From Here?

As recently as 1985 there were more people in the British army than there are today in the army, navy and air force combined. During the Korean war, at the start of the 1950s, we spent 10 per cent of national income on defence. That fell to below 5 per cent following withdrawal from East of Suez in the 1960s, and dropped again after the fall of the Berlin Wall. Since the mid-1980s spending has gradually tailed off towards just above 2 per cent of national income today.

It is that beyond anything else which has allowed for the development of the welfare state, with its ever-increasing spending on the NHS and pensions, and extended coverage of working age welfare, without a continually rising tax burden. Even so, of all the spending programmes not examined in this book, at around £50 billion a year, defence remains the biggest. There is no scope to cut further if we are to maintain our NATO commitment to keep spending at least 2 per cent of national income. Cutting defence as a route to spending more elsewhere has run its course. Indeed, following war in Ukraine, and rising geopolitical tensions, the mood music is for defence spending to rise, not to fall. In fact, Rishi Sunak has pledged to increase defence spending to 2.5 per cent of national income, although frankly that's not a pledge I expect to see fulfilled any time soon by any government.

The pressure on other spending programmes is also upward. Spending on justice, for example – that's running the courts, prisons and probation service, paying for legal aid and so on – was cut by more than a fifth between 2010 and 2020. With court backlogs reaching record levels and criminal barristers striking over cuts to legal aid, that spending can surely only go one way.[1] In autumn 2023 it was reported that judges were being instructed not to send to prison even criminals found guilty of quite serious crimes because we had simply run out of space in the prison system. Pressures on the Home Office (police and immigration) are also severe. Government is looking to increase police numbers by 20,000, after their numbers had fallen to the lowest level in decades. Our £11 billion overseas aid spending has already been cut back sharply from the 0.7 per cent of national income to which we committed, and which we reached for several years before the pandemic struck.

There are other pressures aplenty. Average pay in the public sector remains, in 2023, a long way below where it was in 2010. The 2010s were a dreadful decade for pay in the private sector, the worst in more than a hundred years, but at least average pay crept up. Typical teachers, nurses and civil servants had seen cuts of between 5 and 10 per cent, after accounting for inflation, between 2010 and the start of 2022. That year's huge spike in inflation saw real pay fall again. Everything gets harder when inflation is high.

The combination of energy prices rising, the longer-term consequences of Covid, and lack of economic growth, means that we are considerably worse off than we could reasonably have expected in early 2020. Poor productivity growth in the decade before that, compounded by the effects of Brexit, meant that we had already missed out on a decade of normal economic growth. We have seen some of the consequences in various parts of this book: stagnant incomes, collapsing home ownership among younger generations, falls in the generosity of welfare benefits, cuts in spending on further and vocational education, no increase in spending per school pupil in a decade, a massive widening of the private/state differential in education funding, and the decline in the numbers accessing publicly provided social care.

Spending on the NHS has risen, but much more slowly than usual. It takes an ever-growing chunk of public spending. It still performs dreadfully on many international comparisons, especially when it comes to keeping us alive, in treating heart disease and cancer.

Living standards fell during 2023. We could well be in the midst of the biggest fall in real household incomes seen over any two year period since the 1950s when comparable statistics were first compiled. Interest payments on our accumulated debt are set to reach £100 billion a year – more than we spend on any public service other than the NHS, and more as a fraction of national income than at any time in a generation. And tax, having been pretty steady at around 33 per cent of national income for decades, is set to reach over 37 per cent. That's a huge increase. It means the government will be taking a good £100 billion a year more from us than we have been used to. The consequences in terms of record corporation and income taxes are clear to see. Millions more are being dragged into income tax. The number of higher, 40 per cent, taxpayers is set to reach eight million, double its level at the start of the decade, and four times what it was in the early 1990s.

What's more, these higher levels of tax are almost certainly here to stay. Poor growth, an ageing population, an ever-voracious NHS, and little prospect of big spending cuts elsewhere, are likely to make sure of that. Our politicians need to be honest about that. They also need to do far more to ensure that our tax system is more efficient and more equitable. The bigger the tax burden, the more getting the structure of taxes right matters.

So, we enter the middle years of the 2020s in worse economic straits than at any time I can recall. The financial crash of 2008/09 feels like ancient history, but its effects on our living standards, and on tax revenues and public spending, are clear all around us. Brexit is an ongoing shock to the economy. Covid, a cost of living crisis and fourteen successive interest rate hikes from the Bank of England have made things even more difficult.

Recent economic shocks – the financial crisis, Covid, the energy price spike – have all demonstrated the importance of government's ability to come to the rescue with tens and hundreds of billions of pounds to cushion us from their immediate conse-quences. Government can, and must, bring to bear its firepower to see us through such periods. But each time it does so, debt ratchets upwards, and as each shock makes us poorer it makes it harder to reform and fund our public services.

Worryingly these shocks seem to be coming round more and more frequently. Here's the government's fiscal watchdog, the Office for Budget Responsibility (OBR) from July 2022:

In little more than two years, the UK economy and public finances have felt the consequences of a global health crisis caused by Covid-19, a global security crisis sparked by Russia's invasion of Ukraine, and a global energy crisis brought about by both. In a little over a decade, we have also felt the economic and fiscal consequences of a global financial crisis and the uncertainty created by the UK's decision to leave the EU ... And in the decades ahead, governments in the UK and around the world face perhaps the still greater economic and fiscal challenges of addressing climate change, dealing with the fiscal costs of ageing, and managing all these pressures and risks against a backdrop of potentially weaker produc-tivity growth, higher levels of public debt, and rising interest rates.

It is hard to escape the conclusion that the world is becoming a riskier place.'[2]

That's the reality we need to face up to. As I have stressed again and again throughout this book there are no easy answers, no cost-free solutions, no brilliant wheezes that will give us an easy passage through these perilous waters.

Managing the public finances

It is much maligned, and often rightly so, but I do have a soft spot for the Treasury. In popular imagination, and often in reality, it is seen as the abominable no man of Whitehall, the department that rejects all the demands to increase spending on things we all want more of: health, education, early years provision, pensions and so on. It is an institution with multiple faults, greatest of which is often a lack of deep expertise accompanied by a quite unmerited degree of arrogance. An inbuilt cynicism can also be destructive. Just before I left the Treasury we were informed that we shouldn't be too downcast about the politicians giving the go-ahead for the new Crossrail line in London: the Treasury had delayed it for twenty years and we should take that as a win.

But for all that, somebody, some institution, needs to hold the ring on all the competing demands on our public finances. We can't have everything. And if the politicians and/or the electorate are not willing to sanction higher taxes then those choices need to be made. If the Treasury weren't unpopular it would be doing something wrong.

For any given level of government revenue there needs to be some constraint on what is spent. Exactly what that constraint is at any moment is open to debate, but one constraint must bind in the end – debt can't continue rising forever. The trouble with politics is that working within any constraints which aren't hard and immediate can be difficult. If the bill is to be paid in ten years and the election is next year, let's worry about the bill some other time. The temptations are great. 'Lord make me pure, but not yet' as St Augustine of Hippo famously put it.

It's not your imagination: taxes really do rise straight after elections and not just before them. There is no getting away from the politics. As we noted in Chapter 1, Norman Lamont, chancellor in the early 1990s, famously said of his pre-election Budget in 1992 that it was his worst from an economic point of view and best from a political perspective, whilst his post-election budget was his best economically and worst politically.[3] The former involved tax cuts and promised spending increases that helped win an election despite being unsustainable. The latter included tax rises which, even five years later, helped the Conservatives to their biggest electoral defeat in generations.

Chancellors have faced two problems. The first, to persuade their colleagues, the markets, and us the voters, that they are serious about managing within limited resources. When Kwasi Kwarteng lost the confidence of the financial markets following his extraordinary £43 billion tax cutting 'mini Budget' in September 2022 the consequences were immediate and painful. The pound fell to its lowest ever level against the dollar. The interest rates on government debt rose, and the Bank of England had to intervene to prevent financial Armageddon. Mr Kwarteng seemed not to believe the constraints were real. They are.

The second problem is the need to restrain their own baser political instincts, to cut taxes and increase spending, especially in the run up to elections.

That's why 'fiscal rules' have proliferated in recent decades. These are policy statements setting out medium term fiscal strategy: how much the government is willing to borrow and how much debt it is willing to live with.

Since Gordon Brown first announced his two fiscal rules back in 1997 there have been, on our counting, eighteen such rules, twelve of which have ended up being missed, and junked.[4] Brown's own rules were overwhelmed by the financial crisis. Borrowing hit record post-war levels and debt rocketed towards 80 per cent of national income. George Osborne came in initially aiming for a balanced current budget – i.e. borrowing only to invest. In an unnecessary demonstration of fiscal machismo, he moved to a target of reaching full budget balance – no borrowing at all. He suspended his rules in the wake of the Brexit referendum. More rules, broadly looking for current budget balance, were again suspended in the wake of Covid as borrowing hit new records and debt reached getting on for 100 per cent of national income. As of 2024 debt is at its highest level since the early 1960s.

The appropriate amount of borrowing will change according to the state of the economy and the level of interest rates. That long-term need to stop outstanding debt rising forever isn't enough of a clear target. Virtually every chancellor is of the opinion that he (as of 2023 it's the only senior job in government that has still never been done by a woman) has the magic elixir which will get the economy growing, so why not spend more or cut taxes now to get it on the right path? Then debt will come down. Forgive my cynicism at this point. I've not seen this elixir and I don't believe in it. What has actually happened is that, in principle at least, most economists have coalesced around the view that in 'normal' times we should aim to borrow only for so called 'investment', but not to cover day-to-day spending. In one form or another you can find that commitment in the 2019 manifestos of both Labour and Conservatives, and in statements since by both Labour and Conservative Treasury teams.

That is an imperfect guide to policy, but it makes some sense. There is certainly no need to balance the budget overall, as George Osborne claimed was his intention back in 2015. Along with most other developed economies we run deficits in most years. We have spent more than we have raised in ninety-nine of the 122 years since the start of the twentieth century. The roof has not fallen in. If the economy is growing at 3 per cent a year then we can borrow 3 per cent of national income and debt won't rise as a fraction of national income. Debt fell precipitously after 1945 not because we ran annual surpluses, we didn't, but because the economy was growing fast and deficits were modest.

Borrowing makes sense when spending now delivers benefits in the future. Future generations should share in the cost of financing spending that benefits them. If such spending had to be financed from taxes levied on the current population we'd likely do too little of it. We do too little of it anyway. Public investment in the UK has been below that in nearly all other advanced economies for decades. Since long-term projects should go ahead when the benefits from undertaking them exceed the costs of financing them, when interest rates on government borrowing are low there is a case for more investment spending. As Nick, now Lord, Macpherson who was permanent secretary to the Treasury from 2005 to 2016, put it to me when I interviewed him for a radio programme I made about growth in late 2023: 'with hindsight we probably should have taken advantage of [low interest rates] and borrowed more when times were more stable . . . and invested more'.

One of the great policy errors of the last fifteen years was that it took so long to cotton on to this fact that by the time, in the early 2020s, that investment spending was finally rising again, interest rates had gone up and the public finances were in trouble again. The Conservative government is planning another cut in investment spending from its 2023 level and, as of 2023, the opposition Labour Party is not planning much more.

We are in danger of repeating the errors of the early 2010s when it was chopped, and chopped hard. We saw in Chapter 5 how spending on capital equipment in the health service has not kept up with need. In Chapter 7 we looked at the cuts to the school building programme which Michael Gove, the minister responsible at the time, later agreed was a mistake. The consequences came home to roost in rather dramatic fashion in the autumn of 2023 when hundreds of schools were warned of the dangers of collapsing roofs made from Reinforced Autoclaved Aerated Concrete (RAAC), with many having to close at least some buildings and classrooms. This was at least in part a consequence of the deep cuts in capital spending which Mr Gove has since regretted.

With the focus on levelling up, the under investment in transport and other infrastructure outside of London has become all too apparent. Local authorities have struggled even to repair the roads that already exist. Our economy will suffer from lower growth for years to come as a result of these false economies.

That's all about borrowing in 'normal' times. (Much) more borrowing is right and necessary in abnormal times – pandemics, energy crises and all those things we've had rather too much of recently. In fact, the existence of such shocks is perhaps the most persuasive case for being careful with public finances in normal times. You don't want to go into a crisis with little scope to act. In its 2021 'fiscal risks report', in the wake of Covid, the OBR had this to say:

> ... fiscal space may be the single most valuable risk management tool. Throughout its history, the UK has relied on its ability to borrow large sums quickly in order to respond to major economic and political threats. It was able to do so courtesy of its relatively low levels of public indebtedness, deep and liquid domestic capital markets, and by maintaining the confidence of international investors in its long-run creditworthiness.[5]

Couched in rather bureaucratic language, this is an important statement. We simply cannot prepare for every eventuality.

The next crisis is unlikely to be a pandemic like the last one or a banking crisis like the one before that. We can't be fully prepared for both of those and wars, energy crises, mass unemployment, sterling crashes or whatever else the future may throw at us. What we need is the capacity to respond flexibly when the crisis is upon us, whatever the crisis happens to be, and that means being able to borrow when needed. One reason that rich countries survived better economically speaking than poor countries in the wake of Covid was the much greater fiscal and monetary firepower they had at their disposal.

The last part of the OBR quote is also important. We need to maintain the confidence of international investors. That requires confidence in our political institutions and the rule of law, at least as much as confidence in specific economic and fiscal policies. We throw away that reputation at our peril. Good government is an economic issue, something that will matter to all our living standards, as much as it is a political one. There is an economic cost, a cost we citizens bear in lower living standards, when our political masters play fast and loose with the country's reputation.

If the last fifteen years have taught us anything, it's that making predictions is a mug's game. The financial crisis, Brexit, Covid, the resurgence of inflation, have all come as surprises. They have all had far-reaching consequences for the shape and size of the state. A considerable dose of humility is required when peering into the future. So rather than speculate about different possible futures, how technological advance might change everything, or what the next election might bring, let's focus on just those two big known challenges mentioned by the OBR: climate change and an ageing population. Between them they are plenty big enough.

Climate Change

It wasn't until I joined the Treasury in 2004 that I engaged with climate change properly. That I did so then is because I was fortunate enough to work with Nick Stern, the world leading academic and former chief economist at the World Bank, on his review of the economics of climate change. It turned out to be one of the most influential pieces of work ever carried out by a government official.

The eventual report, weighing in at nearly 700 pages, was not just a compendium of detailed scientific and economic evidence, it was also a call to arms. It has informed climate policy in the UK ever since. It changed Nick's life. He became one of the world's leading advocates for effective climate policy. To a much lesser extent it changed mine too. I was a member of the UK's climate change committee for eleven years.

As Stern put it:

> Climate change is a result of the greatest market failure the world has seen ... the evidence on the seriousness of the risks from inaction or delayed action is now overwhelming ... The problem of climate change involves a fundamental failure of markets: those who damage others by emitting greenhouse gases generally do not pay.[6]

Dealing with climate change, in other words, requires getting the economics right. Get policy right and the world can avoid catastrophic consequences at manageable cost. Do nothing and we face disaster. We are not doing nothing. The bigger risk is getting the policy and the economics wrong. That could lead to costs and consequences that make dealing with the problem unpopular, leading to inadequate action, and ultimately a dreadful outcome for us all. There are few areas where designing policy properly is more important.

'Climate change is an existential threat to humanity. Without global action to limit greenhouse gas emissions, the climate will change catastrophically with almost unimaginable consequences for societies across the world.' Not the words of Greta Thunberg, or a green NGO, or the Intergovernmental Panel on Climate Change (IPCC), or even Nick Stern, but the introduction to a sober Treasury analysis of the costs of reaching 'net zero', published in December 2020.[7] That the Treasury should be saying these sorts of things is an indication of how far the issue has become embedded in policy. With all party support, the government is committed to reaching 'net zero' greenhouse gas emissions by 2050.

That is a big and bold ambition. Don't let anyone tell you otherwise. Those demanding we cease emissions within five years are demanding the literally impossible. Even attempting to do so would be staggeringly expensive and unimaginably disruptive. It would derail effective policy. It would ultimately undermine efforts to combat climate change.

The good news is that we have already made remarkable progress. By the early 2020s UK 'territorial emissions' – those emissions produced within our borders plus our share of international aviation and shipping – were almost 50 per cent below their 1990 levels.[8] A fall of nearly a half in thirty years is not to be sniffed at, though for sure the more difficult half is still to come.

That good news comes with one big caveat. The net zero target is based on that measure of territorial emissions. It doesn't take account of the carbon embedded in our imports. When we buy products from China or elsewhere which are manufactured using greenhouse gas emitting energy supplies then we should also take responsibility. It is the emissions embedded in our *consumption* which really matter. There would be no point importing electricity from another country, generated by burning coal, and proclaiming victory because we are not burning the coal here. On this 'consumption' measure our progress has been less impressive with emissions down on their 1990 levels by closer to a quarter than a half.

National income per head, by the way, has grown by more than 40 per cent over the same period. Reducing emissions and economic growth are not incompatible.

Thus far the fiscal consequences of decarbonisation – i.e. changes to government spending and taxes to achieve climate change objectives – have been remarkably modest. Nearly all the progress has come about through changing the way we generate electricity, first by moving from burning coal to burning gas and more recently through a huge surge in renewable generation, particularly from wind, and also from solar. That hasn't been free, but (pre-energy crisis) it showed up in higher prices, not in higher taxes or higher spending. With appliances becoming more efficient, the impact of the higher prices induced by these investments didn't even show up much in electricity bills.

The cost of wind and solar energy has dropped even faster than the most optimistic promoters of those technologies would have dared guess a decade ago. It is cheaper to produce a kilowatt hour of electricity from offshore wind than from a gas fired power station. That was true even before 2022's surge in gas prices. At least that's true when the wind is blowing or the sun is shining. The problem with renewables is that, currently at least, they can't be guaranteed, which means back-up in the form of fossil fuel powered generation is still needed.

The other great thing about the transition to green electricity is that we the consumer don't notice it. We haven't actually had to do anything. What comes out of the plug hasn't changed.

None of which is to say we are over the finishing line. As of 2020, wind, solar and other renewables produced just over 40 per cent of total electricity generated. Nuclear accounted for another 15 per cent. Gas was responsible for most of the rest.[9] Replacing that gas (and some of the nuclear) isn't the biggest challenge, though. Over the coming decades we are going to have to produce vastly more electricity than we do at present to power all the electric cars we'll have to drive, and the electric heat pumps we'll have to install, as we move away from fossil fuels in other parts of our lives. Government analysis suggests wind and solar generation will likely need to more than quadruple by 2050.[10]

Beyond the power sector the next steps towards net zero are going to be both more expensive and more disruptive. The climate change committee has estimated that around 60 per cent of the emissions reductions required to meet net zero will require some behavioural or societal change.[11] In their words 'the public will need to be engaged'.

We might not notice the electricity changing. An electric car will be more of a change, especially perhaps for those of us without off street parking. Most of the costs of developing electric vehicle technology have been met, internationally, by the private sector. These costs were real, and huge. Public investment in basic science, and various subsidies to encourage take-up, have been important. But governments have not had to bear the bulk of the costs. Their most important policies have been in developing regulations and making it clear that the change will have to happen. It doesn't help when governments flip flop over those regulations. Legislation was in place banning the sale of new petrol and diesel cars from 2030. In 2023, prime minister Sunak unilaterally announced that date would be pushed back to 2035. Labour responded by saying they would reinstate the 2030 date. Not exactly the stable policy environment required for effective decision making by private companies.

As we saw in Chapter 2, whatever the final date, one consequence of this is that the Treasury is set to lose getting on for £40 billion a year in revenues from taxes on petrol and diesel. In fiscal terms that may well turn out to be the single biggest cost of decarbonisation. Now is the time to start addressing it by getting a plan for some form of road user charging under way. That will be much harder to do once we are all driving electric cars and have got used to not paying anything to the taxperson for the privilege.

Getting to net zero will also involve a whole series of other changes in industry and agriculture, but the biggest and most expensive challenge is likely to be the transition away from heating our homes using gas boilers. Getting our homes better insulated, and installing heat pumps we will surely notice. And so will government. That is not a transition that is going to happen without large amounts of public investment.

In total the CCC has estimated that the gross additional costs of investments required to get to net zero, for the economy as a whole, could be around £1.4 *trillion* over the period from 2020 to 2050. On the upside, they estimate that three quarters of that additional cost would be offset by lower operating costs. Low carbon technologies tend to be expensive up front but cheaper to operate than traditional technology. It costs very little to run a windmill once it's built. Electric cars are more expensive to buy but cheaper to run than petrol cars.

Those are whole economy costs, and most of them are due to come from the private sector – through developing the electric cars, erecting the windmills and so on. The OBR's central estimate is that the government might have to fork out around £350 billion over the period, though its contribution could easily exceed £500 billion.[12] Much the biggest element of that is to decarbonise buildings. Not many people are likely to pay to rip out their own gas boiler and replace it with a heat pump (or whatever), and possibly invest in some pretty serious home insulation, without either a large subsidy or government actually paying for and organising the whole thing.

That sounds like a lot of money, but even on the high estimates the cost in terms of extra spending by government doesn't get much over £25 billion in any one year. If that turns out to be the case, then the biggest cost to the public finances will indeed come not through additional investment but simple loss of tax revenues from petrol and diesel. Put all those costs together, though, and we could be looking at a fiscal hit of more than 2 per cent of national income – £50 billion+ in today's terms – over the 2030s and 2040s. To repeat, the obvious way of offsetting a large of chunk of that is to replace fuel duty with another charge for driving.

The bigger challenge to government than the money is the organisation and delivery. As the CCC has observed 'tangible progress is lagging the policy ambition ... greater emphasis and focus must be placed on delivery ... for the UK's climate ambitions to be credible'.[13] It's easy to say we want to reduce emissions, much harder to do.

Ageing population

In 1972, out of every hundred people, one was aged eighty-five or more, and thirteen were aged between sixty-five and eighty-four. The fraction in the oldest group has trebled since then, to nearly 3 per cent by 2022, while the fraction aged between sixty-five and eighty-four has hit 17 per cent. This is a much older country than the one into which I was born a little more than fifty years ago. Roll forward another fifty years and the latest forecasts are that we will be an older country still. It is expected that 7 per cent of us will be eighty-five or more – personally I'll be long gone by then – with 22 per cent aged between sixty-five and eighty-four.[14] These changes have had, and will continue to have, huge impacts on the public finances and public policy, not to mention on politics.

Whilst the past, and present, are broadly known, the future is of course uncertain. Changing patterns of migration, fertility and longevity can change forecasts, and the forecasts have changed rather a lot in recent years. Birth rates are falling much further below 'replacement rates' than expected. To maintain the population at a constant level, in the absence of migration, each woman needs to have an average of 2.1 children over her lifetime. Birth rates have been falling and the ONS thinks that will persist, with women bearing an average of fewer than 1.6 children. That 'represents the lowest birth rate assumed in any set of official population projections published over the past seven decades'.[15] At the same time, while life expectancy is still rising, it is rising at a considerably slower rate than previously forecast. And the most recent projections have net immigration lower than expected. One consequence of all that is that while in 2016 the ONS expected the population in the 2060s to be around 77 million and rising, it now expects it to be around 67 million and falling.

Great, you might think, we're a crowded island; we could do without the population rising. Ignoring the fact that we really are not all that crowded, there are two downsides to this pattern, if it is indeed what happens. First, a smaller population means a smaller economy and all that debt that future generations will inherit will be a bigger problem. Second, and more importantly, a shrinking population means an increasing old age dependency ratio – that is an increase in the number of people aged sixty-five and over relative to numbers aged sixteen to sixty-four. That ratio currently sits at around 30 per cent – there are three older adults for every ten younger adults. It is set on an inexorably rising path. It is due to hit 40 per cent by the mid-2030s and 50 per cent by the 2060s. On the 'upside' the young age dependency ratio is set to fall – the working age population will have fewer children to support.

From a public finances point of view the problem with a rising old age dependency ratio is that working age adults pay most of the tax whilst spending is concentrated on the old. People in their forties on average pay three times as much in tax as they get back in the spending on public services they consume and welfare benefits they receive. Those in their mid-seventies receive three times what they pay, rising sharply for those in their eighties and nineties. More older people relative to people of working age means more spending and lower tax revenues.

Even accounting for the lower costs associated with smaller numbers of children, the long-term consequences are inescapable. Over the next fifty years the OBR suggests that, just to stand still, spending will need to rise by nearly 10 per cent of national income – or around £245 billion per year – to accommodate demographic change and the rising costs of health care. That will entail some big choices. Some combination of tax rises, limiting spending on health and pensions, or cutting other spending will be necessary. Simply carrying on as we are will not be an option.

Can growth save us?

More than a decade of feeble economic growth has made everything harder. There is less money to go around than we might reasonably have expected. Had the economy grown since 2010 at the sort of rate we'd got used to over the previous sixty years not only would we all be better off, but the quality of public services would have been much better than they are.

Faster growth into the future would help a lot. Though perhaps not as much as you might expect. Growth means higher earnings and higher tax revenues. Very handy. Inevitably it will mean higher salaries for public sector workers, taking up some of the additional revenue. It also means greater expectations. What we might have found acceptable in public service provision half a century ago we no longer find acceptable. We expect the quality of public provision to improve in line with the quality of what we experience in the rest of our lives. That's why, when looking over long periods, it is appropriate to compare spending as a fraction of national income. Even if spending on health or education increases in real terms, if it falls as a fraction of national income we will experience it as a drop in quality.

Nevertheless, growth obviously matters for the quality of public services. Our health service is less good than it would have been if the economy had grown more quickly in recent years and we had had more to spend on it. Liz Truss enjoyed the shortest premiership in our history. She was, though, absolutely right to want to focus economic policy on improving growth. While she got the policy monstrously wrong, the ambition is not just right, it is plausible. Whilst we shouldn't rely on it, it is within the gift of government to get productivity up, and to get the economy growing faster. We do know roughly what we need to do. It's one of Whitehall's dirty little secrets: our leaders know what to do, but fail to do it, and quite often don't even try. Here, in broad outline, is what a government that actually wants to deliver growth should do.

First, and most important, ensure maximum political and macroeconomic stability. Provide reassurance to investors that the rule of law, independent institutions, and property rights will be respected. That is top of the list for companies, especially multinationals, thinking about where and whether to invest. If you don't pass that first hurdle, not much else matters.

The constant political shenanigans we have experienced since 2016, with four prime ministers and six chancellors in little more than six years have not delivered this. Occasional attacks from the government on the judiciary, the Bank of England, and the civil service – reaching an apogee in the spiteful and politically motivated sacking of the permanent secretary to the Treasury in September 2022 – alongside an apparent willingness to break the law and resile from international agreements have not helped either.

However entertaining some of this occasionally is, it is economically costly. Bad politics is bad economics. Ask the Italians. Political instability has cost that country dear. It is in danger of costing us dear too.

Second, it really is education, education, education. A well-educated population is the most vital ingredient in a thriving economy. That starts in the early years, especially supporting the least advantaged. It requires effective investment in schooling with well trained, well-motivated, properly rewarded teachers. It means not having an absurdly narrow curriculum from age sixteen. An effective path through technical and vocational training at a high level for a significant fraction of the population is vital. Continued availability of adult education is also needed.

You will recall from Chapters 7 and 8 that we have failed on pretty much all counts over recent years. Closing Sure Start centres, squeezing school funding and teacher pay, narrowing even further the post-sixteen curriculum, cutting spending on further and vocational education. These are not growth-friendly policies.

Third, invest in infrastructure. I've already said it. The big cuts in spending post 2010 were a mistake, and a mistake we will be paying for for some time to come. High quality transport links, a resilient and effective energy system, fast broadband. These are basic building blocks of an effective economy.

Fourth, reform the tax system. The focus is often on rates of tax, but getting the structure right is even more important. Our system for taxing housing is an expensive and costly disaster. Ludicrously high levels of stamp duty and a regressive council tax system gum up the market, make it harder for people to move, and damage the labour market. Our VAT system is insanely and unnecessarily complex and costly for firms to navigate. We seem not to know whether we are coming or going on rates of corporation tax, and continually ignore the importance of getting the base right and hence ensuring there are appropriate incentives to invest. Bizarrely, the corporate tax system incentivises debt-fuelled investment over that funded through equity. Our capital gains tax system incentivises holding on to assets until death, well past the point at which they are likely to be held in their most economically efficient form. As well as creating multiple inequities, our inheritance tax system pushes up the value of certain assets, including farmland and some kinds of shares, in economically inefficient ways. Business rates penalise firms which invest in their property. The fact that we treat incorporated businesses, the self-employed and employees differently for tax purposes distorts choices over legal form, and leads to effort being spent on minimising tax rather than maximising economic productivity. National Insurance contributions are the main villain of the piece here because they are levied very differently on different sorts of income and not at all on interest, rents, dividends, pensions and the rest. Continually raising NICs and cutting income tax rates merely makes things worse.

I could go on.

Fifth, develop the closest and freest possible trading relationship with the European Union. The EU is our biggest, nearest and richest trading partner. Brexit has been, and will be, economically costly. That is a statement of fact, not a mere opinion. The 'harder' the Brexit, the more we put in place barriers to frictionless trade, the more costly it will be. Our trade has suffered. Our trade performance has decoupled from that of other advanced economies. There is little scope to make this up in additional trade with other countries.[16] The OBR estimates that the productivity of the UK economy might be reduced by 4 per cent in the long run.[17] The National Institute for Economic and Social Research (NIESR) comes up with similar estimates.[18] As they put it: 'This is roughly equivalent to losing the annual output of Wales or the output of the financial services industry in London.'

Sixth, sort out the planning system. We need houses where there are high paying jobs, and we need the ability to build roads, reservoirs, wind farms, business premises, where they are economically valuable. Every attempt at reform fails because the vested interests of those who already own their own homes trump the wider needs of the economy and the population. A vast panoply of rules and regulations makes development far slower and more expensive than it could be, and often stops it altogether. The last attempt at reform was dropped in 2021 following the loss of a by-election in the traditional leafy Tory seat of Chesham and Amersham. The minister responsible was fired, despite carrying out the stated wishes of then prime minister Boris Johnson who had promised to reform England's 'sclerotic' planning system.

There is much more that matters. The functioning of our economic regulators, responsible for financial services, energy, water, broadcasting, and telecoms, underpins much economic activity. The Competition and Markets Authority, which promotes competition, investigates mergers and cartels, and effectively sets the rules of the market, protecting consumers from unfair practices, may be relatively little known but plays a central role in managing the economy. Ensuring all these institutions have the right remits and appropriate resources is a core mission for a government concerned about long-term growth.

This is not a book about economic growth and productivity, and each of those topics deserves a much fuller treatment. The most important point is that government could do far more to promote growth, and decides not to. It decides not to in part because, to return to my ongoing theme, there are trade-offs. Tax reform would leave some people worse off. So would planning reform. Effectively we are putting a very high value on the desires of those who are benefited by the current system. Brexit is not just about the economics; we can perfectly reasonably value the additional power that it gives us over certain laws, perhaps especially over immigration, above the value we put on the economic benefits of the single market.

So, it is not just incompetence (though there is plenty of that) that results in our not investing in growth, it is a set of political choices implicitly downgrading growth as an objective relative to other outcomes. At the least we should acknowledge and be transparent about that. In my view we have that trade-off wrong. The long-term consequences of not seeking productivity growth are very serious indeed. We have seen the effects of a decade and a half of poor growth throughout this book.

All this *is* about the long term. Policy needs to look to the future, be consistent and patient, recognise that benefits may not accrue until well after the next election. There's a video from 2010 in which Nick Clegg explains that more nuclear power can't be an answer to problems in the energy sector because it wouldn't come on stream until 2022. Well, 2022 arrived, as inevitably will 2032 and then 2042. That shouldn't take us by surprise. Outside of crises, governments are much more powerful over the long run than over the short run.

Must do better

Let us not despair. We are healthier, better educated and richer than we have ever been. We live longer and in less pain. We support the older generation to a generally comfortable and prosperous retirement in a way which would have been virtually unimaginable fifty years ago. For all its failings the NHS, still free at the point of use, treats and cures more of us than ever before. That nearly half of young people get a chance to experience and benefit from higher education represents a triumph. Our social security system has developed to provide more, and more coherent, support to many low earners than it did at the turn of the century. We still manage to raise vast amounts in tax to pay for all this without widespread evasion or any great sense of injustice. We have adapted to an ageing population, growing international competition, and technological change far better than many doom mongers have predicted. We are making decent progress on climate change. This is still, largely, a well-functioning state and society in which most people are able to lead a good life.

The warning signs, though, are multiplying. In-work poverty has grown and grown, and the safety net is fraying. The welfare of future generations of pensioners looks much less secure. Our education system fails far too many, and especially those from the least advantaged backgrounds. Social care has been a disaster. For the first time that I can remember I really worry for the future of the NHS. Its demise has been forecast too many times to count, but the scale of current pressures is the most worrying in a generation. There is little consensus on either the future role of local government or of the devolved nations.

The repair job starts with honesty about the costs and benefits and trade-offs inherent in any policy decisions. Promising the earth, lower taxes and higher spending, is a way to ruin. Effective policy acknowledges that change takes time, and puts in place long-term strategies to accomplish sustainable change. It recognises the importance of the detail of delivery and values that over rhetoric. It appoints competent ministers and keeps them in post for long enough to get on top of a brief. It values effective management throughout the public sector. It rewards public servants appropriately. It is brave when it comes to confronting vested interests, whether they be taxpayers benefiting from quirks of the current system, homeowners preventing valuable development, or public sector institutions resisting necessary change. It focuses on growth and on the delivery of services.

None of that is easy. But it's not impossible either. We can, and must, do better.

Notes

Introduction: Following the Money

1. Economic and Fiscal Outlook, Table A.7, obr.uk, Mar 2023
2. Earth to Economists: Your Ivory Tower Isolation is Not an Option, *Times Higher Education Supplement*, 25 Sep 2014
3. Hambling, David, How the Great Frost of 1709 Left England's Economy in Ruin, *Guardian*, 17 Dec 2020
4. The Cost of Coronavirus, instituteforgovernment.org.uk, Nov 2020
5. Sunak, Rishi, Updated Statement on Coronavirus, gov.uk, 20 Mar 2020
6. Haldane, Andy, The Beast of Inflation is Stalking the Land Again, *New Statesman*, 9 Jun 2021
7. The difference between the tax and spending numbers isn't entirely made up by borrowing – government does have some revenue streams other than taxes.
8. House Building, UK: Permanent Dwellings Started and Completed, ons.gov.uk, 19 Jan 2022

Chapter 1: Getting Our Hands on the Money

1. Economic and Fiscal Outlook, Table A.5, obr.uk, Mar 2023
2. Richardson, Joseph, et al, *The Rolliad*, J. Ridgeway, London, 1819

3.   Ortiz-Ospina, Esteban and Roser, Max, Taxation, ourworldindata.org, 2016

4.   Joyce, Robert, Pope, Thomas and Roantree, Barra, The Characteristics and Incomes of the Top 1 per cent, ifs.org, 6 Aug 2019

5.   Xu, Xiaowei, Return of Bumper Pay Growth in Finance Fuels New Rise in Earnings Inequality, ifs.org, 4 May 2022

6.   Lewis, Michael, *Liar's Poker*, W. W. Norton & Company, New York, 1989

7.   Number of Individual Income Tax Payers by Marginal Rate, Sex and Age, Covering the Period from Tax Year 1990 to 1991 to Tax Year 2022 to 2023, Table 2.1, gov.uk, 30 Jun 2022

8.   Johnson, Paul and Phillips, David, 50p tax – Strolling Across the Summit of the Laffer Curve?, ifs.org.uk, 27 Jan 2014

9.   Advani, Arun, Koenig, Felix, Pessina, Lorenzo and Summers, Andy, Importing Inequality: Immigration and the Top 1 Percent, Warwick Cage Research Centre, Sep 2020

10. Neidle, Dan, The First Thing We Do, Let's Tax All the Lawyers, Tax Policy Associates, 16 Nov 2022

11. Adam, Stuart, et al, *Tax by Design: The Mirrlees Review*, Oxford University Press, Oxford, 2011

12. HMRC Internal Manual: VAT Clothing, gov.uk, 1 Mar 2022

13. Animals and Animal Food (VAT Notice 701/15), gov.uk, 9 Dec 2011

14. Neidle, Dan from Twitter, 16 Apr 2022

15. McBride, Damian, *Power Trip*, Biteback, London, 2014

16. Mainprice, Hugh, letter to *The Times*, 13 Jun 2006

17. Quoted in Davies, Howard (ed.), *The Chancellors' Tales*, Wiley, London, 2006

18. How Do UK Tax Revenues Compare Internationally?, ifs.org. uk/taxlab

Chapter 2: Getting Our Hands on Even More Money

1.   Economic and Fiscal Outlook, Table A.5, obr.uk, Mar 2023

2.   Window Tax, parliament.uk, 2022

3. Phillip, Hannah, The Tavern Clock: Taxing the Time, fairfaxhouse.co.uk, 2013
4. Johnson, Samuel, *A Dictionary of the English Language: Volume 2*, Longman et al, London, 1805
5. For a survey of all the taxes and how much they raise see the excellent ifs.org.uk/taxlab
6. Johansson, Åsa, Heady, Chistopher, Arnold, Jens, Brys, Bert and Vartia, Laura, Taxation and Economic Growth, OECD Economics Department Working Papers, No. 620, OECD Publishing, Paris, 3 Jul 2008
7. See references in Adam, Delestre and Nair, Green Budget 2022: Ch 6, Corporation Tax and Investment, ifs.org.uk, 21 Oct 2022
8. Howard, Tom, Facebook UK Limits Tax Rise Despite Profits Surge, *The Times*, 15 Dec 2021
9. See: Devereux, Michael and de la Feria, Rita, Designing and Implementing a Destination-Based Corporate Tax, www.etpf.org, Apr 2014
10. The Effect of Incorporations on Tax Receipts, obr.uk, Nov 2016
11. Adam, Stuart and Miller, Helen, Taxing Work and Investment Across Legal Forms: Pathways to Well-Designed Taxes, ifs.org.uk, 26 Jan 2021
12. Lorraine Kelly Wins £1.2m Tax Case Against HMRC Over ITV Work, bbc.co.uk, 21 Mar 2019
13. Agyemang, Emma and Ahmed, Murad, Gary Lineker in £4.9m Tax Battle with HMRC Over Freelance Earnings, ft.com, 6 May 2021
14. Troup, Edward, U-turn on IR35 freelancer Tax Rules, *Financial Times*, 5 Oct 2022
15. Total Wealth in Great Britain, ons.gov.uk, 5 Dec 2019
16. Advani, Arun, Bangham, George and Leslie, Jack, The UK's Wealth Distribution and Characteristics of Highwealth Household, resolutionfoundation.org, Dec 2020
17. Tax Relief Statistics Additional Cost Estimates (May 2022), gov.uk, 3 Aug 2022
18. Lunde, Jens and Whitehead, Christine, How Taxation Varies Between Owner-Occupation, Private Renting and Other Housing Tenures in European Countries, housingevidence.ac.uk, 24 Feb 2021

19. Mill, John Stuart, *Principles of Political Economy, Vol 1*, J. W. Parker, London, 1848

20. Kay, J. A. and King, Mervyn, *The British Tax System*, Clarendon Press, Oxford, 1990

21. Inheritance Tax Review – First Report: Overview of the Tax and Dealing with Administration, Office of Tax Simplification, assets.publishing.service.gov.uk, 2018

22. Neidle, Dan, The Many Holes in Inheritance Tax, and How to Fix Them, taxpolicy.org.uk, 27 Jul 2022

23. Advani, Arun, Chamberlain, Emma and Summers, Andy, A Wealth Tax for the UK, wealthandpolicy.com, 2020

24. Ibid.

25. Japan Urges its Young People to Drink More to Boost Economy, bbc.co.uk, 18 Aug 2022

26. HMRC Tax Receipts and National Insurance Contributions for the UK, gov.uk, 21 Jul 2022

27. Adam, Stuart, Delestre, Isaac, Levell, Peter and Miller, Helen, Tax Policies to Help Achieve Net Zero Carbon Emissions, ifs.org.uk, 2 Oct 2021

28. *Mirrlees Review*, op cit.

Chapter 3: Poverty and Working Age Welfare

1. Benefit Expenditure and Caseload Tables 2023, DWP, gov.uk, 25 Apr 2023

2. Welfare Trends Report, OBR, assets.publishing.service.gov.uk, Jan 2019

3. Bourquin, Pascale, Cribb, Jonathan, Waters, Tom and Xu, Xiaowei, Why Has In-Work Poverty Risen in Britain?, ifs.org, 7 Jun 2019

4. UK Poverty Statistics, Joseph Rowntree Foundation, jrf.org.uk, 2022

5. Beveridge, William H. B., Social Insurance and Allied Services, HM Stationery Office, London, 1942

6. Timmins, Nicholas, *The Five Giants*, third edition, HarperCollins, London, 2017

7.   Welfare Trends Report – May 2022, obr.uk, 24 May 2022
8.   New Ambitions for Britain: Financial Statement and Budget Report March 1998, gov.uk, 17 Mar 1998
9.   Freud, David, Reducing Dependency, Increasing Opportunity: Options for the Future of Welfare to Work, 2007
10. See: Timmins, Nicholas in Seldon, Antony and Finn, Mike, *The Coalition Effect*, Cambridge University Press, Cambridge, 2015
11. Duncan Smith, Iain, Breakdown Britain, Centre for Social Justice, London, 2007
12. Timmins, Nicholas in Seldon, Antony, op. cit.
13. Timmins, Nicholas, Universal Credit: From Disaster to Recovery, instituteforgovernment.org.uk, Sep 2016
14. Freud, David, *Clashing Agendas*, Nine Elms Books, London, 2021
15. Brewer, Mike, Joyce, Robert, Waters, Tom and Woods, Joseph, Universal Credit and its Impact on Household Incomes: The Long and the Short of It, ifs.org.uk, 24 Apr 2019
16. Net Replacement Rate in Unemployment, stats.oecd.org
17. Waters, Tom and Wernham, Tom, Housing Quality and Affordability for Lower-Income Households, ifs.org.uk, 27 Jun 2023
18. Two-child Limit Has Little Effect on Fertility, lse.ac.uk, 6 Apr 2022
19. Timmins, Nicholas, Universal Credit: Getting it to Work Better, instituteforgovernment.org.uk, Mar 2020
20. Ibid.
21. Universal Credit Statistics: 29 April 2013 to 11 Jul 2019, DWP, gov.uk, 13 Aug 2019
22. Waters, Tom and Wernham, Thomas, Budget Measures Bring Number of Families Entitled to Universal Credit to 7 Million, ifs.org.uk, 8 Nov 2021
23. Kay, John, The Basics of Basic Income, intereconomics.eu, Volume 52, 2017 – Number 2
24. Patrick, Ruth, New Welfare Reforms Put Extra Pressure on Single Parents to Enter Paid Work, theconversation.com, 31 Mar 2017
25. Families and the Labour Market, UK: 2019, ons.gov.uk, 24 Oct 2019

26. Codreanu, Mihai and Waters, Tom, How Effective Are Work Search Requirements? Evidence From a UK Reform Targeting Single Parents, forthcoming 2023

27. Rudd, Amber, Hansard, publications.parliament.uk, 11 Jan 2009

28. CPAG Briefing on the DWP's JSA/ESA Sanctions Statistics Release, Supplement; Explaining the Rise and Fall of JSA and ESA Sanctions 2010–16, cpag.org.uk, 17 Aug 2016

29. Avram, Silvia, Brewer, Mike and Salvatori, Andrea, Can't Work or Won't Work: Quasi-Experimental Evidence on Work Search Requirements for Single Parents, Labour Economics Volume 51, Apr 2018

30. Cribb, Jonathan et al, The Cost of Living Crisis: A Pre-Budget Briefing, ifs.org.uk, 22 Feb 2023

31. British Social Attitudes Survey No. 37, bsa.natcen.ac.uk, 2020

Chapter 4: Pensions and the Rise of the Baby Boomers

1. Benefit Expenditure and Caseload Tables 2023, DWP, gov.uk, 25 Apr 2023

2. Public Service Pension Payments (net), obr.uk, 24 Apr 2023

3. Survival to Age 65, Male (per cent of Cohort), data.worldbank.org

4. Period and Cohort Life Expectancy Explained: December 2019, ons.gov.uk, 2 Dec 2019

5. Crawford, Rowena and O'Dea, Cormac, Cash and Pensions: Have the Elderly in England Saved Optimally for Retirement?, ifs.org.uk, 9 Sep 2014

6. Sons of Union Veterans of the Civil War (SUVCW) from Twitter, 3 Jan 2021

7. Pengelly, Martin and Triplett, Irene, Last Person to Collect an American Civil War Pension, Dies at 90, Guardian, 7 Jun 2020

8. Thane, Pat (ed.), The Origins of British Social Policy, Croom Helm, London, 1978

9. Quoted in The Times, Review of Parliament, 16 Jun 2008

10. Dilnot, A. W., Kay, J. A., and Morris, C. N, *The Reform of Social Security*, Oxford University Press, Oxford, 1984
11. Johnson, Paul, General Election 2019 Manifesto Analysis: Opening Remarks, ifs.org.uk, 28 Nov 2019
12. A New Pension Settlement for the Twenty-First Century: The Second Report of the Pensions Commission, The Stationery Office, 30 Nov 2005
13. Pensions Reform: The Pensions Commission (2002–6), instituteforgovernment.org.uk
14. Independent Public Service Pensions Commission: Final Report by Lord Hutton, HM Treasury, gov.uk, 10 Mar 2011
15. Ibid.
16. King, Anthony and Crewe, Ivor, *The Blunders of Our Governments*, Oneworld, London, 2013
17. Johnson, Paul, Flexible Pensions Could Offer a Way Out of the Public Sector Pay Crisis, ifs.org.uk, 10 Oct 2022
18. Broadbent, John, Palumbo, Michael and Woodman, Elizabeth, The Shift from Defined Benefit to Defined Contribution Pension Plans – Implications for Asset Allocation and Risk Management, bis.org, Dec 2006
19. Bourquin, Pascale and Crawford, Rowena, Automatic Enrolment – Too Successful a Nudge to Boost Pension Saving? ifs.org.uk, 18 May 2020
20. Crawford, Rowena, Retirement Saving of the Self-Employed, ifs.org.uk, 16 Oct 2020
21. Pensions at a Glance 2021, oecd-ilibrary.org
22. National Population Projections: 2018-based, ons.gov.uk, 21 Oct 2019
23. OBR Fiscal Sustainability Report – Jul 2018, Chart 3.14, obr.uk, 17 Jul 2018

Chapter 5: Health

1. Autumn Statement 2022: Documents, Tables 2.1 and 2.2, gov.uk, 17 Nov 2022

2. See: engagebritain.org/health-care-matters for multiple stories of experiences with the NHS

3. Hospital Outpatient Activity 2019-20, nhs.uk, 8 Oct 2020

4. Beveridge, William, op. cit.

5. Ibid.

6. Quoted in Cohen, Patricia, William J. Baumol, 95, 'One of the Great Economists of His Generation,' Dies, *New York Times*, 10 May 2017

7. For those that are classed as an emergency or a potentially serious condition that may require rapid assessment, urgent on-scene intervention and/or urgent transport. For example, a person may have had a heart attack or stroke, or be suffering from sepsis or major burns.

8. NHS Performance Summary, nuffieldtrust.org.uk

9. NHS Workforce Statistics, digital.nhs.uk

10. Zaranko, Ben, Pay Compression in the NHS (and Beyond), ifs. org.uk, 1 Jun 2022

11. NHS Workforce: Our Position, kingsfund.org.uk, 23 Feb 2022

12. The NHS Long Term Plan, nhs.longtermplan.nhs.uk, Jan 2019

13. Warner, Max and Zaranko, Ben, Implications of the NHS Workforce Plan, ifs.org.uk, Aug 2023

14. Timmins, Nicholas, Scrapping Prescription Charges: Should it Be a Priority?, kingsfund.org.uk, 24 Sep 2019

15. How Health Care is Funded, kingsfund.org.uk, 23 Mar 2017

16. Appleby, John, What if People Had to Pay £10 to See a GP?, kingsfund.org.uk, 8 Feb 2017

17. NHS 'Will Not Be Free in Future', bbc.co.uk, 14 Apr 2007

18. All figures taken from Warner, Max and Zaranko, Ben, Pressures on the NHS, ifs.org.uk, 10 Sep 2021

19. Britnell, Mark, *In Search of the Perfect Health System*, Palgrave Macmillan, London, 2016

20. Integration and Innovation: Working Together to Improve Health and Social Care for All, Dept Health and Social Care, 11 Feb 2021

21. See: engagebritain.org/health-care-matters, op. cit

22. Hopson, Chris, Frontline Experience Counts More Than NHS Reforms, *Guardian*, 5 Apr 2013

23. Timmins, Nicholas (ed.), Changing of the Guard: Lessons for the New NHS From Departing Health Leaders, nuffieldtrust. org.uk, Mar 2013

24. Independent Inquiry into Care Provided by Mid Staffordshire NHS Foundation Trust January 2005 – March 2009, assets. publishing.service.gov.uk, 24 Feb 2010

25. Timmins, Nicholas, Never Again? The Story of the Health and Social Care Act 2012, kingsfund.org.uk, 12 Jul 2012

26. Atkins, Charlotte, Commons, Hansard, 2 Nov 2005

27. Health and Care Bill: Report Stage, nhsconfed.org, 23 Nov 2021

28. O'Neill, Onora, A Question of Trust: The BBC Reith Lectures 2002, Cambridge University Press, Cambridge, 2002

29. Heitmueller, Axel, Tony Blair Institute for Global Change, institute.global/tony-blair, 29 Jun 2022

30. Tempest, Matthew, Brown and Blair: The Top Five TB-GB moments, Guardian, 19 Jun 2007

31. Kirk, Ashley, Duncan, Pamela and Scruton, Paul, NHS Crisis in Charts: How Covid Has Increased Strain on Health Service, Guardian, 16 Jan 2021

32. Building Back Cancer Services in England, The Progressive Policy Think Tank, 24 Sep 2021

33. COVID-19 and Cancer: 1 Year On, Lancet, Apr 2021

34. Stoye, George, Warner, Max and Zaranko, Ben, Where Are All the Missing Hospital Patients?, ifs.org.uk, 7 Dec 2021

35. Aylin, Paul, et al, What Happened to English NHS Hospital Activity During the COVID-19 Pandemic?, ifs.org.uk, 13 May 2021

36. PHIN Private market update: March 2023, phin.org.uk, 9 Mar 2023

37. What's Behind the Increase in Demand in Emergency Departments?, president.rcem.ac.uk, 6 Aug 2021

38. Heitmueller, op. cit.

39. Anderson, Michael, et al, LSE–Lancet Commission on the future of the NHS: Re-laying the Foundations for an Equitable and Efficient Health and Care Service After COVID-19, Lancet, 22 May 2021

40.   Syed, Matthew, The BBC, the NHS and Oxfam Have a Bad Case of Institutional Narcissism, *Sunday Times*, 23 May 2021
41.   Kirkup, Bill, The Report of the Morecambe Bay Investigation, Mar 2015
42.   Syed, op. cit.
43.   Smith, Stephen, *The Best NHS? Book 1*, Radix UK, York, 2021
44.   Kerr, Sir Ron, Empowering NHS Leaders to Lead, 28 Nov 2018
45.   Dayan, Mark, Gardner, Tim, Kelly, Elaine and Ward, Deborah, How Good is the NHS? ifs.org.uk, 25 Jun 2018
46.   Kirkpatrick, Ian and Malby, Becky, What Do NHS Managers Contribute?, NHS Confederation, 11 Feb 2022
47.   NHS Workforce: Our Position, kingsfund.org.uk, 23 Feb 2022

Chapter 6: The Costs of Getting Sicker and Older

1.   Adult Social Care Statistics in England: An Overview, Table 5, digital.nhs.uk, 17 Nov 2022
2.   DWP spending only. Includes incapacity benefits – including the standard allowance and health element of Universal Credit – disability benefits, carer benefits, industrial injuries benefits, and both Housing Benefit and Universal Credit housing element for those in the disabled, incapacity or carer groups. For those benefits that are devolved during the period the coverage is England and Wales throughout for consistency.
3.   Benefit Expenditure and Caseload Tables 2023, DWP, gov.uk, 25 Apr 2023
4.   Re-imagining Local Care Networks: Neighbourhood Based Care and Wellbeing, Lambeth Council, Nov 2018
5.   Quoted in Rivett, Geoffrey, 1948–1957: Establishing the National Health Service, nuffieldtrust.org
6.   Ritchie, Hannah and Roser, Max, Causes of Death, Our World in Data, ourworldindata.org, Feb 2018/Dec 2019
7.   Razzell, Peter and Spence, Christine, The History of Infant, Child and Adult Mortality in London, 1550–1850, tandfonline.com, 18 Jul 2013

8.   Raleigh, Veena, What is Happening to Life Expectancy in England?, kingsfund.org, 10 Aug 2022

9.   Topping, Alexandra, Macmillan Dismissed Smoke Risk, *Guardian*, 30 May 2008

10. Health State Life Expectancies by National Deprivation Deciles, England: 2016 to 2018, ons.gov.uk, 27 Mar 2020

11. Marmot, Michael, Goldblatt, Peter and Allen, Jessica, et al, Fair Society, Healthy Lives (The Marmot Review), instituteofhealthequity.org, Feb 2010

12. Steventon, Adam, et al, Emergency Hospital Admissions in England: Which May Be Avoidable and How?, The Health Foundation, reader.health.org.uk, May 2018

13. Long-term Conditions and Multi-Morbidity, kingsfund.org.uk

14. Ibid.

15. Boseley, Sarah, Patients with Multiple Conditions Not Getting Best Possible Care, Say Experts, *Guardian*, 19 Apr 2018

16. Powell, Andrew, Disabled People in Employment, researchbriefings.files.parliament.uk, 24 May 2021

17. Blundell, Richard and Johnson, Paul, Pensions and Labor-Market Participation in the United Kingdom, *American Economic Review*, May 1998

18. Banks, James, Blundell, Richard and Emmerson, Carl, Disability Benefit Receipt and Reform: Reconciling Trends in the United Kingdom, ifs.org.uk, 6 Mar 2015

19. O'Connor, Sarah, Left Behind: Can Anyone Save the Towns the UK Economy Forgot?, *Financial Times*, 16 Nov 2017

20. Joyce, Robert, The IFS at 50: The Future of Benefits, ifs.org.uk, 27 Feb 2019

21. O'Connor, op. cit.

22. GPforhire, Shit Life Syndrome, Random Mutterings of a Doctor Up North blog, 25 Apr 2010

23. Cumberlidge, Phil, Sh*t Life Syndrome is the Problem We Can't Medicate, *Mirror*, 7 Aug 2015

24. Cribb, Jonathan, Karjalainen, Heidi and Waters, Tom, Living Standards of Working-Age Disability Benefits Recipients in the UK, ifs.org.uk, 6 Jul 2022

25.   Banks, James, Karjalainen, Heidi and Waters, Tom, Inequalities in Disability, ifs.org.uk, 23 Aug 2023
26.   This definition draws heavily on the report of the Dilnot commission 'Fairer Care Funding'.
27.   Key Facts and Figures About Adult Social Care, kingsfund.org.uk, 2 Jul 2021
28.   Crawford, Rowena, Stoye, George and Zaranko, Ben, Long-term Care Spending and Hospital Use Among the Older Population in England, Journal of Health Economics, 4 Jun 2021
29.   Timmins, Nicholas, The Care Conundrum, *Prospect*, 5 Nov 2020
30.   Ibid.
31.   See: engagebritain.org/health-care-matters, op. cit.
32.   *Kate Garraway: Caring for Derek*, itv.com, 22 Feb 2022
33.   Fairer Care Funding: The Report of the Commission on Funding of Care and Support, The Stationery Office, 4 Jul 2011
34.   Dilnot, Andrew, Dilnot Commission Report on Social Care, kingsfund.org.uk, 13 Jul 2011
35.   Sturrock, David and Tallack, Charles, Does the Cap Fit? Analysing the Government's Proposed Amendment to the English Social Care Charging System, ifs.org.uk, 7 Feb 2022

Chapter 7: Schools

1.   Autumn Statement 2022: Documents, Table 2.1, gov.uk, 17 Nov 2022
2.   Gove Regrets Scrapping Schools Rebuild Programme, Construction Management, constructionmanagement.co.uk, 29 Nov 2016
3.   BBC News, bbc.co.uk, 10 Jan 2008
4.   Drayton, Elaine, et al, Annual Report on Education Spending in England: 2022, ifs.org.uk, 12 Dec 2022
5.   The school systems in Wales, Northern Ireland and Scotland are different. This chapter focuses on England.
6.   Sibieta, Luke, The Growing Gap Between State School and Private School Spending, ifs.org.uk, 8 Oct 2021

7. Sibieta, Luke, What Has Happened to Teacher Pay in England? ifs.org.uk, 11 Jan 2023

8. Rice, Patricia (chair), School Teachers' Review Body 30th report: 2020, gov.uk, 21 Jul 2020

9. One limitation of using more subjective measures of teacher quality (like Ofsted ratings) is the risk of conflating difficult teaching circumstances with poor teacher quality. While Ofsted inspectors try to take school circumstances into account in their assessment, it is of course possible that teachers in better-off schools find it easier to demonstrate the kinds of behaviours that Ofsted is looking for. On the other hand, since pupils will be affected by the teaching quality they actually experience rather than the potential best-case scenario effectiveness of their teachers, these measures still tell an important story about the inequalities experienced in classrooms with different levels of disadvantage.

10. The Evolution of Cognitive Skills During Childhood Across the UK, Education Policy Institute, epi.org.uk, 9 Jul 2020

11. Gibbons, Stephen, McNally, Sandra and Viarengo, Martina, Does Additional Spending Help Urban schools? An Evaluation Using Boundary Discontinuities, Journal of the European Economic Association 16(5), 28 Nov 2017

12. Jackson, C. K., Johnson, R. C. and Persico, C., The Effects of School Spending on Educational and Economic Outcomes: Evidence from School Finance Reforms, Quarterly Journal of Economics 131(1), 1 Oct 2015

13. Rising Class Sizes, National Education Union, neu.org.uk, 14 Nov 2019

14. See: Gurney Read, Josie, Small Class Sizes 'Top Priority for 2 in 5 Parents', *Telegraph*, 14 Apr 2015

15. Kreuger, A.B., Experimental Estimates of Education Production Functions, *Quarterly Journal of Economics*, 114(2), 1999

16. See: Hoxby, C., The Effects of Class Size on Student Achievement: New Evidence from Population Variation, *Quarterly Journal of Economics*, Nov 2000

17. While average class sizes vary around the country, there is no strong relationship between an area's level of disadvantage and its average class size. Indeed, at Key Stage 2, local authorities

with a higher proportion of pupils receiving free school meals tend to have *smaller* class sizes than more affluent areas.

18. Slater, H., Davies, N. M. and Burgess, S., Do Teachers Matter? Measuring the Variation in Teacher Effectiveness in England, Oxford Bulletin of Economics and Statistics 74(5), 2011; Chetty, R., Friedman, J. N. and Rockoff, J. E., Measuring the Impacts of Teachers II: Teacher Value Added and Student Outcomes in Adulthood, American Economic Review 104(9), 2014; Jackson, C. K., What Do Test Scores Miss? The Importance of Teacher Effects on Non-test Score Outcomes, NBER Working Paper nr. 22226, 2016

19. Wiswall, M., The Dynamics of Teacher Quality, Journal of Public Economics, 100c, 2013; Ladd, H.F. and Sorensen, L.C., Returns to Teacher Experience: Student Achievement and Motivation in Middle School, Education Finance and Policy 12(2), 2017

20. Farquharson, Christine, Sibieta, Luke, Tahir, Imran and Waltmann, Ben, 2021 Annual Report on Education Spending in England, ifs.org.uk, 30 Nov 2021

21. Farquharson, Christine, McNally, Sandra and Tahir, Imran, Education Inequalities, IFS Deaton Review: Inequality, ifs.org. uk, 16 Aug 2022

22. Mirza, Heidi Safia and Warwick, Ross, Race and Ethnicity: IFS Deaton Review, ifs.org.uk, 14 Nov 2022

23. Aitkenhead, Decca, Steve McQueen: My Hidden Shame, *Guardian*, 4 Jan 2014

24. Machin, Stephen, McNally, Sandra and Ruiz-Valenzuela, Jenifer, Missing the Mark at GCSE English: the Costly Consequences of Just Failing to Get a Grade C, Centre for Vocational Education Research, 13 Apr 2018

25. Burgess, Simon and Vignoles, Anna, The Covid-19 Crisis and Educational Inequality, Centre for Education Policy and Equalising Opportunities, 22 May 2020

26. Catton, Fitzsimons, et al, Early Childhood Inequalities, Figure 20: IFS Deaton Review, ifs.org.uk, 14 Nov 2022

27. Cottrell-Boyce, Frank from Twitter, 11 Jun 2022

28. Hunt, Emily, Examining Post-Pandemic Absences in England, epi.org.uk, 10 Aug 2023

29. Sibieta, Luke, The Crisis in Lost Learning Calls for a Massive National Policy Response, ifs.org.uk, 1 Feb 2021

30. Callaghan James speaking in 1976, reprinted in Towards a National Debate, *Guardian*, 15 Oct 2001

31. Machin, Stephen and McNally, Sandra, Large Benefits, Low Cost, CentrePiece, Spring 2004

32. Farquharson, Christine, Complicated, Costly and Constantly Changing: The Childcare System in England, ifs.org.uk, 13 Sep 2021

33. Farquharson, Christine and Olorenshaw, Harriet, The Changing Cost of Childcare, ifs.org.uk, 20 May 2022

34. Cattan, Sarah, et al, The Health Impacts of Sure Start, ifs.org. uk, 16 Aug 2021

35. Farquharson, Christine, et al, IFS Deaton Review, op. cit

Chapter 8: Education After School

1. Drayton, Elaine, et al, Annual Report on Education Spending in England: 2022, ifs.org.uk, 12 Dec 2022

2. For DFE Training and Apprenticeship Data see gov.uk/ government/organisations/department-for-education

3. Wolf, Alison, Heading for the Precipice: Can Further and Higher Education Funding Policies Be Sustained?, King's College London, Jun 2015

4. Sibieta, Luke and Tahir, Imran, Further Education and Sixth Form Spending in England, ifs.org.uk, 18 Aug 2021

5. English FE Pay Scales, University and College Union, ucu.org.uk

6. Apprenticeships and Traineeships, Academic Year 2021/22, gov. uk, 8 Sep 2022

7. UK Skills Mismatch 2030 – Research Paper, industrialstrategy council.org, 24 Oct 2019

8. OECD Skills Outlook 2013: First Results from the Survey of Adult Skills, OECD Publishing, 2013

9. Kuczera, Małgorzata, Field, Simon and Windisch, Hendrickje Catriona, Building Skills for All: A Review of England: Policy Insights from the Survey of Adult Skills, OECD, 2016

10. Keep, Ewart, Richmond, Tom and Silver, Ruth, Honourable Histories: From the Local Management of Colleges Via Incorporation to the Present Day: 30 Years of Reform in Further Education 1991–2021, Further Education Trust for Leadership, Jan 2021

11. Britton, Jack, et al, 2020 Annual Report on Education Spending in England, ifs.org.uk, 3 Nov 2020

12. Sibieta, Luke, Tahir, Imran and Waltmann, Ben, Adult Education: The Past, Present and Future, ifs.org.uk, 13 Jun 2022

13. Augar, Philip, Post-18 Review of Education and Funding: Independent Panel Report, Department for Education, 30 May 2019

14. Ibid.

15. Sibieta, Luke, Tahir, Imran and Waltmann, Ben, op. cit.

16. Britton, Jack, Dearden, Lorraine, Waltmann, Ben and van der Erve, Laura, The Impact of Undergraduate Degrees on Lifetime Earnings, ifs.org.uk, 29 Feb 2020

17. Le Grand, Julian, *The Strategy of Equality: Redistribution and the Social Services*, Routledge, London, 1982

18. Wintour, Patrick and Snowdon, Graham, Ministers Admit Plans for Tuition Fees are in Disarray, *Guardian*, 3 Apr 2011

19. Britton, Jack, Dearden, Lorraine, Waltmann, Ben and van der Erve, Laura, op. cit.

20. Belfield, Britton, et al, How Much Does Degree Choice Matter, ifs.org.uk, 11 Aug 2021

21. Augar, Philip, op. cit.

Chapter 9: Levelling Up, Local and Devolved Government

1. Core Spending Power: Final Local Government Finance Settlement 2023 to 2024, gov.uk, 6 Feb 2023

2. Scottish Budget 2023 to 2024: Your Scotland, Your Finances – Guide, gov.scot, 2 Oct 2023

3. Welsh Government Final Budget 2023 to 2024, gov.wales, 28 Feb 2023

4. Announcement by Northern Ireland Secretary, gov.uk, 27 Apr 2023

5. Levelling Up the United Kingdom: Executive Summary, gov. uk, 2 Feb 2022

6. See: People, Population and Community, ons.gov.uk

7. Overman, Henry and Xu, Xiaowei, Spatial Disparities Across Labour Markets, IFS Deaton Review, ifs.org.uk, 2 Feb 2022

8. Britton, Jack, Waltmann, Ben, Xu, Xiaowei and van der Erve, Laura, London Calling? Higher Education, Geographical Mobility and Early-career Earnings, ifs.org.uk, 17 Sep 2021

9. Agrawal, Sarthak and Phillips, David, Catching Up or Falling Behind? Geographical Inequalities in the UK and How They Have Changed in Recent Years, ifs.org.uk, 3 Aug 2020

10. Atkins, Graham, Croydon Council's Bankruptcy is a Warning for the UK Government, instituteforgovernment.org.uk, 26 Nov 2020

11. Ibid.

12. Only One in Five of England's Largest Councils Confident of Preventing Insolvency Without Dramatic Reductions to Services, County Councils Network, countycouncilsnetwork. org.uk, 12 Nov 20

13. Caller, Max, Northamptonshire County Council Best Value Inspection January–March 2018, assets.publishing.service.gov.uk

14. Harris, Tom, Hodge, Louis and Phillips, David, English Local Government Funding: Trends and Challenges in 2019 and Beyond, ifs.org.uk, 13 Nov 2019

15. See Keith-Lucas, B., Government of the County in England, *Western Political Quarterly*, Vol. 9, Number 1, Mar 1956

16. Departmental Overview: Local Authorities Overview 2019, National Audit Office, nao.org.uk, Mar 2020

17. Harris, Tom, Hodge, Louis and Phillips, op. cit.

18. Ogden, Kate, Phillips, David and Sion, Cian, What's Happened and What's Next For Councils?, ifs.org.uk, 7 Oct 2021

19. Ogden, Kate and Phillips, David, The Financial Risk and Resilience of English Local Authorities in the Coronavirus Crisis, ifs.org.uk, 22 Jun 2020

20. Gee, Chris, Market Walk Mall Bought by Chorley Council for £23 million, *Lancashire Telegraph*, 3 Dec 2013

21. Clarence-Smith, Louisa, £1bn Property Drive by Spelthorne Borough Council Riddled by 'Serious Failings', *The Times*, 17 Feb 2021

22. Portsmouth City Council Under Fire for Bailing Out Fruit Importer to Tune of £16.7m, *News* (Portsmouth), 8 Apr 2016

23. In 2022 about 80 per cent of secondary schools and 40 per cent of primary schools were academies or free schools.

24. Children Looked After in England Including Adoptions, gov. uk, 10 Dec 2020

25. LGA: Funding for Almost 10 Million Pothole Repairs This Year Lost From Council Budgets, Local Government Association, local.gov.uk, 9 Oct 2021

26. Barnett, Joel, I Demand that the Shamefully Unfair Barnett Formula is Scrapped, *Daily Mail*, 21 Sept 2014

27. Farquharson, Christine, Phillips, David and Zaranko, Ben, Public Service Spending in Scotland: Trends and Key Issues, ifs.org.uk, 14 Apr 2021

28. Case, Ann and Kraftman, Lucy, Health Inequalities, IFS Deaton Review, ifs.org.uk, 4 Nov 2022

29. Mackenbach, J.P., From Deep-fried Mars Bars to Neoliberal Political Attacks: Explaining the Scottish Mortality Disadvantage, *European Journal of Public Health*, 22(6), 2012

30. FCNI Final Report – More Fiscal Devolution for Northern Ireland?, fiscalcommissionni.org, 19 May 2022

Chapter 10: Where to From Here?

1. Performance Tracker 2021: Criminal Courts, instituteforgovernment.org.uk

2. Fiscal Risks and Sustainability, obr.uk, 7 Jul 2022

3. Quoted in Davies, Howard (ed.), *The Chancellors' Tales,* op. cit.

4. Emmerson, Carl and Stockton, Isabel, Rewriting the Fiscal Rules, ifs.org.uk, 12 Oct 2021

5. Fiscal Risks Report, Office for Budget Responsibility, obr.uk, Jul 2021

6.   Stern, Nicholas, Climate Change, Ethics and the Economics of the Global Deal, Royal Economics Society Public Lecture, November 2007

7.   Net Zero Review: Interim Report, HM Treasury, gov.uk, 17 Dec 2020

8.   Progress in Reducing Emissions: 2022 Report to Parliament, theccc.org.uk, 29 Jun 2022

9.   UK Energy in Brief, Department for Business, Energy and Industrial Strategy, assets.publishing.service.gov.uk, 2021

10. Modelling 2050: Electricity System Analysis, Department for Business, Energy and Industrial Strategy, assets.publishing. service.gov.uk, December 2020

11. Net Zero – The UK's Contribution to Stopping Global Warming, theccc.org.uk, May 2019

12. Fiscal Risks Report, op. cit.

13. Progress in Reducing Emissions: 2022 Report to Parliament, op. cit.

14. Fiscal Risks and Sustainability, Chart 4.1, obr.uk, Jul 2022

15. Fiscal Risks and Sustainability, Para 4.13, obr.uk, Jul 2022

16. The Latest Evidence on the Impact of Brexit on UK Trade, obr. uk, Mar 2022

17. Impact of the Brexit trade Agreement on Our Economy Forecast, obr.uk, Mar 2021

18. The Economic Effects of the Government's Proposed Brexit Deal, niesr.ac.uk, 26 Nov 2018

Acknowledgements

If you have read this you will have gathered that I owe the deepest imaginable debt of gratitude to all my colleagues, past and present, at the IFS. While the book is mine and mine alone, it would quite literally have been impossible without them; much of the research and analysis on which the book relies would not exist without them and their work. My colleagues really are the most exceptional bunch of human beings, the IFS a really quite remarkable institution.

Carl Emmerson, Helen Miller, Luke Sibieta, Ben Zaranko and David Phillips were kind enough to read and comment on versions of my text. All errors and opinions expressed remain mine and should not be attributed to them, or indeed to the IFS corporately.

I should also thank my trustees at the IFS who provide all the support and encouragement I could wish for. I am eternally grateful to the Economic and Social Research Council who are the most important funders of the Institute, and without whom, again, none of this would be possible.

Richard Beswick and Julian Alexander came to me with the idea for this book, for which (I think) I remain grateful. David Boyle provided valuable input.

Index